Battle to Destroy Truth

Unveiling a Trail of Deception

by Claris Van Kuiken

REF Publishing • Manassas, Virginia
1996

DEDICATION

To the only One who so willingly suffered an agonizing, cruel death on a cross, sacrificing His own life in place of mine, and buying me with His own precious blood–Jesus Christ; to my father and mother who taught me that saving Truth; to my children, Lori, Michael, and Hilary, who I pray will love and defend that Truth; and, to all those who diligently seek to preserve and defend the glorious gospel message "that was once for all entrusted to the saints"–to which end this book was written.

SPECIAL THANKS

—To all "the appellants" for their continuing encouragement, support and love: Howard and Jo Stob, Karen and Dean Leensvaart, John and Sharon Tiggelaar, Ken and Ruth Evenhouse and my husband, Si, whose constant help with this computer was a life-saver!

—To Howard Stob and Rev. Neal Punt for their strong example of what it truly means to be an "office-bearer" in the church.

—To friends, Frank and Doreen Voss and Tim Gibbons for listening to the appellants when hardly anyone else would, taking the time to discern for themselves between truth and falsehood, and taking a stand for what they believe in.

—To my wonderful neighbors, Gary and Clara Stob, who always greeted me cheerfully when I came running up their porch and provided me with a cup of coffee and a listening ear whenever I needed to talk, not to mention taking the time to read and constructively criticize many of my articles before they were printed.

—To Samantha Smith whose friendship continues to be a source of strength and sustenance to me, and for her dedication in researching and exposing the false teachings that lay behind the New Age Movement.

PAUL'S CHARGE TO TIMOTHY
2 Timothy 3:10-4:8

You, however, know all about my teaching, my way of life, my purpose, faith, patience, love, endurance, persecutions, sufferings–what kinds of things happened to me in Antioch, Iconium and Lystra, the persecutions I endured. Yet the Lord rescued me from all of them. In fact, everyone who wants to live a godly life in Christ Jesus will be persecuted, while evil men and impostors will go from bad to worse, deceiving and being deceived. But as for you, continue in what you have learned and have become convinced of, because you know those from who you learned it, and how from infancy you have known the holy Scriptures, which are able to make you wise for salvation through faith in Christ Jesus. **All Scripture is God-breathed and is useful for teaching, rebuking, correcting and training in righteousness, so that the man of God may be thoroughly equipped for every good work.**

In the presence of God and of Christ Jesus, who will judge the living and the dead, and in view of his appearing and his kingdom, I give you this charge, Preach the Word, be prepared in season and out of season; correct, rebuke and encourage–with great patience and careful instruction. **For the time will come when men will not put up with sound doctrine. Instead, to suit their own desires, they will gather around them a great number of teachers to say what their itching ears want to hear. They will turn their ears away from the truth and turn aside to myths.** But you, keep your head in all situations, endure hardship, do the work of an evangelist, discharge all the duties of your ministry.

For I am already being poured out like a drink offering and the time has come for my departure. I have fought the good fight, I have finished the race, I have kept the faith. Now there is in store for me the crown of righteousness, which the Lord, the righteous Judge, will award to me on the day–and not only to me, but also to all who have longed for his appearing (emphasis mine).

IN DEFENSE OF THE TRUTH

Wasn't it Aristotle who said, *"Plato I love, but even more Truth"*? The two hundred pages of this book, easily read in one breath, form an important document to be added to the file of the "Battle for Destruction" of the TRUTH. It takes a courageous stand against a deliberate attack, both from the outside and, perhaps unconsciously, inside the Church.

A young lady, defender of the sound doctrine to which her Church officially subscribes, challenges *the absolute relativization of revealed truth*. Written with a pen dipped into the ink of sanctified passion, the document is not content with a dry enumeration of facts. The author is a remarkable exception for a "lay" member of the Church. She is versed in the knowledge of the heresy of the NEW AGE which she denounces, and a couple of its prominent representatives who, curiously, have met with the enthusiasm of some among modern "Christians."

The details of conversations, meetings, "official appearances," telephone calls and random talks are not "trivia." They opportunely bring forth and measure the damages ruining the church from the inside. They carefully substantiate the profound crisis which is befalling the Church. When *"The Betrayal of the Clerics"* (to borrow the title of a famous French book) has become the current, deplorable practice, the author, with a handful of sincere and convinced fellow-believers, does not hesitate to sound the alarm, for the discernment of the spirits is a gift of the Spirit.

In the line of witnesses of the Faith delivered once for all, to the saints, the author is convinced that the defense of the Truth is more vital than the protection of some ministers by their "consistories" or the preserving at any price of the artificial, hence fragile, unity of a denomination. While some without shame will declare: *"My denomination, right or wrong,"* those who truly love the Church of

vi

Jesus Christ, with pain in their hearts, yet unswerving determination of their wills, will challenge the arrogance of church nomenclature and arbitrariness as part of officialdom.

The document witnesses again that, as in the past, some old demons are nowadays haunting the Church of Jesus Christ–those of two channels of Revelation, one serving as a mere facade, the other for the opportunistic jumping onto the band-wagon of modernity, so that some Churchmen may walk, run and fly according to the direction of the blowing wind of history! "Big Brothers" are not the sad privilege of Atheist camps (remember the Great Inquisitor of Dostoevsky). Intellectual terrorism may at times become the regime lording over the pulpit and the narthex, even of Protestant denominations. No wonder we are the afflicted eyewitnesses of the Great Implosion taking place in so many churches–the Decreation, not to mention the assassination, of Christian reality! Again, when short of sound arguments or honest reasons, the bureaucratura will insinuate that the "appellant" has a psychological problem! Does that not remind one of a very familiar trick practiced in the Kingdom of Gulags? TRUTH be easily wiped out, by means of the corrosive, much celebrated, modern heresy of LOVE!

What is also sad is the attitude of those who officially subscribe to the Doctrine, Creed and Church Order, and yet practically behave contrary to the Forms of Unity! The case reported in those pages seems not to be an exceptional one, but rather a sure symptom of a widespread epidemic, plaguing the whole body of the Church.

At the end, the clericatura and bureaucratura may win, according to appearances. While closing the last page, I recalled the wonderful pastoral letter of John Calvin, sent to Gaspard de Coligny, Admiral of France, imprisoned in a Spanish dungeon, as the Chief of French Huguenots. "*Monsignor,*" wrote the great Reformer, "*even if what you did has not been effective, remember that it will count in the eyes of God and his Angels.*" Claris Van Kuiken, and the saints who fought this battle, deserve to receive the same assurance.

A.R. Kayayan
(Retired, French Broadcast Minister, The Back to God Hour)

PREFACE

You are the salt of the earth. But if the salt loses its salti-
ness, how can it be made salty again? It is no longer good
for anything, except to be thrown out and trampled by
men

(Matthew 5:13)

Truth. What is it? Can we know it?

Many Christians have absolutely no clue as to what is taking
place within the Christian community today. While they hear grum-
bling within their particular denomination, and possibly, within the
very church of which they belong, they choose to ignore the symptoms of an underlying deadly cancerous growth.

Some automatically place themselves on the "winning team."
Blind trust leads them to a numbing of the Truth and discernment
fails to break through the coldness of their hearts. Others merely
keep silent and complacent, hoping the turmoil will die down and
disappear in time, remaining what Revelation 3 calls "luke-warm."
Their zest for truth has diminished and the will to stand up for
what they believe in has been weakened to the point of death.

A few years ago, my husband and I had no choice but to remove
our children from the Christian school they were attending. A year
or so later, my family was forced to leave the church we had been
members of for over 14 years. At the same time, we felt conscience-
bound to leave behind a denomination we had grown to love and
been a part of for 40 years, in which we had been born and raised,
the Christian Reformed Church of North America.

I had been portrayed as one being used by the devil to destroy
the church; a lunatic who saw the occult in everything. I was considered to be a devisive, schismatic, negative, narrow-minded fundamentalist, and worst of all, a censor; not by people outside

my church, in the world, but by people inside my church–people I knew and trusted to know the difference between right and wrong, truth and error.

My pastors and elders were convinced I was guilty of destroying the unity of our church. Yet not once did they exercise church discipline out of love and concern for one of their fellow members.

What did I do to bring such heartache to my church? I brought to my pastor's attention, books that were being taught and upheld as Christian literature to our children by the teachers at the Christian school they attended. Books which had also found a home in our church library. Books which, I believed, undermined God's Word, laughed in His face and made a mockery out of His Son, the One who bought us with His own precious blood. These were the works of a renowned author who claims to be a Christian, and continues to have a tremendous amount of influence within the Christian community at large. At the time I first became acquainted with her works, however, I had no idea this was the case.

The conflict that arose was *not* about "what may a Christian read." The heart of our concern was the continual, vigorous defense of our pastors and elders that these works presented a "strong, underlying Christian message," and aided in one's faith and spiritual growth.

An appeal was made to overrule our consistory's (pastors and elders) "conviction" to Classis Chicago South–a group of 17 neighboring CRC churches. Classis adopted a report which declared this author denied:

1. The substitutionary, sacrificial atonement
2. The unique divinity of Jesus Christ
3. The unique authority of Scripture
4. The eternal separation between God and some persons

The question that tore us apart from my church and denomination after a four-year struggle was this: **Can one *deny* the above essential Biblical truths, and still be classified and defended as a Christian author?**

Why was this question the source of such a serious debate which ultimately led to a judicial trial within the church?

That is my story, my experience, which I share with you now. I tell it because there are Christians in various denominations going through similar circumstances. Many, however, do not realize we are in the midst of a spiritual warfare beyond human comprehension. We **must** make every effort to be Biblically literate and well-informed of the subtle ways in which false teachings penetrate Christian churches and schools. I hope, in some small way, my story will encourage you to stand firm in your faith and defend it, as God would have you do, refuting those who blindly seek to destroy it.

Oh, what a comfort it is to know that while many battles here on earth may be "lost," ultimately, the war has already been won by our Savior, Defender, Protector and Victorious King, our LORD JESUS CHRIST–whose "name is above every name" (Philippians 2:9).

INTRODUCTION

I was first introduced to the teachings of the New Age Movement (NAM) by Rev. John De Vries, a pastor in the Christian Reformed denomination and co-author with Erwin W. Lutzer (pastor of Moody Church, Chicago) of *Satan's "Evangelistic Strategy" for this New Age*. It was a warm, summer night in July, 1988. I was scheduled to play the piano for special music at the Cedar Lake Bible Conferences in Indiana, and Rev. De Vries happened to be the guest speaker that night. His topic: the New Age Movement.

There was no doubt that through his experiences and work in India in connection with his ministry, Bibles for India, Rev. De Vries had acquired a keen insight into the beliefs and practices found in Hinduism. As he defined the core beliefs of New Age thought and its relationship to Eastern/occultic mysticism, I found it difficult to believe so many people could be deceived by such a depressing alternative to Christianity. He had opened my eyes to something I hadn't known existed. The trouble was, I thought it only existed *outside* the church. I had no idea, nor could I ever have possibly imagined that fellow members within our denomination and teachers in related Christian schools, had already been deceived by such blatant anti-Christian teachings.

Six months following De Vries' sermon, Diane, my childhood friend called. I hadn't talked with her for some time, but every once in a while we'd get together or talk on the phone to find out how the other one was doing. Excitedly, she told me about her wonderful trip to Sedona, Arizona. Supposedly, in Sedona, there existed "power spots"–places where spirits of the dead dwelled which possessed supernatural energies. An eerie feeling swept over me when Diane told me she had healed her son's injured knee with crystals.

As our conversation continued, she began to complain that all her parents and husband wanted to do was control her. "If they really loved me," she whimpered, "they wouldn't try to control me." She could not understand, for instance, why her husband didn't like her visiting bars and seeing old boy-friends. In other words, she wanted to do whatever she pleased, without feeling guilty about it. But, thanks to those wonderful self-esteem seminars she had been attending, she now felt in control of herself and knew she was really worth something.

I had a good idea my friend was in over her head. Further conversations proved she was entrenched in New Age ideas and had forsaken the God of the Bible. As far as she was concerned, everyone should be able to do whatever they chose to do. After all, the ten commandments were outdated and "God" was only a God of love, not wrath. "He wouldn't condemn anyone," she said with utmost conviction (great theology for those who don't want to feel guilty about anything they do wrong). She further pointed out that no one had the right to impose their beliefs on anyone. As a parent, she would let her son decide for himself what was right or wrong.

Six weeks after this disturbing phone conversation with Diane, my doorbell rang. Standing on my front porch with her little boy beside her was Diane's sister, Brenda. I hadn't seen her for almost 20 years. One look at her troubled face and I knew instantly why she had come. "It's Diane, isn't it?" I asked. She nodded, as her eyes filled with tears.

"You're the only one I know of that was brought up with a strict religious upbringing. I didn't know who else to turn to," Brenda apologized.

I was rather surprised by her remark, (considering what her sister had said about my upbringing), and amazed that God would have led her to me after all this time. Brenda had been given an audio-tape series of Rev. Erwin Lutzer's lectures on the New Age Movement which had been broadcast on WMBI (Moody Bible Institute, Chicago, IL), so she already had a good idea of what her sister was into. But, she came with the hope that we could study the New Age Movement, compare it next to Scripture and together be prepared to converse gently with Diane.

As we talked, Brenda mentioned she had already consulted a relative who was a pastor when she and Diane were on vacation together. He had written her a letter warning that Diane was in contact with spirits (demons) and urged her to find help for her sister. No wonder Brenda was so upset.

Diane had also received *A Course in Miracles*, a New Age "Bible" supposedly dictated by Jesus through medium Helen Schucman, an assistant professor of psychology at Columbia University's College of Physicians and Surgeons. It had been a gift from a man whose parents were good friends with mine. His brother had been in my class in school and they were members of a Christian Reformed church. I don't know if he realized what the channeled book was; I certainly hope he didn't. It may be that he looked at the title and thought it sounded like an interesting, comforting topic. Whatever the case may have been, this "Bible" which closely resembles the Hindu Vedas, and claimed to be "a course in mind training," brainwashed Diane into believing Jesus didn't die for our sins. It had turned her completely against Jesus of Nazareth and consoled her with a god within (Foundation for Inner Peace, Tiburon, CA, 1975, Volume One, pg. 13).

Through the commitment of trying to help her sister, Brenda and I became good friends and several months later, Brenda became a committed Christian. Though she had been brought up in a Presbyterian home and had heard about Jesus, Brenda had not yet accepted Him as her personal Lord and Savior. Her zest for Truth was new and fresh and her enthusiasm for the gospel was highly contagious!

Sadly, her sister Diane remained deeply entrenched in the occult. Her mind and heart were hardened. The Bible was nothing more than one book of many to find God, and Jesus was just an example of what we all could become.

As I continued to research the teachings of the NAM both from a Christian and occult perspective and read how it disguised itself in churches and the school classroom, I began to check the assignments my children came home with from the Christian school they attended. I really didn't expect to find anything wrong in the material the teachers used. I trusted them and felt certain they knew about the NAM and would be discerning enough to spot curriculum and ideas conflicting with Scripture.

Oh, how wrong I had been to simply trust the "experts."

FOREWORD

Sin has its drawbacks. It annoys God–and that can be a serious problem over the long term. The other obvious problem is that sin doesn't work. As ancient Israel learned when it asked Samuel for a king, God gave the people a king and still required the people to meet His standards. Think of the money and worry the people could have saved themselves by being faithful from the start.

These truths have played in my mind since Alexander Solzhenitsyn forced them on me with his account of going to prison under the Communists. Solzhenitsyn argued that those Christians who stood up for their Lord and were killed suffered less than he did for obscuring his faith. The coward pays a price in fear, worry, and harassment–and in the end the coward too must die to self if he is ever to live for Jesus.

The whistle-blower must face this temptation. Perhaps if I remain silent someone else will solve the problem. Maybe everything will go away. How can I challenge family and life-long friends? The tempter who enticed Eve will find some way to package his wisdom to make it more attractive than integrity.

When Claris Van Kuiken came to me with this manuscript she had faced all these enticements to quit. Great and honorable people all over the Evangelical world did not want this story told. One of the greatest Reformed communities in history, her own Mother Church, found itself unable to agree about things an earlier generation would not have even discussed. This was not the time to walk the road Solzhenitsyn spent two decades to find. Frankly, I did not want to believe some of the things she demonstrated.

But this is a story that must be told. This is a time to remember the words of Mordecai to Esther, "Think not with thyself that thou shalt escape in the king's house, more than all the Jews. For if thou altogether holdest thy peace at this time, then shall there enlargement and deliverance arise to the Jews from another place; but thou and thy father's house shall be destroyed: and who knoweth whether thou art come to the kingdom for such a time as this?"

God will deliver His church, but will any of the congregations be Reformed if we sit silently in the palace while the institutions our fathers built rot away around us?

Then Esther told the messengers to return to Mordecai with this answer, "Go, gather together all the Jews that are present in Shushan, and fast ye for me, and neither eat nor drink three days, night or day: I also and my maidens will fast likewise; and so will I go in unto the king, which is not according to the law, and if I perish, I perish" (Esther 4:14-16).

Read the book and face the facts. Claris is right and she will prevail. God always preserves His own. But will the child you placed in what you thought was a Christian school survive? You also may survive, but do you want to pay the coward's price or will you do something?

"The fear of the Lord is the beginning of knowledge: but fools despise wisdom and instruction" (Proverbs 1:7).

Dr. Edwin P. Elliott, Jr.
Reformation Educational Foundation

TABLE OF CONTENTS

Chapter One

DISILLUSIONED

Let no one be found among you who sacrifices his son or daughter in the fire, who practices divination or sorcery, interprets omens, engages in witchcraft, or casts spells, or who is a medium or spiritist or who consults the dead. Anyone who does these things is detestable to the Lord, and because of these detestable practices the Lord your God will drive out those nations before you. . . . The nations you will dispossess listen to those who practice sorcery or divination. But as for you, the Lord your God has not permitted you to do so.

Deuteronomy 18:10-12,14

It was early fall of '89, the beginning of a new school year. My daughter Lori, a freshman at Chicago Christian High School, came home with her usual workload. Among the pile of books she gently laid down on the kitchen table was a novel by Chaim Potok, entitled *The Chosen*. "What's this for?" I asked curiously.

"Oh, it's an assignment for English class."

"I'd like to read it, okay?"

"Go ahead, it's not due for a while," Lori replied, puzzled at my sudden interest in all her homework.

Over the next couple of weeks I read all 271 pages in my spare time. Potok was certainly a gifted writer (he'd have to be for me to continue reading). His story of two Jewish boys, their differences, and the way in which each was treated by his father was captivating.

While Potok's writing was excellent, there was something underlying the story that bothered me. It was the unmistakable theme that we should accept one another for what we believe and be able to incorporate that which is good or "true" from another religious background into our own beliefs, no matter how different the concept may be.

To the orthodox Jews, the Hasidim were considered "heretics." Reuven, the "orthodox Jew" in the story, was enthralled with "gematria"–a form of occult numerology which he learns from the father of his Hasidic friend, Dan. A couple of pages in the book were dedicated to showing the way in which gematria worked. This occult numerology is "a system of divination and magic based upon the concept that the universe is constructed in a mathematical pattern, and that all things may be expressed in numbers, which correspond to vibrations. By reducing names, words, birth dates, and birthplaces to numbers, a person's personality, destiny, and fortune may be determined" (*Harper's Encyclopedia of Mystical & Paranormal Experience,* Gulley, Rosemary Ellen, Harper SanFrancisco, 1991, pg. 409).

Taking a parental interest in his son's newly-found friend, and wanting to explain the differences between the two boys, Reuven's father sits down with him and recounts the history of Hasidism, a Jewish mystical religious movement founded in the eighteenth century by Israel ben Eliezer. Israel was a Ba'al Shem Tov–those Jews who were looked upon as saints. As he describes the beliefs of Hasidism, Reuven's father tells him that Israel didn't study the Talmud, but the Kabbalah (occult works of Jewish mysticism seen today in books of sorcery and witchcraft). He points out that in order to drive away evil spirits, the Ba'al Shem wrote magical amulets, prescribed medicines, performed wild dances, used black candles, screamed, etc. (pg. 100). Because the rabbis had forbidden the study of the Kabbalah, Israel studied it in secret. He was "opposed to any form of mechanical religion." "There was nothing new in what he taught," his father explains. "You will find it all in the Bible, Talmud, and Kabbalah" (pg. 103-104).

The fact that the three of these books were all lumped together bothered me. The fact that gematria was found in the Kabbalah and Reuven ended up learning and enjoying this occult activity bothered me.

Through Reuven's father, Potok also gives his readers a very subtle taste of the occult beliefs found in the Kabbalah:

> God is everywhere . . . and if it seems at times that He is
> hidden from us, it is only because we have not yet learned
> to seek Him correctly. Evil is like a hard shell. Within
> this shell is the spark of God, is goodness. How do we
> penetrate the shell? By sincere and honest prayer, by be-
> ing happy, and by loving all people . . . no man is so sin-
> ful that he cannot be purified by love and understanding
> (pg. 103).

It would be feasible that many students reading this would not see anything wrong with it. If they knew the occult teachings found in the Kabbalah, however, they would know precisely what it meant. The Kabbalah, which has spiritual links with Gnosticism, teaches man is divine and can attain godhood through various stages of occult meditation (techniques used to acquire an altered state of consciousness; see also Appendices D and H).

I wanted to find out more about Chaim Potok and his reasons for writing, so I made a trip to the public library. From reviews of Potok's works, it was clear he was bringing "to American fiction a feeling for biblical exegesis, Talmudic study, and the mystical writings of the Kabbala and the Zohar," the central work in the Kabbala (S. Lillian Kremer, *Dictionary of Literary Biography*, Volume 28, *Twentieth-Century American-Jewish Fiction Writers,* Gale Research Co., Detroit, MI, 1984, pg. 232).

In his work, *The Promise*, a sequel to *The Chosen*, (which I also read), Reuven's thirst for the occult deepens and Potok "turns his attention to Hasidic joy and enthusiasm . . . ." (*ibid.,* pg. 236). Potok's fascination with the occult is seen in even greater detail in his novel, *The Book of Lights.* Western Secular Humanism, Freudian concepts and Marxism also play an important role in Potok's writings. Upon encountering new ideas they were not brought up with, tension and conflict arise among his characters, creating interesting reading. But Potok seemed to be fusing together the best ideas from all these varying sources, teaching his readers a concept I was not thrilled with.

I could see why Mr. Carpenter, my daughter's English teacher, would like to use such a book. Yet, I couldn't help but wonder why he had selected *The Chosen*, which seemed more appropriate for a

college student than for a freshman in high school. Would he be
explaining the occult background of the Hasidim and of gematria?
Would he point out the passages that referred to God and other
ideas in the book which did not coincide with Biblical teaching
and compare them next to Scripture? Or would he leave that up to
the students themselves to discern?

Curiosity got the better of me so I decided to call the teacher. It
was a call I'll never forget. His reason for choosing Potok's book
was that he believed the kids could really relate to the boys in the
story, having been brought up in such "strict CRC" [Christian Reformed Church] homes. (Red flags went up.) It was a book, he
said, that had a universal theme, a theme which taught us to accept
one another for what we believe. (More red flags went up–it all
depended on what he meant by that statement.) I could agree, we
should respect and treat all equally, but I had a feeling something
was about to be compromised, and I had a good idea of what it
would be.

We got into a serious discussion then. I asked if he was going to
point out the occult numerology in the book. He didn't believe there
was any. I asked if he knew the book contained ideas that dealt
with the occult and mysticism. He didn't believe it did. I asked if
he knew where the Ba'al Shem Tov got his powers from. He sneered
and said, "He reminds me of John the Baptist."

"The Ba'al Shem Tov studied the Kabbalah, used magical amulets, things God condemns; his powers couldn't have come from
God," I reasoned, supporting my statement with Matthew 7:21-23.

His come-back took me by surprise. "How do *you* know you
have the corner on truth?" That did it. Now I was upset, but I kept
the conversation as light as I could. We talked about yoga. He
claimed he knew a man who had taken the religion out of yoga. We
discussed Western Secular Humanism. He believed Western Secular Humanism was in the world, not of the world. When I refuted
his statement, he came back with, "Well, maybe parts of it are."
Now I *was* confused. I shook my head realizing I was getting nowhere, and politely ended the conversation. Was he being purposely
annoying because he didn't like having a parent question him? Or
did he really mean what he had said? I just didn't know.

I gathered information concerning Potok, gematria, the Hasidim
and New Age/occult teachings which I presented to the principal
when I told her of my concerns about Mr. Carpenter. I needn't have

bothered. The principal backed him up without question. Though she accepted some of the material I suggested she read, I would never talk with her again.

In the meantime, Lori had come home with an alternative reading list from Mr. Carpenter. Included on his list were *A Wrinkle in Time* and *Many Waters* by Madeleine L'Engle. Also on the assignment list was a little note for me to research her works and to read a "good book on her perspective as a writer." This book was titled *Walking on Water, Reflections on Faith and Art*, a non-fiction work by L'Engle. I guessed the teacher thought it was an especially good book on faith. So I granted his request. I needed to know what beliefs he thought were good. As for Lori, I suggested she stick with reading *The Chosen*.

When I received *Walking on Water*, I read fervently. L'Engle began her gospel message with Carl Jung's concept of racial memory: ". . . his belief that when we are enabled to dip into the intuitive, subconscious self, we remember more than we know." She proceeded to claim: "One of the great sorrows which came to human beings when Adam and Eve left the Garden was the loss of memory, memory of all that God's children are meant to be" (pg. 19).

This was interesting theology. The way I had recalled it, Adam and Eve lost their perfect sinless state, not their memory. Quoting Jung didn't make for a very good start on a book of faith, as far as I was concerned. Carl Jung, whose works are considered to "have paved the way for the New Age,"[1] was a psychologist/occultist who was in contact with disembodied entities (demons) and even had his own Gnostic spirit-guide named Philemon. In his book, *Memories, Dreams, Reflections*, Jung describes his haunting encounter with these spirits whom he credits for having compelled him to write what "might have been said by Philemon" (Vintage Books, New York, 1965, pgs.190-191).

It was quite evident that I was about to be taken on a ride far away from what I had been taught. Oh well, I read on. (Thank goodness for those speed-reading classes I had taken; they were coming in handy). "For the world of the Bible, both the Old and New Testaments, is the world of Story, story which may be able to speak to us as a Word of God" (pg. 54). More interesting theology. The Bible *may* be able to speak to us as *a* Word of God? I thought the Bible *was the* Word of God.

On the same page, L'Engle quoted Clyde Kilby, former professor of English at Wheaton College:

> Meaninglessness inhibits fullness of life and is therefore equivalent to illness. Meaning makes a great many things endurable–perhaps everything. . . . it is not that "God" is a myth, but that myth is the revelation of a divine life in man. It is not we who invent myth; rather, it speaks to us as a Word of God (pg. 54).

This was a rather profound statement by a Christian college professor. But I sincerely believed it was a profoundly wrong one. How could myth speak to us as a Word of God? The Bible was uniquely inspired. Myths were not. To say myth could speak to us as a Word of God seemed to put myths on a par with Scripture. Maybe I was just misreading it.

I read on. "I'm particularly grateful that I was allowed to read my Bible as I read my other books, to read it as *story*, that story which is a revelation of truth" (pg. 60).

Now I was getting just a little bit irritated. The Bible was a revelation of the Truth, not just any "truth" found in a world of fairy tale, fantasy, and myth as L'Engle so convincingly put it. I still wasn't quite sure, though, how to take her freshly-painted portrait of the Bible.

My doubts about her "gospel" increased with L'Engle's candid statement, "I have talked with such a surprising number of people who have had to spend most of their lives unlearning what some well-meaning person taught them in Sunday School, that I'm glad I escaped!" (pg. 58). I wondered what those people had to unlearn. I continued reading, carefully and slowly. She talked of love, of being a Christian, of Jesus, and of God's love for us. How good her comments sounded, but in between all L'Engle's talk about love were unmistakable theological errors–errors so great I couldn't believe the teacher would actually think this was a good book on faith. L'Engle spoke about faith, but the question was–faith in what?

It wasn't the faith one receives after reading or hearing God's Word, because her focus was on one's self. Quoting H. A. Williams, she asserts, " 'Faith . . . consists in the awareness that I am more than I know' " (pg. 162). Faith in ourselves and our capacity to become "co-creators" with God, was her idea of faith. "I know," she insists, "that the human calling is co-creation with this power of love" (pg. 181). No wonder at the beginning of the book she had said we have to remember who we are.

I had read enough New Age literature to know what the term "co-creators with God" meant. Co-creator or co-creation is a person's psychic ability to create their own reality through use of various occult techniques and coming in contact with their Higher Self, or "God." Its use, from an occult perspective, is to transform the world into a state of perfection–what some call "evolution of consciousness."

Probably one of the best New Age works for understanding the occult meaning of co-creation is *The Book of Co-Creation, The Revelation*, by medium Barbara Marx Hubbard (The Foundation for Conscious Evolution, Sonoma, CA, 1993). A firm believer in the human ability to evolve into godhood, Hubbard writes: "I saw humanity, at the next turn of the spiral, gaining the powers of co-evolution and co-creation, just as all our religions told us we would. ('Co-creation' means conscious co-operation with the process, direction and purpose of evolution—the implicate order of the cosmos: God.)" (pg.42). "The Christ 'act'–to do the work that he did–is a new kind of resurrection and transformation at the dawn of the next stage of evolution" (pg. 56). We are at the stage of proto-Christs, just before the flowering of the new pattern; co-creative humans co-operating with other co-creative humans to co-evolve a New Earth (pg. 115). "To work with me to save the world, you must develop your own Christ-consciousness (love) and your own Christ-capacities . . . (psychic powers). Accelerate the co-creative revolution" (pg. 147). In this book, Hubbard channels "Christ" who tells her, *"You have the powers of Christ NOW. This is what I came to Earth to reveal. You can do what I do and even more shall you do. Take this seriously. It is true . . ."* (pg. 63, emphasis mine).

I knew I would have to be careful not to judge L'Engle's teachings by terms she used. Words can often be used by those who have absolutely no clue as to their occult meaning. L'Engle's definition of the word "co-creator," however, was certainly verified when she revealed she went to mystics to learn how to meditate. It was by using techniques of Eastern/occult meditation that L'Engle's character Meg, in her fictional novel, *A Wrinkle In Time*, would "tesser" as L'Engle called it. In *Walking on Water* L'Engle explains,

"For short distances, the people fly; for longer distances they sit and meditate and then (as Meg Murry would say) they *tesser*, and they are there" (pg. 85).

Tessering was a cute and clever name for the occult practice of astral projection or out-of-body experience. This wasn't fiction. It wasn't something L'Engle had created in her own imagination. It was a very real practice known throughout the occult world, and she was advocating its use both in her non-fiction and in her fiction.

L'Engle's idea of faith and the New Age concept of being co-creators could be readily identified in the following paragraphs:

> We were not meant to be any more restricted than Jesus was during his sojourn with us here on this earth. If we take seriously that during the time of his Incarnation he was truly man, truly human as we are, then anything he did in his life time is available to us, too.
>
> Am I suggesting that we really ought to be able to walk upon water? That there are (and not just in fantasies) easier and faster ways to travel than by jet or car? Yes, I am. There are too many stories of mystics being able to move hundreds of miles through the power of contemplation for us to be able to toss them aside (pg. 86).

For L'Engle, humility was a very important ingredient for a Christian, but there it was, that same "we're all becoming gods, but let's be humble about it" mentality found in so many New Age writings.

I finished reading *Walking on Water* in a few hours. Over the next couple of weeks I read it thoroughly five more times. I studied each paragraph and linked her ideas about faith, sin, the Bible, God, Jesus, and so on together from other parts of the book. As I read, I wrote them down putting them into separate categories. It was a good way to get a complete picture of what gospel she was proclaiming. My conclusion was: This book did more to obscure true Christian teachings than to reveal them. And, in the process, it promoted many occult teachings as well.

There was one passage in the book that made me shudder–it still does, every time I read it. To describe God's love for us, L'Engle quotes favorably from Dostoyevsky's book, *Crime and Punishment*, and informs her readers:

> Then Christ will say to us, "Come you as well, Come
> drunkards, come weaklings, come forth ye children of
> shame. . . ." And he will say to us, "Ye are swine, made
> in the Image of the Beast and with his mark, but come ye
> also." And the wise men and those of understanding will
> say, "O Lord, why do you receive these men?" And he
> will say, "This is why I receive them, O ye of under-
> standing, that not one of them believed himself to be
> worthy of this." And he will hold out his hands to us and
> we shall fall down before him . . . and we shall weep . . .
> and we shall understand all things! Then we shall under-
> stand all things! . . . Lord thy kingdom come (pg. 68-69).

I looked up Revelation 14:9-12 where God's angel proclaims:

> If anyone worships the beast and his image and receives
> his mark on the forehead or on the hand, he, too, will
> drink of the wine of God's fury, which has been poured
> full strength into the cup of his wrath. He will be tor-
> mented with burning sulfur in the presence of the holy
> angels and of the Lamb. And the smoke of their torment
> rises for ever and ever. There is no rest day or night for
> those who worship the beast and his image, or for any-
> one who receives the mark of his name. This calls for
> patient endurance on the part of the saints who obey God's
> commandments and remain faithful to Jesus.

"Wait a minute," I thought. We weren't made in The Image of
the Beast. We were made in God's image. For those who worship
the Beast and his image and take his mark, there is eternal damnation, not eternal life! Could it be L'Engle was saying everyone would
be saved? (I'd find out sometime later that that was exactly what
she was saying.)

Lori's teacher refused to talk with me about L'Engle's writings
even though he had suggested doing so after I researched them.
Dismayed at his refusal, I decided to talk with my pastor, thinking
he would be willing to read the book and possibly talk to the teacher,
especially since his children attended the same school. He had been

kind enough to compliment my concern when our children were reading Potok's book in a sermon, and had also tried to help my friend Brenda, whose sister was deeply involved in the occult.

My meeting with him didn't turn out the way I had expected. I was shocked when he quickly and valiantly defended L'Engle's belief that we can do anything Jesus did by going to mystics and learning to meditate with Scripture. For support he quoted 1 Corinthians 13:2 where the apostle Paul, using hyperbole, states, "faith can move mountains." I pleaded with him to take the book home and read the paragraph in its full context. He refused to do so. I read a couple of other disturbing sentences to him, but each time he quickly backed L'Engle up. I was deeply disappointed in his apparent lack of discernment and unwillingness to verify that what he was hearing was *not* taken out of context.

The next Sunday, I walked into the church library and sitting propped up on the shelf as if to say "READ ME!" was L'Engle's book, *Trailing Clouds of Glory, Spiritual Values in Children's Books*. I hoped this book would prove to be a better source of Biblical knowledge than *Walking on Water* since it was meant for children as well as adults. I signed it out and took it home. In between her short stories lay an abundance of false teachings:

> In Kenneth Grahame's *The Wind in the Willows*, when Mole and Rat had the numinous experience of their vision of the Great God Pan, that opened the gates of another heaven for me, too. And surely Christ was there (pg. 106).

I quietly whispered to myself, "I don't think so." The god Pan is known to be the "high god" in witchcraft. So it didn't surprise me at all that she lambasted churches for their condemnation of witchcraft and then supplied a small excerpt from Ursella Le Guin's book, *The Wizard of Earthsea,* which promoted sorcery (pgs. 62-63).

I guess one could believe Christ would be in the same heaven as the horned-god Pan if they believed God and Satan were One, or that all paths or religions lead to God. In the paragraph preceding the above statement, L'Engle states:

> I have a white china Buddha sitting on my desk, given

THEY CALLED IT CHRISTIAN

Woe to those who call evil good and good evil, who put
darkness for light and light for darkness, who put bitter
for sweet and sweet for bitter.

Isaiah 5:20

The days and weeks that followed were busy ones. Trips to the
library, reading, researching, long-distance phone calls and visiting bookstores took up more time than my family was used to.
McDonalds would sometimes take the place of a tasty roast, mashed
potatoes with gravy and fresh beans, and the laundry was done,
well, when it got done. As long as there were clothes to wear, I
didn't worry about it. I was getting behind in doing the housework,
but it just didn't seem important to me. After all, my house would
be standing long after I was gone and I figured if everyone pitched
in things would be fine. Unfortunately, they didn't take it quite as
well as I had hoped.

One morning I received a phone call from my former pastor
who had accepted a call to a church in Michigan. I considered him
a good friend and was glad to hear from him. Strangely, he asked
if I was all right, thinking I might be ready for a nervous breakdown. I asked where he got that idea from. He told me he had heard
some things that made him think that. When I inquired as to who
he had talked with, he refused to tell me. Two weeks later, I called
him back. After a little persuading, he admitted Rev. Erffmeyer
had called him to find out if I had ever caused trouble when he had

been the pastor of Orland Park Christian Reformed Church.

Not long after this, rumors were being circulated among church members that I was reading New Age and occult into everything and ready for a nervous breakdown. It hurt to know fellow members of the congregation could so willingly take part in gossip without bothering to find out the facts for themselves.

Sometime later, I received another phone call. This time it was Dave Larsen, an elder in our church and Dean of Students at Trinity Christian College (Palos Heights, IL). He asked if I would be willing to bring my concerns about L'Engle's works before the church education committee. I excitedly agreed to do so, but when he asked if I would abide by the committee's decision and be satisfied with their conclusions, my enthusiasm dwindled. I was beginning to sense a fierce defense for L'Engle, and an answer that was already decided upon.

Because of the rumors that had been spread, and my experiences with the teacher, principal and pastor, my confidence in the leadership of our church and Christian schools at this point was fading fast. I began to reconsider meeting with the education committee. How I wished there was someone I could trust to ask whether or not I should go through with it. Suddenly, Rev. Lutzer's name came to mind. Since he had co-authored *Satan's "Evangelistic Strategy" for this New Age,* maybe he had read L'Engle's works. I wanted, no, I *needed* someone to confirm I wasn't as crazy as people were making me out to be.

Fortunately, Lutzer was in his Chicago office when I called. He was very pleasant and easy to talk with. He hadn't heard of L'Engle before so I asked him if he had time to discuss some of the passages in her works. Whether he had the time, I'm not sure, but he made the time, for which I was grateful. His reaction was quick and tone of voice was filled with authority. I'll never forget his words: "Either your church has very little discernment or it is already New Age." He encouraged me to go ahead and present my findings before the education committee. I hesitated for a moment, then mentioned I was already being classified as a trouble-maker. "We're going to be called trouble-makers," he replied most assuredly.

Towards the end of our conversation, Lutzer provided me with the phone number of someone he thought might be of help. Her name was Samantha Smith, a researcher and public speaker on the

New Age. I made a long distance phone call to Colorado where she lived, quickly introduced myself and proceeded to describe what had happened with my daughter's teacher and my pastor. Her genuine interest and caring tone was the total opposite of what I had experienced from those within my own church and school. She informed me that she had received many calls about L'Engle's works and promised to send some information to me. I told her about all the research I had done, so we decided to exchange information whenever possible. That one simple phone call was the beginning of a long friendship and resulted in the writing of *Trojan Horse, How The New Age Movement Infiltrates the Church*, in the years ahead.

By this time I thought I had gathered enough documentation for anyone to be able to see the deception of L'Engle's works. I drafted a letter and recommendations for the committee to review, which I had been asked to do. I provided several of the most damaging quotes from her works and described her affiliation with the Cathedral of St. John the Divine in New York City. I talked with television personality, John Ankerberg, who considered this "Episcopal" church to be one of the "most occult places in the country." Other Christian authors and researchers also acknowledged the church as such. L'Engle not only attended there, she preached sermons from this church's pulpit and was also the librarian and author-in-residence. (Note: A detailed report of the New Age\occult background of St. John the Divine can be found in *Trojan Horse*, Scott, Brenda, & Smith, Samantha, Huntington House Publishers, Lafayette, Louisiana, 1993, pgs. 61-108.)

While one might consider her affiliation with St. John the Divine as "guilt by association," I hoped those on the education committee were smart enough to put all the information I provided them together, not just take one thing in and by itself. Definitions of New Age/occult terms were also provided along with a suggestion to watch the excellent Christian film exposing the New Age movement, GODS OF THE NEW AGE (a Rivershield Film Ltd. Production).

My sister-in-law Karen, who had been helping me with some of my research, was also concerned and kind enough to go with me to present the matter before the education committee. So far, she had been my sole supporter and together we had met with Rev. Erffmeyer on two different occasions. I was not in the habit of making speeches or confronting elders and teachers, so her presence and help were greatly appreciated.

At the meeting with the education committee, I explained that in *A Wrinkle in Time*, children are whisked off by what L'Engle calls "guardian angels," taken to a medium, and gaze into her crystal ball. This enables the children to receive information that helps them find their missing father. In an effort to reveal the deception taking place in this particular part of the book, I quoted from Leviticus 20:6, "I will set my face against the person who turns to mediums and spiritists to prostitute himself by following them, and I will cut him off from my people." I emphasized the fact that, therefore, angels sent by God would *never* bring children to a medium. I counted on the committee to see how terribly confusing and dangerous this could be for children, especially since L'Engle was portrayed as a "Christian" author.

"*A Wrinkle in Time* is just fiction," remarked one of the committee members who happened to be a Bible teacher.

"But, L'Engle is putting her *theology* through her fiction," I tried to explain.

I read from *Trailing Clouds of Glory* where L'Engle states: "All my life through stories, those I read, and those I write, I have been building (intuitively, rather than consciously), a theology . . . the word about God. . . ."

Rolling his eyes in disbelief, the Bible teacher muttered, "You mean to tell me you're saying L'Engle is putting a theology in her fiction?"

Noting his great interest, I simply said, "yes" and let it go.

Much more could have been said about this book, which I fondly re-titled, *A Wrinkle in Theology*, but time was spent on describing New Age thought since the committee members seemed to have very little knowledge about it. I was also worried that if I presented too much information, they'd simply close their minds to anything I had to say.

Both Karen and I now spoke to them of our concern about *Trailing Clouds of Glory.* Dave Larson argued that many missionaries come back from foreign places with artifacts like Buddhas and place them in their homes. I wondered if he was just saying that in defense or if he really knew this for fact. I couldn't fathom missionaries wanting an idol for display in their homes. And even if they did have one, I was pretty certain they wouldn't claim it could be a better Christ figure than the crucifix.

It was becoming rather obvious that we were definitely not on the committee's most popular list. L'Engle had it hands down, as did Mary Beth Bootsma, our church librarian and wife of the president of Trinity Christian College. Mary Beth was invited to our meeting since she, we found out, was the one ordering L'Engle's works for our church library. Now when she talked, the education committee listened. After all, we were just a pair of housewives, what did we know? Her defense of L'Engle was intimidating, despite the fact she didn't have any documentation to support her statements and didn't seem to know anything about the New Age Movement.

We left the meeting discouraged, but hoped the material we handed out would convince them of the seriousness of the issue.

Decision of the Church Education Committee

Several weeks passed before we finally received a copy of a letter addressed to the elders from the education committee (dated January 16, 1990). Eagerly, I read the committee's recommendations:

> Only materials which critically evaluate the occult and the New Age Movement from a Christian perspective have a place in the church library. Further, it is the committee's judgment that this is the library's current practice.

Their grounds for this were: "Occult beliefs and practices are condemned in Scripture and the confessions" and that "Both in the library's statement of purpose and material selection process, care is given to evaluate all materials from a Christian perspective."

Sounded good so far, until I read point 2:

> It is the committee's judgment that the writings of Madeleine L'Engle do not promote occult beliefs or practices and are not part of the New Age Movement. Rather, her writings contain a strong, underlying, Christian message. Therefore, there is no reason to remove them from the church library.

My mouth dropped. A strong, underlying, Christian message? I could agree her message was hidden underneath and lying, but it was definitely *not* Christian. What were their grounds for this unbelievable conclusion? I continued reading:

    a. L'Engle professes her faith in Jesus Christ as Savior.
    b. Her works have been endorsed by many evangelical Christians, reviewed in evangelical periodicals such as *Christianity Today* and *The Banner* [the CRC's "official" magazine-CVK], housed in a special collection at the Wheaton College library, and included in reading lists developed by Christians for children.
    c. Although her works contain elements of fantasy, imagery, and symbolism, this is not sufficient evidence to link her with the New Age Movement. Because the New Age Movement is eclectic in nature, believing everything and nothing as it draws from many sources, there is no evidence beyond individual interpretation to link L'Engle to the New Age Movement. The writings cited by Claris and Karen at our meeting and in the printed materials can be understood differently than their particular interpretation. It is our judgment that, taken as a whole and in context, the works of L'Engle can be understood and appreciated in a positive light.

This was a nightmare. I had no idea to what extent L'Engle was known within the Christian community. I, personally, had never heard of her before. Questions raced through my mind. Did they understand that just because someone claims Jesus is her Savior it doesn't necessarily means she is a Christian? Didn't what she believed concerning Jesus Christ count? Many leaders in the New Age Movement claim to be Christians and say Jesus is their Savior. Did the committee know that? I had not yet come across L'Engle's statement of faith, but I was determined to find out where she said this and in what context it was used.

Then it hit me. How could so many Christians be promoting her literature as Christian? Could we have been so utterly wrong in our assessment of L'Engle's writings? We didn't believe so, and if we weren't, we couldn't begin to fathom the outcomes of what this meant for thousands in Christian communities around the country.

I couldn't understand why the education committee had denied L'Engle promoted occult beliefs and practices in her works. There simply was no question about it. In the *Encyclopedia of Children's Literature Review* I found at the public library, many writers supported our assessment. I had given the information to Dave Larsen. Hadn't he shared it with the other members? Had he even bothered to read it?

There was yet another problem. Reading over point c, I realized the elders would think all we had dealt with were L'Engle's fictional novels. We had supplied them with much more–factual documentation and many quotes from her non-fiction. Then again, what did the committee mean by their statement, ". . . there is no evidence beyond individual interpretation to link L'Engle to the New Age movement"? Didn't it matter if some people saw her writings as anti-Christian? Shouldn't it be of any serious concern? Or should everyone just decide for themselves what interpretation was right or wrong?

While the NAM draws from many sources, it does have its own core set of identifiable beliefs by which one can evaluate and determine if a person's teachings coincide with New Age thought. To say it was simply a matter of interpretation was to say no one could know what she was teaching. But an author writes with a purpose–a theme he or she wants to get across to their readers. What good would a book be if it was so confusing both Christians and occultists could claim it belonged in their camp? There was only one "good" thing I could think of, deception.

I felt the letter was misleading and might very well have been written so purposefully. Time would tell. I turned to the next page which contained a letter from the church librarian describing the purpose and function of the church library. The library's primary purpose was to "aid in developing a consciousness toward Christian faith and growth." Under the selection criteria was the question, "Is the book true to biblical teachings and the doctrinal position of our church?" Karen and I gathered this meant L'Engle's works were considered Biblically sound, an idea that alarmed both of us tremendously.

A few days later, I received a letter from the clerk of the church council (council is made up of the pastors, elders and deacons). It thanked us for the concern we had for our children and the reading

materials that were available to them. Though the full council had
never met with us, the elders "unanimously approved of the Education Committee's recommendation" (letter dated 1-24-90).
Sometime later, I talked with an elder who informed me that none
of the elders, with the exception of those on the education committee, were given the information we had provided. The council had
supported the committee's decision without knowing what they were
defending.

Upset by the decisions of both the education committee and elders, we wrote a rather long letter to the elders with additional
documentation linking both L'Engle and her writings to the NAM
and numerous quotes from her non-fiction. In our letter, we asked
for a meeting with them to discuss L'Engle's works. This we were
granted. We also asked for a list of references read by the committee and biblical back-up for their decision. This we never would
receive.

Chapter Three

DEFENDING THE WRONG CHRIST

Jesus answered, "I am the way and the truth and the life.
No one comes to the Father except through me. If you
really knew me, you would know my Father as well."
John 14:6-7a

There is no limit to the ways in which Christ can speak
to us, though for the Christian he speaks first and most
clearly through Jesus of Nazareth.
Madeleine L'Engle, *A Stone for a Pillow*, pg. 169

When an author promotes beliefs and practices God forbids, it seemed perfectly logical to conclude their beliefs concerning God, Jesus Christ, the Holy Spirit, etc. would no doubt be different from what Scripture teaches. *A Stone for a Pillow*, the book the education committee used to claim L'Engle was a Christian author, was now on my priority list. I ordered it from Family BookStores and anxiously waited for its arrival. Hopefully, this book would reveal whether L'Engle believed Jesus was her Savior from sin, or if He merely showed the way to what we all could become.

In the meantime, I continued to research the occult, the New Age Movement, and L'Engle. By this time, I was receiving several New Age magazines and had acquired a number of books by New Age authors as well as an assorted array of occult books dealing with sorcery, witchcraft, feminism, psychic powers, mysticism, etc. I had already read a few Christian books exposing New Age beliefs and practices, but I was compelled to look at it from both sides myself. Comparing what L'Engle taught both to Scripture and to the occult, one could readily see what category her works fell into. There were no ifs, ands, or buts about it.

I read the two books that followed *A Wrinkle in Time* in what is called L'Engle's "Time Trilogy." Combined with *Wrinkle, A Wind in the Door* and *A Swiftly Tilting Planet* unveil L'Engle's knowledge and approval of the occult as the children in her novels meet with additional spirit guides (demons) and develop their psychic abilities which are said to be "God's gift" (*A Swiftly Tilting Planet*, pg. 130). It literally sent chills down my spine when I read the childrens' spirit guide, who called himself their "Teacher," bowed down to their pet snake, Louise the Larger, and announced, "She is a colleague of mine. . . . She is a Teacher" (*A Wind in the Door*, pg. 66). You didn't have to read New Age/occult material to know who those "Teachers" worked for.

As I have already stated, this was not simply fiction. The book, *H. P. Blavatsky and The Secret Doctrine*, edited by Virginia Hanson, (The Theosophical Publishing House, Wheaton, IL, 1988, pgs. 6-15) is one occult source I read which made perfectly clear L'Engle's definition and portrayal of these "Teachers" coincided precisely with New Age occultism. It appeared L'Engle's writings were purposefully written to subtly and slowly introduce her readers to the world of the occult, and at the same time, discredit the authority of the Bible.

By the end of *A Swiftly Tilting Planet*, L'Engle had introduced her reading fans to this domain of darkness in a most unique fashion. Scrying (a form of divination), mediumship, astral projection (out-of-body experience), clairvoyance, communication with the dead, the use of runes (letters of a secret magical alphabet–used in magic and divination), were just a few of the occult practices seen throughout her works and given the false portrayal of being Christian.

Curious now as to what happened in *Many Waters*, the other novel suggested by my daughter's teacher, I went to the store and bought a copy. It wasn't much better. By sending her characters back in time to the backdrop of Genesis, L'Engle re-tells (and distorts) the Biblical account of Noah and the flood. In the process, she undermines the unique inspiration of God's Word, and filters in a feminist touch (pgs. 168-169).

You could always find a sermon beneath the story. Throughout the novel, the children encounter spiritual, angelic beings called seraphim which are good, and nephilim, the threatening fallen angels. Both have the power to transform themselves into varying creatures, and vice-versa. L'Engle's names for these beings were so strange and different, I wondered where she might have gotten them. After supper, I went to the library hoping to find out why L'Engle compared the rape of Leda by the mythical god Zeus, with God, in the form of Gabriel, having intercourse with Mary (resulting in Christ's birth).[1] When I walked into the library, I noticed a book entitled, *The Dictionary of Angels*, by Gustav Davidson propped up on top of a bookcase (Macmillan Inc., New York, 1967). Instinctively, I picked it up and searched for the name, Rofocale, a mosquito in the story. Here was the description given:

> Rofocale—more usually called Lucifuge Rofocale, prime minister in the infernal regions, according to the *Grand Grimore*. Rofocale has control over all the wealth and treasures of the world. His subordinate is Baal (a king, ruling in the east). Two other subordinates are Agare (one of the dukes in Hell and formerly of the angelic order of virtues) and Marbas (pg. 246).

I knew the *Grand Grimore* was a textbook on magic. I looked up another character, Eblis, the dragon\lizard:

> Eblis—in Persian and Arabic lore, Eblis is the equivalent of the Christian Satan. As an angel in good standing he was once treasurer of the heavenly Paradise. . . . There is a tradition that the great grandson of Eblis was taught by Mohammed certain *suras* of the Koran (pg. 101).

These were names of demons! I paged through to find the name of Aariel, a seraphim:

> Aariel ("lion of God")—the name of an angel found inscribed on an Ophitic (gnostic) amulet alongside the name of the god Ialdabaoth (q.v.), [Rf. Bonner, *Studies in Magical Amulets*] (pg. 1).

L'Engle may think Aariel is a seraphim (good angel), but this was no more an angel than was Rofocale or Eblis!

I found many more names though, not all of them, but I didn't need any more. I was thoroughly astonished at what I was reading.

In *Many Waters*, L'Engle skillfully intertwined her gospel message:

> There seemed a healing in the calling of their names.
>
> Although the circle of seraphim was outside that of the nephilim, when they spread their great wings to the fullest span the wing tips touched.
>
> Likewise, the nephilim raised their wings, turning so that they faced the seraphim, and the glory of their wings brushed.
>
> "Brothers," Alarid said. "You are still our brothers" (pg. 126).

"Angels" and "fallen angels" were depicted as brothers. Was I wrong to think L'Engle meant God and His angels and Satan and his host of demons would eventually be reconciled? I'd find out when I received *A Stone for a Pillow.*

As I previously mentioned, I firmly believed anyone who could reflect such a positive view of occult beliefs and practices could not possibly believe in the same God I grew to know and love from the Bible–and, yes, even from those teachers in Sunday School!

Did L'Engle's affirmation that Jesus was her Savior mean she believed He died in her place in order that she might be saved from sin?

What I found brought tears to my eyes. Not three pages into the book, L'Engle began her feminist-induced assault on God the Father and Jesus' death as a sacrificial payment for sin, preparing her readers to accept a different Christ:

> Did Jesus have to come and get crucified, because only if he died in agony could this bad-tempered father forgive his other children?
>
> We got into a good discussion, then. The teen-agers did not really like their cartoon god. They were ready and

willing to hear *another point of view*. We talked about
astrophysics and particle physics and the interdependence
of all Creation. But I suspect there may have been in their
minds a lingering shadow of God as a cold and unforgiv-
ing judge (pg. 12, emphasis mine).

Bad-tempered father? Cartoon god (with a little g)? Is that what
she thought of the righteous and just God of Scripture? Whatever
happened to Romans 2 and all the many other texts throughout the
Bible that speak of God's righteous judgment? L'Engle also neglected to mention I John 4:10: "This is love; not that we loved
God, but that he loved us and sent his Son as an atoning sacrifice
for our sins." And for some reason, the fact that Jesus willingly
laid down his life of his own accord (John 10:17-18) was also left
out.   I wondered if L'Engle just couldn't quite fit that in with her
own theology, so she decided to throw those texts out.

Granted, there may be some "pastors" preaching hell-fire and
damnation without ever mentioning God's abundant love and complete forgiveness of sins through faith in Jesus Christ and His atoning sacrifice on the cross. This would confuse parishioners who
don't test what they hear, into believing God is a "cold and unfor-
giving judge." But the picture L'Engle left her readers with was
incomplete as well. In fact, it was the totally opposite picture. For
L'Engle, God was just a God of love, no wrath, no condemnation.
Neither picture is accurate. For while God is just, he is also com-
passionate and forgiving–the only requirement being that we repent and believe in His Son, in who He is and what He did for us
(John 3:16, Acts 2:38-39, 3:17-23, Hebrews 9:27-28, 10, etc.).
Maybe we can't understand it, but we'd better believe it!

It was obvious L'Engle wanted those teenagers and her readers
to believe in her own version of "God." That being the case, her
Jesus *had* to be another Jesus and her gospel, a "different gospel"
(2 Corinthians 11:4). I kept reading, searching for clues as to what
she believed concerning Jesus Christ, when I came upon this disheartening passage:

In a vain attempt to make people see God as an avenging
judge, theologians have even altered the meaning of
words. Atonement, for instance. A bad word, if taken
forensically.

A young friend said to me during Holy Week, "I cannot cope with the atonement."

Neither can I, if the atonement is thought of forensically. In forensic terms, the atonement means that Jesus had to die for us in order to atone for all our awful sins, so that God could forgive us. In forensic terms, it means that God cannot forgive us unless Jesus is crucified and by this sacrifice atones for all our wrongdoing.

But that is not what the word means! I went to an etymological dictionary and looked it up. It means exactly what it says, at-one-ment. I double-checked it in a second dictionary. There is nothing about crime and punishment in the makeup of that word. It simply means to be at one with God. Jesus on the cross was so at-one with God that death died there on Golgotha, and was followed by the glorious celebration of the Resurrection (pg. 23).

This was an unmistakable denial of the substitutionary, sacrificial atonement, and this was the book our church librarian, education committee and elders had claimed presented a strong, Christian message? My stomach turned. L'Engle had sliced out the heart of the gospel, added in her own piece of apple pie topped with whipped cream, and delicately seasoned it with a pinch of rat poison. How sweet it is to think God won't punish those who deny His Son and His ultimate sacrifice for our sins. But how deadly that thought is! Snow White eating the poisoned apple comes to mind.

Reading Shirley MacLaine and other New Age/occult authors, I recognized the redefinition of the substitutionary atonement to mean at-one-ment, or union with God (reaching a state of godhood). But I had to make sure that's where L'Engle was taking her readers. Since the atonement was redefined, it necessarily followed she would also redefine sin, judgment, heaven, hell, the second coming, Jesus Christ, etc.

I read a few more sentences and there was the first one. "And what is sin?" L'Engle asks her readers. "It is not frivolous to say that sin is discourtesy. . . . Sin, then, is discourtesy pushed to an extreme, and discourtesy is lack of at-one-ment" (pg. 23). Sin is not discourtesy, it's disobedience–disobedience to God. True, sin will estrange you from God if you don't ask for forgiveness, but that is the *result* of sin, not sin itself. A subtle, but very important difference. In the channeled work, *A Course of Miracles*, sin is seen as mistakes we make because of our lack of being at-one with God. In the *Manual for Teachers*, it concludes:

> For true perception is a remedy with many names. Forgiveness, salvation, Atonement, true perception, all are one. They are the one beginning, with the end to lead to Oneness far beyond themselves. True perception is the means by which the world is saved from sin, for sin does not exist (pg. 81).

> The name of Jesus is the name of one who was a man but saw the face of Christ in all his brothers and remembered God. So he became identified with Christ, a man no longer, but at one with God. Jesus became what all of you must be (pg. 83).

So far, L'Engle's concepts fit pretty well into the New Age category. I also remembered reading her attempt at debunking the Biblical truth that sin was inherited from Adam in *Walking on Water*: "When we do wrong we try to fool ourselves (and others) that it is because our actions and reactions have been coded into our genetic pattern at the moment of conception" (pg. 180).

L'Engle's novel, *A Ring of Endless Light*, made her belief unmistakable:

> Adam thus bequeathed us his death, not his sin. . . . We do not inherit the sins of our fathers, even though we may be made to endure their punishment. Guilt cannot be transmitted. We are linked to Adam only by his memory, which becomes our own, and by his death, which foreshadows our own. Not by his sin (pg. 80).

Scripture is clear: "Therefore, just as sin entered the world through one man, and death through sin, and in this way death came to all men, because all sinned. . . ." (Romans 5:12).

Bits and pieces put together from her other works helped to fuse together a solid picture of where L'Engle was truly coming from.

Now I was coming upon another piece to the puzzle. In chapter three of *A Stone for a Pillow*, the last judgment was being redefined. No longer was it seen as a time when God poured out His wrath against those who denied His Son and persecuted believers. No, God's judgment was a time of "celebration" for the whole world to rejoice in: "For God's judgment is atonement, at-one-ment, making us one with the Lord of love," L'Engle claimed (pgs. 61-62). She presented quite a different picture than Jesus did in Matthew 24, or that seen in 2 Thessalonians 1:6-10, 2 Peter 2 and 3, Jude 1, Revelation 1:7, and chapters 14-19.

Though L'Engle's puzzle pieces didn't fit into Scripture, they surely came together in the demon-channeled book, *A Course in Miracles*, where the Last Judgment is seen as "a final healing rather than a meting out of punishment" (Volume One, pg. 30). In *A Course, the Manual for Teachers* states: "Salvation is God's justice. . . . God's Judgment is His justice. Onto this,–a Judgment wholly lacking in condemnation; an evaluation based entirely on love" (*ibid.,* pg. 47). L'Engle's philosophy was right on target.

Of course, if there was not going to be a final and just judgment of wrath, it meant all would be saved. Forty pages further into the book, I read, "The judgment of God is the judgment of love, not of power plays or vindication or hate. The Second Coming is the redemption of the entire cosmos, not just one small planet. . . . All will be redeemed in God's fullness of time, all, not just the small portion of the population who have been given the grace to know and accept Christ" (pg. 117). Sewing up all the loose threads in L'Engle's gospel (including ideas from her other books), I was seeing a very clever way in which to say humanity will eventually reach a state of perfection–godhood.

While giving the appearance of being so benevolently tolerant, L'Engle had absolutely no tolerance for any Christian or group of Christians who claimed to know *the* truth. "Are we looking for evidence that our Christian group is *the* group, with *the* truth, or are we looking for at-one-ment?" she asks in such a way that one could easily be made to feel guilty for defending her faith (pg. 67).

L'Engle wasn't squabbling about minor insignificant issues here. No, there was much more behind that statement than met the eye. She wasn't just talking about issues being disputed between various "Christian" denominations. She was implying that "truths" found in all the different religions were so many paths to find one's way to God. How else could all people be saved without Jesus having to die for their sins? Her beliefs became clearer in the pages ahead.

Her insistence that we should "shed our idea of God as being someone Out There, separate from all that has been made, and begin instead to think of God within all Creation, every galaxy every quantum every human being. . . ." revealed her interest in Eastern mysticism. On the next page, she made a rather peculiar remark, "If God created everything, if the Word called all things into being, all people are part of God's loving concern. The incarnation was not only for the Jews. Or the Christians. Christ did not come to save Christians, but to save sinners" (pgs. 86-87).

Of course, God loved what he had made. I could agree with the first part of what she said. But on the second, she was dead wrong. Mary called her son Jesus because he would "save *his* people from their sins" (Matthew 1:21, emphasis mine). When the jailer asked Paul and Silas, "Sirs, what must I do to be saved?"–what was their answer? " 'Believe in the Lord Jesus, and you will be saved–you and your household' " (Acts 16:31). Weren't both Jews and Gentiles called Christians if they accepted Christ as their Saviour? Yes, they were (Acts 11:26). A better statement for L'Engle to make would have been, "Christ came to save those sinners who would come to believe in Him–Christians."

I took offense when I read, "It's seductively pleasant to think that God loves Christians better than Buddhists or Hindus." Her portrayal of Christians as those "who feel they can't be happy in heaven unless they're watching the tortures of the damned in hell" didn't do much for me either (pg. 87). Christians, at least the ones I know, don't rejoice at the thought of others suffering eternal separation from God. Why else would they bother to tell people about Christ, and in the process, be ridiculed and mocked–even by this very author? That "minority, small, but growing," who disagree with L'Engle's old, yet newly spun gospel, are cast into the mold of being holier-than-thou, bigoted, frightened people who see the devil in everything. It wasn't hard to reason L'Engle would do this since, as she points out in many of her works and lectures, there is always someone who sees the occult in her works (I wonder why), and even the devil in her:

The people who are looking to see if they can accuse

someone of being in league with the Devil frighten
me. . . . There aren't many of them, yet, but I met or heard
one or two every place I went. They are powerful, and
they claim to be Christians, to be even better Christians
than those of us who are looking for Christ, for love,
rather than Satan (pg. 68).

I wondered if the readers of this book would see through this
veil of deception. Would they understand Christians tell people to
repent and believe because of their love for Christ and His com-
mission for them to do so, not because they are so much better than
everyone else? Would they know there is indeed a devil, masquer-
ading as an angel of light, who was a liar and murderer from the
beginning, who would like nothing more than for people to think
Christians are the ones in league with the devil (2 Corinthians 11:14,
John 8:44)?

I was burning with anger at the mockery of my God who had
been dubbed a tribal, cartoon, bad-tempered, patriarchal "god"
throughout this book, yet I felt sorry for L'Engle who had been just
as deceived as Eve. It was obvious she had made a deliberate choice
not to believe God's Word. Her thoughts on the Bible became a
little more explicit now in *A Stone for a Pillow*:

That limited literalism which demands that the Bible's
poetry and story and drama and parable be taken as factual history is one of Satan's cleverest devices (pg. 81).

Alas, Lucifer, how plausible you can be, confusing us
into thinking that to speak of the Bible as myth is blasphemy. One definition of myth in the dictionary is parable. Jesus taught by telling parables. Did Jesus lie? Blaspheme? (pg. 82).

While it is true that Jesus sometimes taught in parables, the whole
Bible is not a parable. If the recounting of what took place thousands of years ago, including the birth, death and resurrection of
Jesus Christ is not factual history, then there is no Christianity. It
is God who would want us to think that the Bible accurately recorded history. It is God who foresaw that some will turn away
from sound doctrine and turn aside to myths (see I Timothy 3).

L'Engle had switched what God would have us believe, to what Satan would have us believe.

This was pure confusion for the reader and a detestable scorn of God Himself. I still hadn't come across the passage where she claimed Jesus Christ as her Savior, but I had a feeling it was coming soon after reading this interesting admission:

> Two young women who run a Christian bookstore in the Midwest wrote me that they were concerned as to whether or not I accept Christ as my personal Saviour. Even when I assured them that I do, they were not at all convinced that I was one of them. And perhaps the Christ I accept, by the grace of the Holy Spirit, is different from the Christ they want me to accept. But God made us all in our glorious complexity and differences; we are not meant to come off the assembly line alike, each Christian a plastic copy of every other Christian (pg. 90).

Then, there it was, L'Engle's tongue-in-cheek statement of faith:

> I accept Christ as my personal Saviour only because of this loving, unmerited gift of the Spirit. Christ within me and within all of Creation. . . . Through the power and love of this Spirit, I accept Jesus as my Saviour, the light of my life, and the light of the world (pg. 91).

This was definitely an affirmation that she accepted Jesus or Christ as her personal Savior, but Savior from what? She had already denied that Jesus was our mediator; that He died in order to save us from our sins and the wrath of God. Her words were chosen well–"I believe that God loved us so much that he came to us as a human being to show us his love" (pg. 91). Jesus helped many people. He taught them what love was, but the most important aspect of Jesus' love, the ultimate kind of love, the sacrifice of one's life for another, she denied.

L'Engle's need to advise her readers that God was not "Out There" but "in and part of all creation" (pg. 98), and that Christ was "within all of Creation" was more an affirmation of panentheism, a kissin' cousin to pantheism (all is God) rather than Christianity. Her vigorous defense of Pierre Teilhard de Chardin (pg. 74-75), considered a "patron saint of the New Age Movement," and the endorsement of the New Age labeled book, *The Tao of Physics*, by New Age physicist Fritjov Capra, as well as Eastern mysticism (pgs. 191-192), gave her mixed bouquet of beliefs away.

I could see how easily it would be for one who didn't know and/or believe the Bible to think this book presented a strong "Christian" message. But, there was much more to L'Engle's gospel that could not be discounted. Her words were contradictory, confusing, and the ridiculing worsened:

> As to who goes to heaven, there seems to be considerable division. Some churches are holding adamantly to a heaven for Christians only. Other churches are asking questions, wondering if this judgmental (if not forensic) attitude toward heaven is true to the love of God. . . . For me, Gandhi is a Christ figure. I'll be perfectly happy to go wherever he goes. If you want to call that hell, that's your problem (pg. 166).

Of course, since L'Engle makes it known that she doesn't believe in a literal heaven and hell (pg. 165), it really didn't matter who went where, because no one would really go anywhere, anyhow.

If guru Gandhi could be a Christ figure to her, if Buddha could be a better Christ figure to her (as seen in *Trailing Clouds of Glory*), what Christ was she talking about?

The next sentence told me all I needed to know: "There is no limit to the ways in which Christ can speak to us, though for the Christian he speaks first and most clearly through Jesus of Nazareth" (pg. 169).

I shook my head. "No," Ms. L'Engle, I thought, "Christ *is* Jesus of Nazareth, He doesn't speak *through* Him, nor does he speak through Buddha, Saint Shinran, or Attila the Hun!" L'Engle cushioned her blasphemous statement with "Indeed, my icons would be idols if they did not lead me to follow more closely in Jesus' steps" (pg. 169). For me, it was quite clear that L'Engle was not following more closely in Jesus' steps, at least, not the Jesus I had learned about from the Bible. Indeed, her icons *were* idols.

This "Jesus" L'Engle spoke of had an aspect other than what was taught in Scripture. She suggests to her readers: "When I am informed that Jesus of Nazareth was exactly like us except sinless, I block. If he was sinless he wasn't exactly like us. That makes no sense. . . . I want Jesus to be like us because he is God's show and tell, and too much dogma obscures rather than reveals the likeness" (pg. 176).

No wonder L'Engle didn't like too much dogma or doctrine–she wanted to teach something other than what God already made clear to us. Jesus was "without sin; "he "committed no sin" (Hebrews 4:15, 1 Peter 2:22). If Jesus were a sinner, He wouldn't have had the authority to forgive sins (Matthew 9:6) or been able to save us from our sins.

How mighty generous it sounded of L'Engle to include everyone into heaven. And oh, what a guilt trip she was giving those who believed God's Word. L'Engle even had a name for those who dared to accept the notion that God would condemn anyone, "the echthroi," the Greek word for enemy (pgs. 215-216).

L'Engle's assertion that "666 will return to God" (pg. 195) and that "if in the fullness of God's time, Lucifer and Michael are again friends, there will be no more echthroi" (pg. 239), supported what had been said in *Many Waters*. I hadn't just been reading more into her book of fiction than what was there.

I read the book in its entirety and straightway brought it over to Karen. I read the first few pages out loud to her. She wept. I read L'Engle's denial of the substitutionary atonement. Both of us now had tears in our eyes.

What I've mentioned here is only a taste of L'Engle's perversion of the gospel. Her feminist agenda was also promoted in the book. She claims God is adrogynus–both female and male (a Gnostic/Eastern idea based on the concept of the yin-yang–the union of opposites) and put in a good word for the goddesses Ishtar, Astaroth and Diana (pgs. 182-183). (This, and other more detailed information can be found in Appendices G & H.)

Her gospel was a strange and foreign one. Her Jesus was a different Jesus; her spirit, "a different spirit." I no longer had any doubts in my mind concerning L'Engle's beliefs, and the more of her non-fiction I read, the more convinced I became.

A few weeks later, I would find *The Irrational Season* in our church library. On page 88, I came across another sarcastic gem that added credence to her denial of Christ's sacrifice for us. L'Engle explained that one of her students suffered all her life because her Church taught her she was "born so sinful that the only way the wrath of God the Father could be appeased enough for him to forgive all her horrible sinfulness was for God the Son to die in agony on the cross." L'Engle continued this poor student's story on pages 96-97:

> My young friend who was taught that she was so sinful the only way an angry God could be persuaded to forgive her was by Jesus dying for her, was also taught that part of the joy of the blessed in heaven is watching the torture of the damned in hell. A strange idea of joy. . . . I know a number of highly sensitive and intelligent people in my own community who consider as a heresy my faith that God's loving concern for his creation will outlast all our willfulness and pride. *No matter how many eons it takes, he will not rest until all of creation, including Satan, is reconciled to him. . . .* (emphasis mine).

I had a hard time believing this student was taught that "the blessed" enjoyed watching those being tortured in hell," but L'Engle was certainly right about one thing, I did consider her faith as heresy.

In the days ahead, I bought as many non-fiction works as I could. *A Circle of Quiet, And it was Good, Sold into Egypt, Two-Part Invention* and others that I would read in the future, all pointed to a god who was both male and female, good and evil, God and Satan—a "Christ" who was an energy force found in all of us who would eventually evolve us into godhood. (You don't have to take my word for it. In fact, I wouldn't want you to. Read her works yourself if you can't believe this is what was being defended as "Christian" to our children as well as to adults.)

I looked up interviews with L'Engle and heard them on radio and television. I read many of her articles and reviews of her works as well as reviews she had given other authors and works such as Gary Zukav and his New Age labeled book, *Dancing of the Wu Li Masters.* In her review of this book, L'Engle writes: "*It is easy to tell from the books which have spoken most deeply to me where my own mind is turning at the moment*" (*Commonweal,* Volume 109, Issue 21, 12-3-82, pg. 666, emphasis mine). It was also easy for me to tell where her mind was and what she believed from her endorsement of the book.

I found that L'Engle endorsed several New Age authors and they endorsed her. There was no doubt L'Engle was deeply influenced by the New Age Movement and the occult, even though she fervently and repeatedly denied so in her works. Why she denied it, and to this day still does, is anybody's guess. I knew one thing though: L'Engle wholeheartedly believed occult ideas and practices condemned by God were to be desired and practiced.

Footnotes

1. This is seen in L'Engle's non-fiction work, *A Cry Like a Bell*, Harold Shaw Publishers, 1987, Wheaton, IL, pg. 47).

Chapter Four

AN EARNEST APPEAL

Salvation is found in no one else, for there is no other
name under heaven given to men by which we must be
saved.

Acts 4:12

Gandhi said, "Religions are different roads converging
upon the same point. What does it matter that we take
different roads as long as we reach the same goal?". . . .
God, unlike some organized religions, does not discrimi-
nate. As long as you reach out to Her, She will go the
better part of the way to meet you. There are an infinite
number of roads to reach God. . . .

M. Scott Peck,
Further Along the Road Less Traveled, pg. 155

I was nervously, yet eagerly awaiting the upcoming meeting with
the elders. With *A Stone for a Pillow* in hand, I felt confident the
elders would recoil in disgust when I read from the book, see the
deception of L'Engle's works, and wisely decide to pull the books
from the church library. But on March 16, 1990, the Sunday prior
to our meeting, once again something happened to shake my confidence in our leadership. While preaching a sermon entitled, "Live
a Life of Love," our co-pastor, Rev. Cornelius (Corky) De Boer,
quoted glowingly from M. Scott Peck's book, *The Road Less Traveled*, without so much as a hint that there was anything wrong with
Peck's misguided, self-produced theology.

I wasn't upset that De Boer had quoted from a different source other than the Bible. That wasn't the point. It was the way in which he quoted from the book, as if it was a most compatible friend to Scripture. How many people in the pews would think that book might be a good source to read? Worse yet, how many would consider it to be a Christian book? Peck claims to be a Christian, as does L'Engle.

While Peck may have some interesting insights into people's psychotic behavior, he picks and chooses whatever he likes from various different religions and combines them to produce his own gospel–like his friend, Madeleine L'Engle. Whatever works for him is good. Like L'Engle, whatever he can't cope with, such as the doctrine of eternal damnation and the substitutionary atonement, he throws out. He "simply cannot accept the view of Hell in which God punishes people without hope and destroys souls without a chance for redemption. He/She wouldn't go to the trouble of creating souls, with all their complexity, just to fry them in the end" (*Further Along the Road Less Traveled*, Simon & Schuster, New York, NY, 1993, pg. 171).

The reason Peck doesn't have to believe in eternal damnation is because he doesn't believe the Bible is the only *authoritative* book on matters of faith. "Indeed," he says, "the Bible is a collection of paradoxical stories. . . . It is a mixture of legend, some of which is true and some of which is not true. It is a mixture of very accurate history and not so accurate history. . . . It is a mixture of myth and metaphor" (*ibid.,* pg. 107). Being fans of New Age guru Joseph Campbell, whose work, *The Power of Myth*, has swept many off solid ground, both Peck and L'Engle share his enthusiasm for myths–found in all different legends, religions, stories, etc. (See Appendix I for more detail concerning this.)

In *The Road Less Traveled* (written prior to Peck's supposed conversion to Christianity and his newer work, *Further Along the Road Less Traveled*), Peck states:

> For no matter how much we may like to pussyfoot around it, all of us who postulate a loving God and really think about it eventually come to a single terrifying idea: God wants us to become Himself (or Herself or Itself). We are growing toward godhood. God is the goal of evolution. It is God who is the source of the evolutionary force and God

who is the destination (Simon & Schuster, 1978, pg. 270).

It is my vision the collective unconscious is God (pg. 282).

Since the unconscious is God all along, we may further define the goal of spiritual growth to be the attainment of godhood by the conscious self. It is for the individual to become totally, wholly God. . . . This is the meaning of our individual existence. We are born that we might become, as a conscious individual, a new life form of God (pg. 283).

After hearing this book being used as a guideline on love and support for De Boer's sermon, my question was this: Did De Boer think Peck's theology was a help-mate–compatible with Christianity? Or, had he just innocently neglected to mention Peck's New Age gospel was in dire need of a heart transplant?

Sometime later, I found out *The Road Less Traveled* was a new addition to the church library. It was also among the many books placed on the table in the narthex of the church to be purchased and used for evangelism in conjunction with the Stephen Series–an adult education program on caring.

To say the least, I was more confused than ever. I really didn't believe the co-pastor would actually defend Peck's teachings. They were even more blatant than L'Engle's works. But I wasn't about to let that sermon go over my head and pretend it never happened. I decided to ask him what he thought about M. Scott Peck at the elders' meeting.

Karen and I prepared as best we could for the meeting and were thankful that our husbands had decided to read L'Engle's works and support us. Sharon, a mutual friend of ours, also came along mainly to witness what was said, and she knew her presence would be greatly appreciated. There were seventeen elders and only five of us which, when confronting them with a decision they had made, would be a trifle bit intimidating.

The night of the meeting, we all walked timidly into a room of cold-staring elders. We were greeted, it seemed, more like strangers, rather then people who had been members of the church for more than fourteen years. As Sharon put it later, "I'm glad I kept my jacket on. The chill in the air could have killed me."

I glanced quickly around the room and noticed that Rev. Erffmeyer was not present. De Boer was to take over the meeting. He announced emphatically that we had forty-five minutes in which to present our concerns, and *only* forty-five minutes. This sure helped to make us feel right at home. I looked for a moment at my notes and began by explaining that in L'Engle's fiction, children were developing psychic powers. I went briefly through *Walking on Water* to show occult teachings were not just in her fiction. So far, this was going over like a lead balloon. No one seemed interested at all in what I was saying, nor did they act like it mattered in the least. De Boer kept glancing at his watch to let us know every so often just how much time we had left.

Dave Larsen and pastor De Boer were about the only ones who commented. Most the other elders remained silent. I took out *A Stone for a Pillow*; my last hope. Slowly, with as much expression as I could, I read L'Engle's denial of the substitutionary atonement. Surely, the elders would pounce on this one. Alas, with the exception of Dave Larsen, all remained quiet.

"That's taken out-of-context," he assured all there without further reading of the book. The reaction I had hoped for never happened. Before we knew it, our time was just about up. I read one more passage, this time from *The Wittenberg Door* magazine where L'Engle states, "The Bible is not a moral book, it is not an ethical book. It is a magnificent storybook. . . . It doesn't give any answers, it just tells more stories" (Dec., 1986, pg. 24).

Finally, someone other than Dave Larsen spoke up. It was Howard Stob, a person I thought highly of—most people did. "If that's what she really is saying, I'd like to see that."

"I'll get the documentation for you," I promised.

Because I had been accused of misreading L'Engle and taking her words out-of-context, I asked the elders if they had read any of her books. Larson informed everyone that he had read part of *Walking on Water*, and another elder said he had read *A Wrinkle in Time*. But, when I asked him a couple of questions concerning the medium in the story, he refused to answer saying he didn't realize he was going to be tested on it. It appeared he was afraid to speak out against the book, but maybe it was just my imagination. No other elders indicated they had read her works.

Our time spent, Pastor De Boer arose from his chair and began walking out, signally the meeting was now finished. He wasn't about to give us any more time then we had been allowed. Upset by his apparent lack of sensitivity to our concerns, I blurted out, "You quoted M. Scott Peck from the pulpit Sunday, what do think of him–do you know who he is?"

"I know who people *think* he is," he smugly retorted.

His answer left me dazed and silent. For the first time, I had the most horrible feeling our pastors knew exactly what Peck taught, and possibly believed it.

Before we departed for home, we literally begged the elders to read L'Engle's works, call for more information if they needed it, and to examine her works with us.

That night, I couldn't sleep. I kept thinking of all the people who were reading L'Engle's works and believing them to be the words of a wonderful Christian author. In my mind, I went over everything I said at the meeting with the elders, wondering what would have opened their eyes to the deception in her works. (I hadn't understood yet, that it wasn't my job to convict, just present what I knew.)

Then my thoughts shifted to the children. L'Engle's books had been used for over seventeen years in the Christian school classroom and by the defense of our librarian and the teacher, one could see the devastating outcome. In the inside cover of *Trailing Clouds of Glory, Spiritual Values in Children's Books*, it states: "Madeleine L'Engle has now focused her creative eye on literature for and about boys and girls. She shows us, not subjects, but spiritual themes." And that was exactly what the children were learning, a spiritual theme in complete and utter opposition to God's Word; a theme that could destroy their eternal souls–a theme that switched good for evil and evil for good and came under the disguise of being "Christian." The whole notion made me sick.

Tired, but unable to sleep, I prayed that I'd get through to at least one elder. It was about 5:00 a.m. when Howard Stob's name came to my mind. He was the only one who had shown any real interest at all. I was somewhat scared that he might not feel free to come over, and then I thought of his wife, Jo. She had written me several notes expressing her appreciation for my piano playing in church. I desperately needed to talk to someone who would listen to everything that had taken place over the past year and a half. Though I didn't know her very well, I felt she was the one whom I should call and could trust.

I couldn't wait any longer. It was 8:30 a.m. when I called her on the phone. The genuine kindness I could hear in her voice made me feel relaxed and comfortable. I apologized for calling so early in the morning, and tried to explain that I really needed to talk to Howard, but was worried he wouldn't be willing to come over. She asked why I would think such a thing, and then everything spilled out. I kept that poor woman on the phone for three hours telling her what had happened from the time my daughter had come home with *The Chosen* to the end of the elders' meeting the night before. I read from L'Engle's works and told her of the decision made both by the education committee and the elders. Stunned, she promised me she would talk with Howard and try to persuade him to come over. I breathed a sigh of relief and thanked God for leading me to her.

A couple of days later, Jo called to let me know she and Howard would be coming over the following Sunday afternoon after his weekly visit to the nursing home (part of his volunteer work as elder). It hadn't been easy; he didn't want to come, but she persisted until he reached the conclusion that it was his duty as an elder of the church to listen to what I had to say.

After church Sunday morning, I gathered together some of the documentation I had given the education committee along with a few of L'Engle's books, some occult works to back up my reasoning, and, of course, the Bible. My husband, Si, sent the kids downstairs and we sat at the dining room table with Howard and Jo talking over a cup of coffee. I could tell Howard's mind wasn't focused so much on what I was saying, but on trying to convince us that what we were doing was wrong. He chided, "You should be reading more of your Bible," just as Rev. Erffmeyer had said at one of my meetings with him. I thought it a bit strange that both Erffmeyer and now Howard Stob should know just how much I was reading my Bible; they weren't with me at home. Seeing the slightly perturbed look on my face, Jo politely asked her husband to listen to what I was saying. Thank goodness she had decided to come with him.

With each piece of documentation I laid out in front of him, Howard became more interested, and at the same time, acted more confused. Last, but not least, I placed *A Stone for a Pillow* on the table and asked him to read the page I had read out loud at the elders' meeting where L'Engle redefines the atonement. Appalled at what he had just finished reading, Howard asked, "If this is what she actually believes, how can she be so well-endorsed by the pastors and elders?"

That was a good question. Apparently, because of a hearing loss, he hadn't heard that passage very well at the meeting. Also, for some reason, he had been under the impression the books in question were just fiction like *Tom Sawyer*. He didn't realize there was a theology worked into them, or that L'Engle's non-fiction works were included in our concern. That's why he couldn't figure out what all the fuss was about. Now, he knew.

I asked him to take *A Stone for a Pillow* home so he could read it in full context and compare it next to Scripture. Because he took his office as elder seriously, he wholeheartedly agreed to do so. After he finished reading and studying the book, we would meet again.

Encouraged by the outcome of our meeting with Howard, I began to call the rest of the elders to see if they would be willing to meet and discuss L'Engle's works. With each phone call came a resounding "No!" Two elders I called weren't at home, but their wives didn't hesitate to decline for them. One went on to let me know that because I didn't have a college degree I couldn't possibly know what I was talking about.

Discouraged, but not quite ready to give up, I called two more elders. One was kind enough to meet with Karen and me at his house. He seemed to understand what we showed him, but we didn't feel he would be willing to stick his neck out–and we were right. The other elder, Ken Mels, also invited us to his home. I had played for his daughter's wedding and thought he was a kind man who knew his Bible well. With an armful of books and other documentation, we drove off in eager anticipation thinking he had invited us over to discuss our concerns.

When we arrived at his home, he led us into the kitchen. After we were all seated I asked, "Why do you think we are doing this?"

"I don't know, it seems to me you're wasting a lot of God-given time," Mels replied in a rather low, gruff voice. I tried to explain the seriousness of the matter–that L'Engle's works were being accepted within the Christian community and taught as Christian literature to our children at all levels in the Christian schools. Yet, we believed her writings undermined Scripture and taught a different gospel.

"If the experts accept her as Christian and her works as Christian, that's good enough for me. I talked to people I know and respect who are in the literary field and they say her writings are perfectly acceptable," he coldly remarked.

I could feel the tension building in the room as I pulled out *A Stone for a Pillow.* "Would you please read this?" I asked.

He refused vehemently. "I'm *not* literary, I'm *not* a reader."

After some gentle persuasion, I finally convinced him to read the page where L'Engle claims all people will be redeemed. He read it, seemed puzzled, read it again and was silent. Peering up from his dark-rimmed reading glasses, he broke the silence. "If that's what she is really saying, I'd have to disagree, but that's one page out of a book and you can't go by that."

"Then take the book and read it in full context," I pleaded. This was a legitimate appeal to his conclusion–I thought.

He snapped back, "No! I'm *not* going to. It's a waste of my God-given time!" It was a waste of an elder's God-given time? Wasn't this exactly what our elders were supposed to do–watch, protect and guard the flock against false teachers? And where on earth was all his anger coming from anyway? Karen and I were absolutely floored by his reaction.

"How much of the Bible are you reading?" he now asked accusingly. I wondered where he got that question from–it seemed to be the question of the year. He continued, "I think you're reading things into it that just aren't there." (Now there was a comment that was totally out-of-line, since he admitted he hadn't read any of her works.) "What are you teaching your kids by doing this?"

I tried to remain calm. Thoroughly upset, Karen was unable to speak. I answered his question for the both of us: "Discernment, dare to be a Daniel, expose false teachings . . . and I've read my Bible more now than ever before. . . ."

"I don't think much of what you're doing. It's a terrible waste of time. Did you ever think maybe the devil was using you?"

That comment ripped down through to the bone. "No, we have total peace of mind," was all I could think of to say.

"I'm glad," he sarcastically answered.

Instead of leaving well enough alone, I decided to show Mels *The Door* interview where L'Engle states, "the Bible doesn't give any answers, just tells more stories." He pushed it away. This elder never had the slightest intention of listening to what we had to say. He proceeded to warn us that he was watching who we talked with at church and that we were picking on the most vulnerable people.

I took that to mean people who we felt were stupid enough to believe what we were falsely dishing out.

Now I felt like a criminal being scoped out by the police. So far, I had only talked to a very few of my close friends about the books at my home, only after I had received the letters from the education committee and the elders. For that matter, was it wrong to discuss a book with your friends–a book which you felt could be hurtful to members of the congregation? I couldn't believe what I was hearing.

I tried to explain that it wasn't our intention to cause division in the church (as we had been accused of) and that unity is founded on sound doctrine.

"You're just digging up dirt on L'Engle," Mels cut in–as if two housewives, each with three children, had nothing better to do with their time.

Trying to say anything more would definitely not help the situation. I managed to thank him for having us over as Karen and I were shown the way out. We drove away from his house stunned by the attitude displayed. There wasn't a reasonable explanation for what had just taken place. We thought back to the elders' meeting. There too, we felt as if *we* were on trial, not the works of Madeleine L'Engle. What was going on?

I remembered my prayer that we would get through to at least one elder. I placed my hope in Howard Stob. Jo told me for the following two weeks since they had come over, he had gone upstairs to his room every night after supper to read and study. Once more we gathered around my kitchen table. This time, however, there was a changed expression on his face. He shook his head sadly, but by the sheepish grin on his face, I could tell he was in agreement with our conclusions. His sadness stemmed from the realization of the tremendous enormity of the problem and the tragic consequences that would surely follow.

"In no way is this woman a Christian author," he pronounced.

One elder is what I had asked for, and one elder is what I had been given! Such a pronouncement was not an easy one to make for him, nor was it for us, but it was absolutely necessary. Howard promised to present his findings to the elders at the next consistory meeting which would take place on April 17, 1990.

Before he left, I asked him why he had been so reluctant to come over the first time. Was it because it had been suggested to the elders that I was reading occult or New Age into everything and maybe, perhaps, a little nuts? I needed to know. "Something like that," Howard hesitantly mumbled, not wanting to reveal any "private" information discussed at an elders' meeting.

We shook hands, and as we did so, I could feel the warmth of a like-minded friend. "Surely," I thought, "this humble, God-fearing man who is so highly respected in the church will get through to the rest of the elders."

****

NOTE: It wasn't until a few years later, that I would find out why the elders had reacted in the way they did. The coldness, the disinterest, was not in our imaginations. Before our very first meeting with them on March 20, 1990, Rev. Erffmeyer and Bruce Ireland, a Bible teacher at Southwest Christian School and a member of the church education committee, had written a "report" to them. Among other things, it stated:

1. Pastor Erffmeyer has sat down for many hours with Claris (and Karen) and gone over the writings of Madeleine L'Engle page by page, listening to the objections. I have found no passages with New Age teachings in these writings. Many times Claris and Karen do not understand the statements in their context. [Remember, Erffmeyer refused to read her works in full context and had gone over only a few passages in the book at the time–CVK].
2. Mary Beth Bootsma has made an extensive research of Madeleine L'Engle's writings and not found them to be filled with New Age teachings. [Mary Beth indicated she didn't know much about New Age teachings and never provided documentation to the committee to support her conclusions.–CVK]
3. All members of the Education Committee are familiar with Madeleine L'Engle's writings and have found her to be a Christian author not promoting New Age teachings. . . . [Again, no documentation or Biblical reasoning for their findings was presented to the elders–CVK.]

It was indicated in the report that they had contacted both Gospel Truth Ministries and the Christian Research Institute in California. The Christian Research Institute said they had never had anyone bring Madeleine L'Engle's writings to them challenging that they were New Age writings. [I called and this was true, but they did have a report on M. Scott Peck that was right on target– CVK].

According to Rev. Erffmeyer, Joel Groot from Gospel Truth Ministries stated that L'Engle "is in the 'camp of Christian Authors' and that 'she is NOT New Age.' " [I called Joel Groot. He told me that he remembered talking with someone from my church, but if that's what they had written it was a very misleading statement since he told them he hadn't read L'Engle's books since he was in college–CVK].

At the bottom of their report, a P.S. was added:

It is important for the Elders to know that I received a call from Gary Meyer from CCHS [English teacher at Chicago Christian High School–CVK] stating that on Sunday, February 25, Claris Van Kuiken approached the 9th Graders from our church who are in his class at CCHS, and told them not to read Chaim Potok's book, THE CHOSEN, as assigned in English class because it is satanic and not Christian in nature. She did this before, after, and during our worship services. It is upsetting to see how she uses the time before and after and during worship services to be devisive, to not only approach adults who come here for worship and edification, but she is also now approaching students and encouraging them to defy and disobey the authority in the school. People should be able to come to church for worship and upbuilding, not to be approached in this way.

The first time I read this note, my temper flared. I had never been approached by Gary Meyer or Rev. Erffmeyer as to the truth about it. The only true statement in it was that I had talked with some 9th graders. It was on a Sunday night. I had come to church with my daughter Lori, and Karen met me in the narthex. Jo Stob stood close by. A student Lori's age came up to me and asked what I had against *A Wrinkle in Time* because it was his favorite book. I explained a couple of the errors in the book as his friend looked on. A few girls walked up and asked what I thought of Ouija boards. I told them they could be dangerous. That was the end of the conversation. I sat with Karen that night. I didn't talk to these boys or anyone else during church services. I never stated *The Chosen* was satanic or told them they couldn't read it. My own daughter read it and took the test. Why would I tell someone else's child they couldn't read the book?

For Rev. Erffmeyer to tell the elders I was encouraging students to defy authority and causing devisiveness in the church without approaching me first was, as far as I was concerned, a purposeful way to discredit me. Without ever confronting me about the matter, the elders took this mis-information as pure fact.

I include this note out of order to shed some light on events in the chapters ahead.

Chapter Five

AN UNFORGETTABLE LECTURE

> For the time will come when men will not put up with
> sound doctrine. Instead, to suit their own desires, they
> will gather around them a great number of teachers to
> say what their itching ears want to hear. They will turn
> their ears away from the truth and turn aside to myths.
>
> 2 Timothy 4:3-4

> Myths make us more alive. . . . God gives us the truth;
> we do not "have" it, and when we think we do, we are
> often close to sin.
>
> Madeleine L'Engle, "The Mythical Bible"

A few days following Howard's visit, I was surprised to receive
a phone call from an elder who thought it might be a good idea for
Karen and me to hear Madeleine L'Engle speak. She was going to
be presenting a lecture entitled, "The Plausible Impossible" at
Wheaton College–the "Harvard of Evangelicals." He hoped this
would convince us that we had misjudged her teachings. His daughter had several of her autographed books at home and thought highly
of her. I appreciated the phone call and made plans with Karen to
drive up to Wheaton.

We left early on the evening of March 30th so we'd be guaran-
teed a good seat, and it was a good thing we did. The auditorium
of Armerding Lecture Hall quickly filled up with students, teachers, pastors and parents. The stairways were lined with people waiting for their first glimpse of this renowned "Christian" author.

Outside the hall, adoring fans strained to see what was happening, anxiously awaiting L'Engle's arrival. And then she came–with long, flowing, dark print dress and some type of talisman or amulet hanging around her neck.

Dr. Joe McClatchy, who taught Modern Mythology at Wheaton, gave the opening welcome:

> She understands the Christian faith in its international and inter-philosophical context. She understands music and makes music. She understands silence and prayer. She understands the family. Best of all, she understands myth and the truth of myth. She understands the principle put forward so convincingly by physicists like Hawking and Greenstein, but she does them all one better. She understands it as a Christian myth-maker, that it undergirds myth. She understands, in other words, that myth, as storied and worshipped, is the nature of things. Madeleine, welcome back to Wheaton, where you belong!

Taking her place in front of the microphone, she returned the compliment. "Well, . . . it's good to be here, good to be home. To see so many old friends and make, I hope, many new ones."

Applause echoed throughout the room. Within a few minutes time, we could see this woman, who stood on stage with students surrounding her, gazing up into her face, had a tremendous amount of influence at Wheaton College. She was obviously well-known and loved by many there. Doubts filled my mind. Could I have been wrong about her works? No, I didn't think so. Yet, I couldn't fathom how this many people at an Evangelical college could be blinded by her works. I noticed Ken and Mary Beth Bootsma, the president of Trinity Christian College and his wife, sitting in the audience. I hoped they would hear something, anything, that would upset them.

L'Engle began her speech with that famous age-old question, "What is truth?" Probing her audience she inquired, "What do we mean by truth? Is there a difference between truth and fact? Do we, in our society, get hung up on literalism?" I had read enough of her works to know exactly where she was leading her audience, and I didn't like it. Not knowing what to do, I squirmed in my seat as she turned Truth into "myth."

In some of her works, L'Engle chides those who fear fiction, especially adults who won't let their children read fairy tales. (I don't know of any adults like this, but I guess there must be some.) So she asked her listeners, "Is this rather general fear of fiction not so much a fear that fiction is not truth, as a fear that fiction *is* truth?" Clever question. I wondered if anybody else was catching on to what she was doing.

Amid stories of her great-grandmother and several cute jokes that had almost everyone in stitches, she constructed her theology like a seamstress weaving in and out a beautiful sweater from soft, white sheep's wool. The Bible was simply story, "searching for truth rather than fact, and searching more deeply in story." The Bible, Greek and Roman myths, fairy tales, fantasy and myth, were all lumped together as "truth." Although she never came right out and said it bluntly, her idea that the Bible is not to be taken literally, but to be looked upon as any other story, religious books such as the Koran or Upanishads, and even her own fiction, came shining through. If anyone had read *A Stone for a Pillow*, they would know this was exactly what she meant–and I was sure many of them had.

Toward the end of her lecture, L'Engle asked, "Can those who are a part of that great cloud of witnesses which has gone before us, be in two places at once?" Answering her own question, she said confidently, "I believe that they can." Everyone sat in silence as L'Engle told them of the time she was with her eldest daughter and family on a boat. She had gone to sleep in the cabin and after a while had "slid into wakefulness" to find Hugh, her deceased husband, in bed with her. She believed he had come to inform her of the death of Cannon Tallis, a friend she knew from The Cathedral of St. John the Divine.

I looked around the room. Did anybody understand what she was feeding them? Didn't anyone realize she was advocating communication with the dead which God forbids? Not a gasp, not a sound, until L'Engle explained how her "mathematical and rational and eminently reasonable" daughter Josephine had even thought this was possible. Then, there was laughter. LAUGHTER! Echoing in my ears, it grew louder and louder until it turned into a hideous mockery of God's Word.

"The Plausible Impossible:" no wonder she had chosen this title.

It was so very fitting for a speech that would seduce people into believing her fiction, which promoted occult practices, was just as reliable and reasonable as God's Word.

Karen and I glanced at each other, wanting to say something, anything, but we were too upset to know quite what to do. We had never encountered anything like this before. We didn't want to come on too strong and look like a pair of fundamentalist lunatics. So, we waited, trying to gain our composure and hoped for an opportunity to calmly ask some questions.

L'Engle shared her belief that it is the child within each of us who is able to recognize the truth in stories, the mysterious, the ominous, the unexplainable (a typical New Age theme). She asserted that we should never fear the plausible impossible because it would "open up that truth which will make us free." I wondered if anyone knew what "truth" she was speaking of. Ending her speech with the words Jesus spoke about Himself was a deception of the worst kind. Seeing her receive a standing ovation convinced me more than ever as to just how crucial it was to expose her teachings and affiliations with the New Age Movement.

Finally, there was time for questions and answers. I glanced at all the people there, waiting to see if someone other than Karen and I knew what she was teaching and was brave enough to speak out against it. Then, a man sitting towards the middle of the room introduced himself as a minister. "Here it comes," I thought to myself, counting on him to refute what L'Engle had purported. Instead, he politely thanked her for teaching him not to take the Bible literally and went on to share with the audience that he now taught his congregation this. I sunk back into my chair, shaking my head, unable to grasp what had just been said. This was definitely not what I had expected to hear at the college known as "The Harvard of Evangelicals."

My courage was draining fast and my stomach didn't feel so great either. More questions, more laughter, until one petite lady seated several rows behind us stood up. "MS. L'ENGLE," she said loud enough for everyone to hear. "In your book, *A Wrinkle in Time*, in chapter five, . . ." [laughter from audience] "I'm a Christian parent, too. I'm a little bothered that you have our Lord Jesus on the same level as Gandhi and Buddha." My heart pounded. Instantly, I knew this woman was of like mind.

Somewhat taken aback, L'Engle answered, "We know St. Paul,

we know that all things work together for good. . . ."

Obviously distressed, the lady cut her off. "No, no, NO!" But Jesus is not on the same level!"

L'Engle asked if she could please finish her quote while more laughter sounded from the audience. She quoted Romans 8:28-29:

> We know that all things work together for good to them that love God, to them that are the called according to the Scriptures. For whom He did foreknow, He also did predestine to be conformed to the image of His Son that He might be the firstborn among many brethren.

This was an interesting answer. Buddha was not a brother of Jesus. To say such a thing would be similar to saying the stone god Baal was a brother to the Almighty God who condemned idol worship (Exodus 20:3-4, Judges 6:25, etc.). And what was this game she was playing? Why was L'Engle defending herself using a verse from Scripture that taught predestination, a doctrine she herself scowls at in *A Stone for a Pillow*? There, L'Engle states:

> I shudder at the once widely-accepted theory that God preordained us all before we were born for either heaven or hell, and nothing we did would change this predestination. What kind of god would predestine part of his creation to eternal damnation? This is surely not consistent with God's creation in the early chapters of Genesis, when Elohim looked at all that had been made and called it good, very good. And yet this brutal theology used to be widely accepted and taught, a kind of spiritual terrorism (pg. 187).

What a contradiction! Nothing like using bits and pieces from Scripture only when it suits your own purpose.

The brave woman spoke up again: "But you say He's a light. You quote out of John, 'And the light shineth in darkness, and the darkness comprehended it not.' You said, 'Jesus why of course, Jesus! But go on Charles, there are others that are great lights. All your great artists.' Then you go on and compare Jesus. . . ."

Now it was L'Engle's turn to cut her off. "I'm not comparing Jesus with anybody!" she barked.

". . . with Leonardo Da Vinci, Shakespeare. No, He's not on the same level! I question that as a Christian," the lady replied, frustrated.

L'Engle turned the accusation around. "No, that's *you* putting Him on the same level."

"No! No!! That's your–that's your writing, Ms. L'Engle!"

Applause filled the air, but I couldn't quite figure out who the applause was for. I kept poking Karen to ask a question, too afraid to ask one myself. She surprised me by raising her hand and asking, "Do you believe the imagination is reliable, totally reliable?"

"Nothing is totally reliable on this earth, we have to test what comes from the imagination to see if it's from the Holy Spirit or if it's from the Imitator. And the only test that I have come across which seems to be perfectly valid is, does it have in it anything of the temptations that Satan offered Jesus on the mountain? And if it does, I know it's not the Holy Spirit."

Good diffusing answer. But, what about comparing what comes out of the imagination next to Scripture? Timidly, Karen asked her one more question. "Do you believe that God abhors mediums, witchcraft, magic and the like?"

I didn't think the question was so funny, but L'Engle managed to make a joke out of it compelling everyone in the audience to laugh. Skirting around the issue without ever really answering the question, she defensively added that she knew nothing about the occult. L'Engle was honest enough to admit she had been asked before why she used the occult in her works and continued to explain that "the word occult means hidden." "Certainly," she contended, "John's Revelation is occult. Certainly books like Daniel and . . . ."

That was enough for me. This author who so blatantly promoted and defended witchcraft, communication with the dead, goddess worship, and every other form of occultism in her works, knew exactly what she was doing. To deny she knew anything about the occult was ridiculous. Any author who could write like she did, knew her stuff. To downplay the occult and compare it to books of the Bible was outrageous. Yet, she gained the audience's approval and had them all laughing in their seats, as if the whole thing was just a big misunderstanding.

My head was spinning, so instead of asking a question about her non-fiction, which would have been the best thing to do, I first stated that in her book, *A Wrinkle in Time*, "angels" bring her characters to a medium. I proceeded to explain that they look into her crystal ball and receive information, and are also given talismans by these so-called "angels" to help them. I further noted that talismans were magical amulets. Because L'Engle had made it clear in her answer to Karen, that she didn't have the medium looking into the future (as if that made a difference), I asked, "How do you account for the fact that God says do not even consult a medium or you will be cut off from my people" (Leviticus 20:6)?

"'Cause I didn't think it as being a medium! She's a character who was a happy medium," L'Engle chuckled. (More laughter sounded from the audience.) As for talismans, L'Engle maintained there was nothing wrong with them, "as long as you know that it is a way to God; it is not a way to you."

"Talismans are another way to God? I don't think so," I mumbled under my breath, but loud enough for the people in back of us to hear.

In agreement with L'Engle, someone shouted "AMEN!" and once again applause echoed throughout the room. She had done it again. My nerve was gone and asking more questions would only do more harm then good at this point.

A student now asked a question about "kything," the word L'Engle uses to define mental telepathy, communication with the dead, plants and trees, etc.

"In order to be willing to kythe, you have to be willing to be vulnerable," L'Engle answered without providing a definition as to what "kything" was. I guess it was understood by L'Engle that most people there knew what it meant from reading her works. But I still had my doubts as to whether or not that student recognized "kything" was occultic in nature and prohibited by God.

L'Engle politely answered a few more questions and was then whisked off to catch her flight. As Karen and I arose from our seats to leave, an older man came up beside us, scolding us for questioning L'Engle's beliefs. "You have no right to judge another person," he scowled.

I looked up at him and simply said, "The Bible teaches us to expose false teachings." I didn't know what else to say, nor was there an opportunity to say more.

Outside the auditorium, a male student approached us and asked what we had against L'Engle. (They must have been paying more

attention than we thought.) We explained we had nothing personally against her, but that her works contradicted Scripture and proceeded to show him some examples. We discussed her writings for
almost an hour and he promised to look into it further. Karen was
still talking to him when a short woman (about my size) brushed
past us, turned suddenly, and stopped short. I stared at her for a
moment and asked, "Aren't you the lady that asked the question
. . . ?"

"Aren't *you* the lady that asked . . . ?" she broke in. We both
laughed at the same time, relieving a considerable amount of built-
up tension. I found out her name was Jackie Schaefer and she had
come all the way from Michigan to hear L'Engle speak. Her daughter attended Wheaton College and had been upset by some of the
things that were being said by professor McClatchy during class.
Jackie had also studied some of L'Engle's works and believed they
promoted New Age/occult beliefs and practices. We talked as I gave
her some information I had taken along, and we exchanged phone
numbers.

On our way home, Karen and I repeatedly went over what had
been said that night, wondering how Christians could be so completely mesmerized by an author who willfully turned Truth into
myth, fact into fiction, and Light into darkness.

Chapter Six

BLIND TRUST

Now the Bereans were of more noble character than the Thessalonians, for they received the message with great eagerness and examined the Scriptures every day to see if what Paul said was true.

Acts 17:11

I'm not a reader. I'm not going to waste my God-given time. If the experts believe she is a Christian author, that's good enough for me.

Elder, OPCRC

It was only a few weeks until the next elders' meeting at which Howard would present his assessment of L'Engle's works and ask the elders to reconsider their previous decision. Aware of the cold and hostile attitude already being displayed towards me, he was somewhat intimidated and nervous about sharing his thoughts. Nevertheless, he was not willing to compromise a situation that might, in any way, bring dishonor to his Lord.

Needing as much support as we could possibly get, I placed a call to Rev. John De Vries, as elder Ken Mels had suggested I do. At first, his tone of voice lacked the enthusiasm I had hoped for. It was rather obvious he had already talked to someone about our situation. Immediately after I read a few passages from L'Engle's works, however, his tone deepened to concern and he willingly promised to read some of her works and any documentation I could send him.

Letters of Encouragement

It was Saturday, April 12, just a few days before the elders were to meet, when the mailman handed me an envelope with a Bibles for India return address on it. Eagerly, I tore it open to find two letters; the first, a personal letter addressed to me, and the second, a copy of a letter De Vries had written to his friend, Ken Mels. A wave of relief rushed through me as I read:

> Dear Claris,
>
> Thank you so much for sending me the information on Madeleine L'Engle's books. I have reviewed her writing and in my estimation, not only is she New Age, but her writings are probably more dangerous than average because they are so cleverly disguised as Christian. . . .
>
> Thank you so much for your alertness and your concern, Claris. Please be encouraged and do not give up in trying to root this material out of our churches and schools. Last weekend I met a beautiful young mother of three children who 8 months ago was very close to suicide because of her involvement in the demonic and occult. She probably became involved through writings similar to the ones of L'Engle. By God's providence this woman is in a church that knows what she has come out of. She has a small cluster of women who are in contact with her each day, praying for her as she continues to suffer demonic attacks. I have wondered after reading this material of L'Engle what confusion would come in her mind if she would find books like this in a church library. I was especially impressed with L'Engle's statement that the white china Buddha statue that she has in her home is more of a symbol of Christ than the crucifix. It is on page 106 of *Trailing Clouds of Glory*.
>
> Thanks for your concern. I realize that it gets very difficult at times, but just be reassured that the New Age is not what people think it is. It is deadly and demonic and is causing not only great psychological disturbance, but is leading multitudes astray. I also believe that it is the

top side of the evil of Satanism throughout the United States.

May God bless you.

In His Service,

Rev. John De Vries.

Tears filled my eyes as I read the letter to Ken which was written in stronger language than my own. De Vries warned, "I believe that L'Engle is a good example of the methodology that the devil uses in disguising his message by wrapping it up in some Christian terminology. I believe her books are deadly and have absolutely no place in a Christian church's library."

His letters of support and encouragement meant a great deal to Karen and me, and especially to Howard, who could not begin to fathom why his pastor and fellow elders could not and/or would not see anything amiss in her writings.

That night, I called Rev. De Vries to thank him for giving up so much of his time for us. During our conversation, he informed me that he had talked with Ken who said he would be sharing his letter with the consistory (pastors and elders). We were all confident the letter would change the hearts and minds of the elders creating a new desire to study the matter thoroughly.

A Disturbing Elders' Meeting–April 17, 1990

It was late, around eleven o'clock on the night of the elders' meeting, when the phone rang. It was Howard. "What's the matter–how did the meeting go?" I asked, somewhat afraid to find out.

"It didn't go very well," was all Howard managed to say. He was obviously distraught about something. His voice was broken as though he was in defeated agony.

"Didn't Mr. Mels read John De Vries' letter?"

Not sure of how much he was able to tell me because of the confidentiality of elders' meetings, he hesitated to answer my question. Being the persistant and stubborn person I can be, and sensing Howard needed someone to talk to, I questioned him again. As long as this was not a personal matter concerning anyone other than ourselves, what could it hurt? Finally, Howard answered softly, "No, the letter wasn't read. Someone said De Vries disclaimed his letter."

"What?" I asked in disbelief. "He couldn't have. I just talked with him a few days ago. He told me he had talked with Ken and that he would be reading his letter to the elders. He thanked me again for sending him the material and said he couldn't believe how deceptive her writings were. What's going on?"

Howard didn't know, and I surely didn't know, but I was determined to find out. It hadn't been until the end of the meeting (I found out later), when Howard saw that Mels was not going to bring up De Vries' letter, that he took the copy I had given him and put it in view of the other elders. Then, and only then, did Mels come forward to say De Vries had written a letter, but in fact, had also disclaimed it. By the time he finished and asked the elders if they wanted it read, not one raised their hand. Why should they? The letter was no longer valid anyway.

The final decision made by the elders that night was to hold to their previous decision. The books were to stay in the library because they were in fact, not harmful to the Christian faith, but a blessing.

The little bit of information Howard had provided me with proved to be more disconcerting than I had bargained for. The next day I decided to call Rev. De Vries to find out if he had indeed disclaimed his letter. Before I had the chance to call him, he called me to let me know how very disappointed he was in the elders' decision and that he stood behind his letter. He had already talked with Rev. Erffmeyer who had informed him of their stand.

Rev. De Vries was terribly disappointed in Erffmeyer and the elders, but was absolutely dumbfounded when I told him his friend hadn't bothered to read his letter and someone had maintained he had, in fact, disclaimed it. To let all know that he stood firm behind his letter, Rev. De Vries promised to write a series of articles exposing L'Engle's works for *The Outlook*, a conservative Christian Reformed magazine. He was true to his promise.

Agree to Disagree: An Unholy Compromise

On April 19, I received an official letter from the elders. It is a letter of such significance that I print it in full. Please, read it carefully.

April, 1990 (no date given, but postmarked April 18)

Dear Karen and Dean, Claris and Si, and Sharon,

This letter explains to you our decision with regard to our mutual concern. It is written in the hope that you will believe that we have sincerely considered your appeal and that we have prayerfully sought the leading of the Lord in this matter.

Disputes between believers are never easy matters. As Paul writes in I Corinthians 6, these situations occur, but can and must be resolved for the sake of unity in the church and our witness to the world. Are we as elders competent to make such decisions? In the same passage Paul suggests quite strongly that we are equipped by God for this purpose.

We agree on many things, and share much about the faith in common. We, like you, are concerned to "not believe every spirit, but test the spirits to see whether they are from God, because many false prophets have gone out into the world." We, like you, are convinced that the church ought to promote literature which builds faith and does not undermine it. We also share a mutual promise to "submit to the government of the church" and "its admonition and discipline."

We have given your appeal fair and careful consideration, first through the advice of our Church Education committee, and then through your direct appeal at our March, 1990 elders meeting. In addition, you have spoken individually with many elders since the March meeting, and our pastoral staff has met with and listened to you on numerous occasions both in person and over the phone.

Our decision remains unchanged. We again concur with the earlier decision and endorse the stand of the education committee.

Several factors have gone into our decision. First, we also have consulted those familiar with the New Age teachings and the writings of Madeleine L'Engle. It is our conviction that she is a Christian author, and that her work is not harmful to the faith of children or adults. Further, there is reason to believe that her writings have in fact been a blessing to many in appreciating God's gift of creativity, imagination, wonder, and awe.

Both sides in this "dispute" have consulted outside authorities. Several differences in the advice of these authorities have surfaced.

A very significant one has to do with what Reformed Christians believe about reading literature and involvement in culture. We hold with the historic Reformed view that one is called to read all literature, both Christian and non-Christian, with critical discernment, recognizing that not all that is Christian is good or wise and not all that is non-Christian is without merit. God works his grace as he wills, and often gives insight through those who don't know him. Books in our church library are carefully examined from this Reformed point of view, and are selected on the basis of their potential for building the Body of Christ. Our reading of the authorities in this regard leads us to endorse L'Engle's works as appropriate and not harmful.

Another has to do with whether or not L'Engle is or isn't a professing Christian. Again, you cite authorities who would say she is not. It is our belief that she is, both because of her own profession and because of the many instances where evangelical Christians point to her as an example of a Christian author. While we admit to the fact that she would likely not believe all that our Christian Reformed expression of the faith would hold, we do believe that she "acknowledges that Jesus Christ has come in the flesh", the apostle John's test of orthodoxy in testing the spirits of the age.

Finally, we realize that both sides in this dispute have lined up authorities. On both sides we have committed Christians with differing opinions as to the interpretation of L'Engle's writings, her standing as a Christian, and whether or not she is a proponent of New Age thought. All sincere and knowledgeable; each committed to Christ and his kingdom. It serves no cause but Satan's to continue pitting one Christian against another.

It is clear to us that each side will not be persuading the other. What is equally clear is that the discussions must come to an end and we must move on. We have made this decision in good faith, in prayer, and on the basis of information we have considered trustworthy. It is time to put this dispute behind us and work together.

The Lord has blessed Orland Park CRC in many ways, and continues to do so. There are many exciting ministries which would benefit from your energies and gifts. It is our prayer that we can work together as God's people on other challenges and opportunities, and we thank you for being concerned about the spiritual welfare of our congregation.

Paul always considered disputes in the church in the context of a unity which honors our Lord. It is this unity to which we call ourselves and all of you. We may agree to disagree, but we do so only and always as brothers and sisters in Christ.

In His Service,

The Elders Orland Park Christian Reformed Church

The letter sparked a fire in us that would not go out until we got some answers. Unity. Unity with whom, what and how? I Corinthians 6 was talking about disputes over property. I began looking up all the passages in the New Testament that referred to unity, divisions in the church, sound doctrine and false teachings or teachers. There was no question that sound doctrine was the solid foundation on which unity rests. Without it, true unity would never be achieved.

In a plea to his fellow elders, Howard Stob observed:

The apostles never took a neutral position where basic truth was concerned. The apostle Paul never had unity as a goal. When he went into a synagogue, the old testament church, he declared a message, and that message left a trail of split churches. The only unity he looked for

was unity on his side and on God's terms. He made judgments as to what agreed with his message, and what did
not agree. He made judgments on the same basis we are
doing now. Jesus was the only name on the list. Paul called
himself a doulos; that is, a slave of Christ Jesus. A slave
had an owner. The slave gave up his selfish thinking and
his will so that his might imbibe the mind and will of his
owner. . . . Unity in the church is a by-product of being
on the side of truth under Christ Jesus. We cannot unite
under false doctrine. Judgments must be made. We must
know when to unite and when to divide. Light and darkness are incompatible. . . . Wheat and weeds might grow
in the same field, but finally they will be separated. We
must identify what belongs to the world's kingdom, and
what belongs to Christ's kingdom (Howard's confirma-
tion of resignation from office to the elders, dated March
25, 1991).

What did our elders mean by "agree to disagree"? Were we to
agree that some see certain teachings as heretical and blasphemous,
but others in the church called them Christian, so forget about it?
And how could we forget about it when these works were being
taught to our children as an example of Christian literature? I had
already seen the consequences of L'Engle's teachings at Wheaton
College. There was no way I could leave this alone. Such strong,
differing views of L'Engle's works meant something was terribly
wrong.

As I read the letter over again, I stopped short with dismay at
the elders' words, "It serves no cause but Satan's to continue pitting one Christian against each other." Is that what they thought we
were doing–helping Satan? I could almost see the devil smiling.
What better tactic could there be than to make one think those who
saw error were helping him. All we had done was to bring to light
an author's teachings and compare them to Scripture. We had no
intention of pitting people against each other. And really, why should
it have? Didn't we all believe the same essential truths of Scripture?

I noticed none of the passages we had read to the elders had
been taken apart, scrutinized or supported with Scripture. It seemed
they felt more comfortable with changing the issue to a matter of

what we should or should not read, even though the education committee had said books which promoted occult teachings didn't have a place in the church library. What was worse, while declaring Christians must read with "critical discernment," they claimed L'Engle's writings built up the Body of Christ. As far as I knew, most of the elders hadn't read any of her works. Why hadn't they read at least one book of non-fiction each with critical discernment and given us Biblical reasons why L'Engle's writings fit the body of Christ? Was it because they all felt it was a "waste of God-given time"?

It appeared the elders' decision had been made exclusively by their "reading of the authorities" who agreed with their previous decision and whom they deemed "trustworthy." Those who disagreed, I took it, were not trustworthy, or maybe just their information wasn't.

To "agree to disagree" was an unholy compromise; one certainly unworthy of office-bearers whose duty it was to keep watch over the flock and be on guard against those who distort the truth (Acts 20:28-31). Direction had to be given by the overseers of the church to guide the congregation into Truth. A choice had to be made of which interpretation was right or wrong. As the apostle Paul forewarned:

> You cannot drink the cup of the Lord and the cup of demons too; you cannot have a part in both the Lord's table and the table of demons. Are we trying to arouse the Lord's jealousy? Are we stronger than he? (1 Corinthians 10:21).

Blindly Following the Leader

There was one question that still haunted me. Had Mels somehow misunderstood De Vries? Or had he purposefully tried to keep De Vries' assessment hidden from the other elders?

It was Saturday, April 21, 1990, 6:30 p.m. Karen stopped by. We had decided to call our elder and listen to his explanation of why De Vries' letter had not been read. I was not going to tell him I had already talked with Rev. De Vries or with Howard Stob. I wanted to hear first-hand from his point of view what happened at that elders' meeting. I didn't like doing this, but I needed to know; we all did. With Karen listening in, I dialed Mels' number and soon there was a low-pitched voice on the other end saying "hello." My first inclination was to hang up, but it was too late. I had already said "hello" and told him who I was.

"Ken, I just want to ask you a few questions. Did you read John De Vries' letter at the elders' meeting?" (Nothing like getting right down to the nitty-gritty.)

"No, I read it and Rev. Erffmeyer read it."

"Did you say anything about it?"

"Well, I talked to John De Vries and John said he wrote the letter in haste. He said that he read a part of her book and well, wasn't really sure if she was New Age or not, and that he wasn't sure if her books should be in the library or not. He said he wished he hadn't even written the letter."

"Oh, John De Vries said all this when you talked with him?"

"Yes," Ken asserted.

"I talked with Vernon Boerman [a teacher at Illiana Christian High School whom Ken had said I should also speak with–CVK]. He said it would be naive to think there was no New Age thought in her books. Then he gave me a copy of a speech he said his daughter had used as a faculty speech in New Jersey. He asked me to see what I thought of it. He said, 'Maybe you'll think there is New Age thought in it, maybe you won't. I'd like your opinion.' I read it and knew it was L'Engle's speech and told him his daughter could be charged with plagiarism. I don't know if he knew this or not, but it seemed pretty suspicious to me. . . . Oh, he was nice enough, but cagey and contradictory. You couldn't tell where he was at. . . ."

"Well, that's Vernon," Ken agreed.

"The elders say in their letter that they talked with 'experts' who know New Age writings and L'Engle's writings. Who are they? They weren't written down."

"You just mentioned two of them."

"But John De Vries was for us."

"Well, I didn't make it sound like that at the meeting."

"Why?"

"Well, you know John, every five years he is into something different. Right now he is into New Age. . . . John is seeing it in everything."

"Oh? He's reading it into everything?" [I repeated to make sure I heard right].

" Yes."

"You know Ken, John called here Wednesday and told me he was very discouraged with the decision the elders made and that he stands behind his letter." There was a long pause here.

"Uh, . . ." (another long pause) "that's possible. . . . Gerda Bos is another one I talked to and Jenni Hoekstra. . . . They said there was nothing wrong with her writings."

"John De Vries knows New Age thought and has had much more experience. . . ." Mels was not listening, nor did he care. "There's no point in continuing this conversation. Good-by, Ken," I said sadly.

"Good-bye."

Thoroughly disgusted, I looked over at Karen and my husband who had come upstairs and were now sitting at the kitchen table. They were as utterly confused and upset as I was. It was incomprehensible to us how a friend of Rev. De Vries' could say the things he had without knowing the first thing about New Age thought, without taking the time to read so much as one of L'Engle's works, without comparing them to Scripture, and without a desire to do so. As an elder, he was responsible for the well-being of the church, but his responsibility along with the oath he had taken didn't seem to be taken very seriously at all. He blindly followed the leader, who trusted the "experts," who blindly followed the deceived.

Chapter Seven

A QUESTION OF JUDGMENT, DISCERNMENT AND CENSORSHIP

Watch out for false prophets. They come to you in sheep's clothing, but inwardly they are ferocious wolves. By their fruit you will recognize them. Do people pick grapes from thornbushes, or figs from thistles?

Matthew 7:15-16

The whole concept of judging . . . is abhorrent to the Reformed Christian.

Pastors and Elders of
Orland Park Christian Reformed Church

We all assumed from the elders' letter to us which spoke of promising "to submit to the government of the church" and "its admonition and discipline," that we would be put under church discipline if we continued in our efforts. I welcomed the idea. If they did so, I might believe what the pastor and elders were doing was out of love and concern for us. As parents, we discipline our children because we love them and want them to grow up knowing right from wrong. As our Father, "the Lord disciplines those whom he loves" (Hebrews 12:6). So far, I had not seen anything that remotely resembled love and concern. If discipline took place, the matter would go before the congregation, and maybe that's where the whole matter needed to be—out in the open.

Almost every night for the next couple of weeks, Karen and I

69

worked on a reply to the elders. We wanted the letter to be as force-
ful and as much to the point as possible without sounding mean-
spirited. This was somewhat difficult to do considering the fact our
pastors and elders were holding high the works of a woman who,
as far as we were concerned, denied every essential tenet of the
Christian faith.

Point by point we refuted their letter and provided many verses
from Scripture warning of false teachers and of the elders' duty as
office-bearers to guard the church of which they were overseers.
Once again we quoted from L'Engle's non-fiction works and from
M. Scott Peck's book, *The Road Less Traveled,* where he states, "It
is for the individual to become totally, wholly God . . . ." We also
included a number of things that had happened personally and how
we felt about them. Though that was not our main concern, *all* the
elders needed to see to what extent a false teacher was being defended.

I reminded them I had been told we were out on a witchhunt,
looking for a conspiracy and that the devil could be using us; that
we had been called unloving and unChristian and were being
watched; that we had a "narrow" view of Christianity; had been
accused of slandering L'Engle, and that so far, no Biblical basis
had been given for their judgment of "Christian." The elders' statement that they had "prayerfully sought the leading of the Lord in
this matter," and had given our appeal "fair and careful consideration," hardly seemed an appropriate or accurate one.

The letter was perhaps a bit more blunt than it should have been,
but I didn't see any point to seasoning the letter with wishy-washy,
superficial niceties to protect their ego. We ended the letter by saying if our words sounded harsh it was because we had written it
with a lot of frustration, but it was also written because we cared
about them. It would have been much easier for us just to leave our
church and attend somewhere else. While the personal aspect of
this matter did hurt, it was a minor issue in comparison to what we
saw as an eternal life or death issue. The hurts we could handle; the
consequences for not saying anything, we could not.

We sent the letter May 1, 1990, and received a very short reply
toward the latter part of June. It simply stated the elders reaffirmed
their decision, but because they realized there were still strong feelings on our part, they would continue to pray for the Lord's healing for all involved.

Now, what were we going to do? To stay in a church whose leaders could hold such writings to be Christian was out of the question. Yet, we longed to stay. Hoping the consistory's decision concerning L'Engle's works was more a matter of pride and/or unwillingness to put much effort into the issue than anything else, we decided to appeal the matter to Classis Chicago South (a broader assembly of 17 neighboring Christian Reformed churches).

More late nights, more study, more McDonalds and pizza for supper. This was not an easy task. Karen and I worked on the appeal together but knew little about all the particular procedures involved. We were told classis would not even consider an appeal asking it to reverse a decision on whether or not some literature or author was Christian or not. We couldn't come out and say our consistory no longer held to the tenets of the Christian faith. It would sound absolutely preposterous. The only decision the elders had made which we could ask to have reversed was their judgment to keep the books in the library. So we began our appeal asking classis to reverse that decision, which we explained in the next paragraph was based on the fact they believed L'Engle's writings gave a strong Christian message.

Little did we realize when we wrote the appeal, "CENSORSHIP" would become the center of the controversy. Our main concern was not that L'Engle's books were in the church library, but that they were being called "Christian." If they were found under a section labeled "Occultism" or "New Age," that would be a different story. But as it was shown us, Christians nowadays don't like to label anything. It's not polite or "politically correct" to say something isn't right and give it a label. Everyone should make up their own mind. Right? I don't think so. Haven't Christians who hold to the wonderful truths of Scripture been labeled? Where's the "political correctness" in that?

The next few pages of the appeal contrasted L'Engle's writings and Scripture under four separate categories: Denial of Biblical Authority, Denial of the Substitutionary Atonement, Denial of Eternal Damnation/Universalism/Satan's Redemption, and Denial of Jesus as the Christ and only way to Salvation. Information on the occult in comparison to her works was also included. We also quoted the purpose of the church library from the library criteria that was given us. We hoped classis would conclude our consistory was wrong in its premise for keeping the books in the library, which then in turn would tell us, depending on how our consistory responded, where they stood with their own beliefs.

On July 18, 1990, we sent out our appeal to Classis Chicago South, only to have it rejected. The classical chairman, Rev. Neal Punt, pastor of First Christian Reformed Church of Evergreen Park, IL, called to ask if he and Rev. John Dykstra, pastor of Oak Lawn CRC, could come over to clarify why our appeal had been denied. As they sat at the dining room table with us sipping some hot coffee, they explained if our appeal had gone before classis without first seeking advice from the church visitors, classis would judge our appeal was not properly before them and dismiss it.

We agreed to meet with the church visitors (two CRC ministers from other churches who acted as counselors or mediators when a problem arose in the church). As we were talking, I got the distinct impression they didn't realize the seriousness of the appeal. I handed a copy of *The Irrational Season*, another book of L'Engle's I had found in the church library, to Rev. Dykstra and explained that this is what our elders were upholding as good "Christian" literature. I watched his face as he read the concluding paragraph of the book:

> But his love is greater than all our hate, and he will not rest until Judas has turned to him, until Satan has turned to him, until the dark has turned to him; until we can all, all of us without exception, freely return his look of love with love in our own eyes and hearts. And then, healed, whole, complete but not finished, we will know the joy of being co-creators with the one to whom we call (page 215).

I'll never be able to put into words the look that came over his face. "Rev. Punt, read this!" he exclaimed.

Rev. Punt didn't want to take the time to read it, but Dykstra kept pushing the book in front of him. Finally, he held it up right in front of Punt's face. "READ THIS, READ THIS!" he urged, upset at what he had read.

Slowly, Rev. Punt reached for the book. As he read L'Engle's summary of her theology, a look of complete puzzlement came over his face. From that moment on, we knew God had opened another door.

The Issue Made Clear

Our meeting with the church visitors was scheduled for September 6, 1990. Still an elder, Howard carefully wrote up his lone, dissenting position so that the church visitors would have no question as to the cause of our dilemma. Because the issue would continuously be camouflaged, concealed, and changed by the elders over the next few years, I'm printing Howard's letter as written. This I do so you, the reader, can see in the chapters ahead to what length our consistory and many others went to defend this writer:

Elder\Church Visitors' Meeting, September 6, 1990

Madeleine L'Engle is a prolific author. Her books contain her Christian perspective. She is teaching a type of Christianity.

What is the issue here? My view of the issue is:

1. Do her books convey an underlying, acceptable, Christian message?

2. Are they in basic and general harmony with what is taught at OPCRC?

Obviously, we don't expect any author to be letter perfect. We give any artist certain literary freedoms to express their views.

That she is a spell-binding artist of considerable talent is not in question. She has a large part of the Christian community mesmerized with her profound insights into the Bible. All the people gathered in this room presenting the majority elder reply are proof of that. The standing ovation she received at Wheaton College, Calvin College, and the Christian Academy in Japan, are proof of that. They all answer the two issue questions in the affirmative.

It would seem unlikely that such a vast majority could be wrong, and a lone and isolated voice of dissent here and there could be right.

Anything this obvious and this accepted should make the task of the church visitors a simple one.

What possesses me to give a lone, dissenting vote on these two issues? Is it super Christian pride that I see something no one else does? Just the opposite is true. That pride had to be surrendered and put to death in order to take a most unpopular position.

Everyone here believes that Christ Jesus died for their awful sins. I'm the only one here who believes that Madeleine L'Engle, in her books, teaches the exact opposite and that she teaches it clearly and unmistakably.

Everyone here believes that because Jesus died for our awful sins–and we believe it–by that faith we are joined to Him eternally for eternal life. But if we reject Jesus and the atonement, eternal death awaits us–eternal hell–no more reprieves. So important is this good news that we send missionaries all over the world to say to the Buddhists, Hindus and those who worship the sun or reptiles that Jesus is the Way. He loves you. Turn to Him. Repent of your sin. He offers life. This is my story, this is my song. What praise and hallelujahs it brings around the world when people come to Jesus.

Madeleine L'Engle takes this all away from me. Clearly, and in no uncertain terms, she rejects Jesus as the Way, the Truth and the Life. She states that all who worship the sun will be saved–all will be saved. In fact, there is no literal heaven or hell.

My negative vote cast against Madeleine L'Engle, her books and her writings are because I perceive her literature to deny every basic, foundational doctrine I believe, and I can't bend that far. To me it's a different and foreign and strange gospel. To me her writings not only are not edifying, but are repulsive, dangerous, subversive and treacherous. To defend her writings as being Christian, in my opinion, is to defend error.

Howard Stob.

The Issue Confused

Karen, Si and I also thought we had made our concerns clear to the church visitors. At the end of our meeting, one church visitor, Rev. Cal Hoogendoorn, pastor of Palos Heights CRC, assured us the issue was now "crystal-clear" to him. He even prayed for the Lord to bless our work–a prayer which I had hardly expected. We believed he understood the seriousness of the matter and hoped for a quick resolution.

A week after our meeting, we received a letter from Rev. Hoogendoorn and Rev. Tony Van Zanten (Roseland Christian Ministries, Chicago, IL), which would be sent to Classis Chicago South for information. They listed their observations as to what both we and the elders perceived the problem to be and proceeded to provide a rather familiar opinion of their own. They wrote:

> In the judgment of the church visitors, whether one believes L'Engle's works are Christian or New Age need not be seen as central to the concern. As a matter of fact, one can question whether any piece of literature is completely biblical, agrees with all the doctrinal teachings of any Church, and satisfies the standards of orthodoxy. . . . The issue is not, in our judgment, whether a book is Christian, but whether in reading any book the reader critically evaluates the work against the Scriptures. The Elders have made an acceptable decision (Letter from CV to Elders & Appellants, 9-11-90).

Did we ever say one could not read a book other than those which agreed with everything in Scripture? No. Had the elders ever critically evaluated L'Engle's works against Scripture? No. So how could the church visitors conclude they had made an acceptable decision? While saying the issue had been made perfectly crystal-clear, their letter had missed the point altogether. The question was, why?

Another meeting with the church visitors was set up so we could meet face to face with the elders and discuss our differences. The church visitors would moderate the meeting. According to their rules, *"The standard for determining success would not be who 'wins the argument' but the demonstrations of concern for the unity of the church as evidenced by the willingness to listen and learn from the hearts of others*." (Letter dated 10-10-90, emphasis mine).

It wasn't hard to figure out what the outcome of that meeting would be. With the elders' position of "let's agree to disagree" for the sake of unity of the church, our position looked pretty dim. This wasn't a game in which a bunch of silly, immature adults had to win or else. However, a right or wrong answer was demanded. Had the elders been right in their assessment that these works were Christian, or did they undermine Scripture and teach a different gospel? And what about the church library criteria, didn't that count?

On November 27, 1990, we sat with the elders and church visitors, not knowing quite what to expect. At the beginning of the meeting, the clerk of the elders read a prepared written statement affirming the elders' unyielding position (this was denied to Rev. Punt at a later date). So much for discussion. Rev. Erffmeyer attended this meeting, but was not at all enthused about answering the questions we asked. The elders refused to see the new information I had found concerning L'Engle and M. Scott Peck. And all pastor De Boer could say was that L'Engle's books fit the church library criteria. Because our discussion was at a stand-still, the church visitors laid out the following options:

A. Agree to Disagree [on the doctrinal aspects of L'Engle's works–CVK]
B. Initiate an informal, voluntary study group to critically review L'Engle's writings, without beginning with preconceived agendas and conclusions.
C. If Elders and Appellants cannot resolve, to bring the matter to Classis (letter dated 11-29-90 from church visitors confirms this).

To agree to disagree would be to compromise our strongly held beliefs. Plan B is what we had asked for all along. We hoped the elders would agree to study L'Engle's works with us. They refused. The only option left was plan C; bring the matter before classis.

With no other alternative possible, I took out a newly written appeal (Appendix A) at the end of our meeting and handed it to the church visitors. Rev. Punt, as classical chairman, had suggested I do so if we didn't make any progress at our meeting. If we waited, our appeal would not be on the next agenda for the January session of Classis Chicago South and would be delayed for several months.

Much to our surprise, we were fiercely reprimanded for this action by the church visitors in front of the elders, and in their report to Classis Chicago South, they wrote:

> As Church Visitors we are disappointed and greatly disturbed by the action of the Appellants. While giving the appearance of seeking resolution, providing a ready made and newly written appeal betrays their presence at and the purpose of the meeting. We can only conclude that they are not interested in resolution and reconciliation with the Elders (letter from church visitors, dated 11-29-90).

Did these church visitors really think we would go through all the trouble we had over the past year if we didn't want reconciliation with our elders and our church? As I continued to read the report, I noticed something of far greater significance. These words stood out above everything else:

> In obedience to Matthew 7, no one may harbor a judgmental spirit. Whether author, reader or critic, care must be taken not to attack someone else's speck before addressing personal blindness.

It was bad enough the church visitors had misjudged our motives, but under this new line of reasoning lay a whole new argument for the elders to use as part of their "defense." I wasn't positive if the church visitors meant we couldn't judge an author's teachings to be un-Christian, but it was the only thing that made sense because of the context in which it was written. When we received the elders' response to our appeal (Appendix A), there was no doubt that was precisely what the church visitors had meant and our elders used it to their advantage.

The Elders' Response–December 4, 1990

In their response, the consistory (pastors and elders) first questioned classis' "obligation and duty to evaluate books in church libraries and declare them to be heresy." They also provided a chronology of events in an effort to show "countless hours, and much thought and prayer went into making this decision."

Quotes by Mildred Zylstra, English professor at Calvin College in Grand Rapids, Michigan, were used to support their conclusion that L'Engle was "a sincere Christian from a different background." Zylstra's analysis was: "To read *A Stone for a Pillow*, is to listen to the ideas of an interesting, intelligent, vitally Christian woman. Her faith permeates all her books." The consistory also informed classis that seven out of eight church libraries in Classis Chicago South carried L'Engle's books and reported the CRC's magazine, *The Banner*, had repeatedly included favorable reviews of L'Engle. This only strengthened our concern.

Much of the problem, the consistory noted, had to do with our personal "interpretation" of L'Engle's writings. Out of all the quotes we had supplied, only one under the category of "Denial of Eternal Damnation/Universalism/Satan's Redemption" was taken and supported by Scripture. As to whether or not all would be redeemed, including Satan, our consistory said: ". . . we refer to Romans 8:19: 'The creation waits in eager expectation for the sons of God to be revealed.' Romans 8:22: 'For we know that the whole creation has been groaning as in the pains of childbirth right up to the present time.' This sounds similar to the quote on Page 3 [of our appeal–CVK], 'The Second Coming is the redemption of the entire cosmos, not just one small planet.' "

For our consistory to use Scripture in such a way was hard to comprehend. As Howard Stob would later say in his resignation as elder, "It is a misuse of Scripture, totally unworthy of those who want to exalt Christ Jesus" (Letter of Resignation from Howard Stob to the Council of Orland Park CRC, March 5, 1991).

Did our consistory actually believe it was possible for Satan and all people to be redeemed? Or could it be they purposely ignored all of the other quotes by L'Engle we had provided in their attempt to defend her "Christianity"? There was yet one last possibility. Maybe, they thought this theory was compatible with Christianity, even though they themselves did not agree with it.

These questions had to be answered because, in our eyes, to claim Satan and all people will be saved is to call God a liar, the Bible untrustworthy, and the substitutionary, sacrificial death of Jesus Christ, needless (since L'Engle denies he came to mediate between God and man). While we were accused of taking things out-of-context, that is precisely what our elders were doing, or at least the pastor and few elders that worked closely with him. I wondered if all the elders had taken the time to read our appeal or if some had just tossed it in the wastebasket. Then again, had all of them even read their own response? If not, they were still all responsible for what was written.

For the appellants, the summary of the elders' response was a complete disregard of their office as elder and of God's Word. It stated:

> Many of the statements in the appeal are taken out of context or are interpreted differently by different Christians. Some are misunderstood by those who wrote this appeal. We have verbally tried to point this out to the appellants on several occasions, but they refuse to listen or acknowledge that there may be different ways to interpret L'Engle's works. They firmly maintain that they are the final authorities on L'Engle [that was never said–CVK].

> We do acknowledge that there are many problematic passages in L'Engle's writings. There are many things that she says in a way that we would not say them. L'Engle is clearly not a Christian Reformed Church writer. The issue is whether, as a whole, her writings are written from a Christian perspective, and whether they are useful for Christian readers. This is where we differ from the appellants.

> We believe very firmly in the fact that God gives the gift of discernment to His people. We believe that God does gather, defend, and preserve for Himself a chosen people, through His Word and Spirit. The Word and Spirit of God cause us to read a variety of literature which we do not always agree with completely, but which we read critically, as Reformed Christians. As the Church Visitors have reminded all of us, we must read all literature with an eye to testing it against the Scriptures, and agree with literature in so far as it is in harmony with the Scriptures. This has always been the Reformed Perspective on Literature.

> While we agree with the appellants that many parts of

> L'Engle's writings are not Reformed, *we strongly feel that*
> *no one has the right to judge another person as to their*
> *Christianity. God alone is the judge. Each Christian*
> *falls short of complete purity of doctrine. L'Engle is no*
> *exception.*
>
> *The whole concept of judging L'Engle as to whether she*
> *is "Christian" or not, is abhorrent to the Reformed Chris-*
> *tian* (emphasis mine).

How could our elders, whose sworn oath and duty it was to "reject all errors," "refute and contradict" them, and "keep the Church free from such errors," possibly make such a declaration? They had made the firm, staunch judgment that L'Engle was indeed a "Christian author" and her works a blessing. Why were we not allowed to test her teachings by Scripture and make the judgment that her writings were not Christian and harmful to the body of Christ? We are called to "test everything" (I Thessalonians 5:21).

To speak of the gift of discernment and testing literature against Scripture, and in the same breath say it is abhorrent to judge whether one is a Christian or not, is completely contradictory. The discernment God graciously gives causes His people to make judgments; right or wrong, true or false, Christian or not-Christian. What was this rhetoric our consistory was using? Discernment and judgment cannot be separated.

There is a type of judging that is wrong, as seen at the beginning of Matthew 7, that is, to judge hypocritically or self-righteously. But we had made it clear to our pastors and elders that her salvation was in God's hands, not ours. They knew what we meant. I could imagine false teachers having a celebration the day our consistory announced we couldn't judge teachings to be Christian or non-Christian. Had they forgotten Paul's ceaseless warnings to the Ephesian elders?

> Keep watch over yourselves and all the flock of which
> the Holy Spirit has made you overseers. Be shepherds
> of the church of God, which he bought with his blood. I
> know that after I leave, savage wolves will come in among
> you and will not spare the flock. *Even from your own*
> *number men will arise and distort the truth in order to*
> *draw away disciples after them.* So be on your guard!

Remember that for three years I never stopped warning
each of you night and day with tears (Acts 20:28-31,
emphasis mine).

Now, redefining the issue, diffusing its clarity, the consistory
claimed: "The real issue here is: What are we as Reformed Christians able to read? Can we read only that which agrees totally with
our own theological viewpoint? That would be a fundamentalist
and not a Reformed Perspective on Literature. We are called to
critically evaluate all literature from our Reformed Perspective. As
we evaluate all that we read in the light of God's Word, we believe
that God's Word and Spirit will guide us to discern truth and error."

I couldn't help but wonder if they really thought the appellants
believed Christians should read only that which was in agreement
with Reformed thinking. It was a ridiculous assumption if they did.

Censorship. It's a dirty word to many Christians. "Let the children decide for themselves what is right and wrong," they say. But
they forget, God our Father was the first censor. Parents love, guard
and protect their children. They give them food, not poison. Would
they purposely buy them *The Satanic Bible* and tell them it was a
good Christian book to model their life after? Would they put
Playboy or *Playgirl* under their noses and tell them it's a Christian
magazine? Would they give them these things at all? I doubt it.
But, they might read an interesting fantasy novel or watch a good
science-fiction thriller together with their children and if they see
something that disagrees with God's Word, point it out and show
them why it's wrong.

As parents protect their children till they're old enough to dis-
tinguish right from wrong, the leaders of the church should protect
their flock. Not by telling them what they can or cannot read, but
by letting them know what teachings are in harmony with Scripture. The word "censorship," I believe, has been screamed out and
used many a time to one's own advantage whenever his or her own
misguided beliefs are exposed. Maybe that's why L'Engle uses it
to discredit those who expose her works.

Our elders had been consistently told what the issue was. The
fact that they maintained differing interpretations were possible so
we must "agree to disagree" was disturbing. To acknowledge there
are differing interpretations of an author's writings, therefore, not

one interpretation can be right or wrong, is known as "deconstruc-
tionism." As Dr. David Thibodaux, English professor at the University of Southwestern Louisiana observed:

> Ultimately, it becomes pointless to read or write anything
> because, according to deconstruction, no one will ever
> be able to know what we were trying to say, nor will we
> ever be able to know what anyone else was trying to say"
> (*Political Correctness*, Huntington House Pub., Lafayette,
> Louisiana, 1992, pg. 22).

The elders' reasoning was a sad one, but it made perfect sense.
After all, if there are differing interpretations and you cannot make
judgments, how can there be a right or wrong answer? Their response to our appeal reinforced our commitment to see this matter
through, difficult as it was for both sides.

Chapter Eight

SERMONS THAT DIVIDE

I urge you, brothers, to watch out for those who cause
divisions and put obstacles in your way that are contrary
to the teaching you have learned. Keep away from them.
For such people are not serving our Lord Christ, but their
own appetites. By smooth talk and flattery they deceive
the minds of naive people.

Romans 16:17-18

From the time of our first appeal to Classis Chicago South, the
appellants (as we were now formally called along with our friends
who supported us), became acutely aware of an increasingly vigorous defense of Madeleine L'Engle's writings. As the elders noted,
articles had appeared in *The Banner* defending L'Engle's Christianity and chiding those who exposed her teachings. They included
one entitled, "Madeleine L'Engle: A Passion for What's Real," in
their response to our appeal.

This particular article was written by Mary Boerman Lagerway,
a Bible teacher at Eastern Christian High School in North Haledon,
New Jersey. She is the daughter of Vernon Boerman, the teacher at
Illiana Christian High School, (Lansing, IL) who had told Karen
and me that one would be naive to think there was no New Age
thinking in L'Engle's works. (Presently, Mary is teaching Bible at
Illiana.)

Lagerway gave a ringing endorsement of *The Irrational Season*
and *A Stone for a Pillow* without providing so much as one particular problematic passage she knew would be of concern to many

Christians. Lightly dismissing the "charges" that L'Engle's writings promote New Age thought, Lagerway defended her by saying: "L'Engle herself confesses to be a Christian in magazine interviews and public speeches. To hear her speak is to be assured that Jehovah is her God . . . her writing speaks . . . clearly of God's grace and his salvation."

Did Lagerway support her assumptions with Scripture? No, there wasn't one verse used and compared to L'Engle's ideas, which wasn't at all surprising. Yet, her readers were to assume, "It would be tragic to lose this Christian writer to a fad label just because she doesn't write in an overtly Christian enough way for some" (*The Banner*, October 1, 1990, pg. 13).

One has to stop here a minute and ask, "What is a Christian enough way?" How much of a difference can one accept before the meaning to the word "Christian" is totally lost?

Continuing her defense, Lagerway cried, ". . . a great misunderstanding has occurred. These books predate the New Age movement and the scientific concepts that she deals with . . ." (*ibid.,* pg. 13). Well, one of two things was certain. Either she had no idea what New Age thought was, where it came from, and how subtle it could be, or she knew exactly what she was doing.

The damage unfortunately, was already done. A fog would cloud the vision of those who would read, "Don't let . . . the accusations ('sounds New Age to me') scare you off. Find out for yourself about this talented Christian writer who dares to deal with real life." Trouble is, most people wouldn't bother to read the books in question, but they would not hesitate to join the ranks with Lagerway against the opposition–"right-wing conservatives."

Howard and I were thoroughly upset with the article so we both wrote a full rebuttal to *The Banner*. Several passages from L'Engle's works that denied the substitutionary atonement, eternal damnation, etc. . . . were listed and compared to Scripture. I also included occult connections in her works and information on New Age thought. Neither one of our rebuttals was printed.

For the next several weeks, short responses to Lagerway's article appeared in "The Voices" section of the magazine. This was unusual since most of the time, responses were only printed up to a couple of weeks after an article was printed. One which appeared in the November 26, 1990 issue, read: "I am grieved by people who accuse her of being New Age. New Age teachings may be something to fear and fight, but I don't believe we should go on witch hunts against fellow Christians. I think Satan laughs when we do."

Someone from my church liked this answer so much they took an iridescent yellow marker highlighting the words, cut it out and put it in my mailbox at church. While not proving their accusations, these people complained of censorship, fear, self-righteous judging and of witchhunting. Why couldn't they see Satan laughs when Christians insist there are no false teachers among them? We had taken Scripture and tested L'Engle's works—where was their proof?

Battle lines were forming. No longer was this an issue in our church alone. It was widespread, throughout the denomination. Never would I have imagined that reading *Walking on Water* would lead to such a monumental division. Unfortunately, those people in the pew who didn't bother to find out the facts and discern for themselves what was going on were caught in a battle for the mind.

Recently, I watched Oprah Winfrey, one of Chicago's famous talk show hosts, interviewing a woman who had come out of a cult. The deprogrammer who helped her find her way out of the cult was also on and described methods of mind control. He pointed out that the female pastor of the church this woman attended would not allow anyone to criticize her. Those who dared do so were pegged as "Satan's helpers." This, he explained, was a form of mind control. It brainwashes a person into believing anything the pastor says without question and puts them down in the process. The members are, therefore, conditioned to respond in a certain manner. The deprogrammer knew what he was talking about. Though the situation was a bit different, I was seeing a similar thing happening from the pulpit in our own church.

After our first appeal had been sent to Classis Chicago South and to our consistory, I asked permission to have Samantha Smith come and speak on the New Age Movement at our church. Permission was flatly denied. Somewhat surprisingly, she was allowed to speak at Chicago Christian High School in Palos Heights, IL, the school my daughter attended.

Just before Sam began her lecture, I walked into the teacher's lounge to get some coffee. As I opened the door, I noticed a huge stack of copies of Mary Boerman Lagerway's article lying on a shelf. Obviously, somebody wanted all the teachers to read it.

Approximately fifty or sixty people showed up that night, but neither of our pastors nor any of our elders were there. (One elder, however, did come to Sam's lecture the night before held at Tinley Park Reformed Church.) I believe only one or two teachers from Christian High came to hear Sam speak. I had a feeling the reason for the lack of attendance had something to do with the sermons that were being delivered from the pulpit, along with all the gossip that had been spread in the church and school.

A few weeks before Sam was to come, about the time of our first appeal to classis, Rev. Erffmeyer had begun a series of messages on Nehemiah. The Sunday before her lecture, his morning sermon was entitled "Examining the Walls." He spoke of how all of us, like Nehemiah are, at times, faced with an "impossible situation about someone or something that really disturbs you." "Nehemiah," he continued, "simply waits and prays and turns it over to God. . . . He waits for direction from God. And that's the mark of a great spiritual leader."

He suggested as Nehemiah looked around and saw the walls in ruin, "so today in our lives, the walls of testimony so often are in ruin." He gave examples of how the testimony was broken in the country and in churches when "Jesus says to us as a church, you want to be Bible-centered, you want to be orthodox. . . ." This was a switch. Wasn't he defending blasphemous teachings as Christian? Something was coming now, I could feel it. And something did.

> Do you hold grudges against other people? There are people that do that. When you hold a grudge for a while, you can take the middle part of that word and put an "m" in front of it, and you see what people sling when they hold a grudge. They sling mud at other people. It's not enough simply that you're hurt, but you want to sling mud at those other people. You want to get back at that person who hurt you. Or you have this free floating anger and that free floating resentment in your life *where you begin to simply attack people no matter who they are.*

"Did it matter who they were?" I thought. You could hear the anger in his own voice. It was almost as if he was putting himself in Nehemiah's place. Was he the great spiritual leader no one should question, or as he put it, attack? Visibly distraught, Erffmeyer spoke with intensity:

> Satan is always there. Rebuilding is difficult, because Satan always, always, has someone there to discourage you in that rebuilding in your life. It happened here for Nehemiah. In verse 19 Sanballet and Tobiah ridiculed us, they mocked us. Satan had people right there mocking and ridiculing Nehemiah and the people. . . . Rebuilding will always be difficult. It's never easy because Satan always always, has someone there to discourage you.
> . . .

I wondered if I was reading more into this sermon than what was really there, until he closed with these dividing words:

> *One man said to me, "You know what? I never talk to a certain group in the back of the church anymore. I won't go over there, because you know what happens when I go there and I hear the dirt that they sling just after I've come out of worship?" He says, "that's not good for my spiritual life. I walk away from that group. I won't talk to them anymore." And I say, praise the Lord for that man and for his soul!*
>
> *Because we're not here to sling mud at each other. . . . We're here to worship God and to be positive and rebuilding. . . . Satan will always say through someone else, "Let's rise and destroy! Let's rise and destroy!"*

While I knew that I and my "group" were not the ones slinging dirt in the back of church, I knew what many in the congregation were going to think. While Erffmeyer spoke about people who slung dirt, he had passed on to the elders false information about me without even confronting me to find out if what he heard was true. While he talked about keeping the church orthodox, he defended false teachings. A lump formed in my throat. I couldn't sing the ending song. We had been accused of dividing the church and had been told Satan could be using us. Did he have us in mind when he spoke those words with such animosity?

I thought about his sermon over and over again. Sanballet and Tobiet, who ridiculed Nehemiah, were not inside the church or inside one's own congregation. Never in all my life had I heard such a sermon, or one that even closely resembled it. The appellants and others who heard his analogy felt it was a terrible abuse of his office and misuse of Scripture. As to its effect, after church some people came up to Sharon and remarked, "Boy, your group really got hit from the pulpit!" Was it because they knew Erffmeyer was talking about us? No. It was just assumed from everything that had been said about us.

Sam had been staying at my house and went to church with my family the Sunday following her lecture (9-30-90). If there was any doubt left in the appellants' minds these sermons were being used against us, or anyone else who criticized Erffmeyer, there was none left now. The sermon was entitled, "Facing the Opposition," based on Nehemiah 4:1-9. This time, it started from the very beginning:

> . . . I have to say to you this morning that whenever and wherever God is working and moving in a mighty way, there will always be opposition . . . there are always, always, going to be those that oppose the work of God. Even though he is doing the work of the Lord, the enemy opposes him, and Satan uses people to discourage him, even as Satan uses people sometimes to discourage us as we want to build for the Lord. . . . Sanballat is used by Satan, and so often Satan does that yet today. He tries to discourage us through the insults and through the opposition of people who he uses in our lives.

> You see what happens, the critic resists change when it happens. The critic can't stand change when it occurs. *. . . It can happen in a church, it can happen in a denomination when a church is doing the work of the Lord. . . . Critics stay together. They kind of form a special group that is in opposition to the will of God. . . .*

> Satan will always have those that will oppose what God can do in our lives to bring change. It can happen *within* the church that is building for the Lord, that is really

moving forward in the Spirit's power. *People of God, there will always, always, be the critics like Sanballat and Tobiah that will say, "Who do those people think they are?" They question your motives. They question your character when you serve the Lord. They will do anything. Satan uses them in his warfare to try to discourage us.*

What was Nehemiah's reaction? Notice first of all . . . he prayed. . . . Did he try to get even with his enemies? Did he try to argue with them? No. Did he try to debate with them and say, "Well, I want you to agree with us that the wall is wonderful?" No. He didn't even debate with them. Did he get so angry that he simply lashed out at them? No, not at all. . . .

. . . *You know how to stop an argument? You simply close your mouth.* You know, so many people think that they have to respond back to every criticism. . . . Don't argue back to the opposition. . . . Did Jesus argue with those who opposed Him? No, he simply kept doing the work of the Lord. We could learn from Jesus.

Was this the reason Rev. Erffmeyer had kept as silent as possible at our meetings? And what did he mean, critics within the church resist change–change to what–a new color of the carpet? A new song? A new theology, perhaps? It does make a difference. The message of his sermon came across loud and clear. Anyone who dared to question or criticize the work of the Lord–via Rev. Erffmeyer–were Satan's helpers out to destroy the church.

His sermons on Nehemiah continued into October. "Facing Tricky Traps" (10-28), was the title of another based on Nehemiah 6:1-14. Once more he began, "Satan seeks only to destroy you. . . . Satan is alive and active today. . . . Satan uses any tactic and any device. He uses people to discourage you. . . . Satan never stops."

During the second part of his sermon, "Misrepresenting our Motives–Slander" (vs. 5-9), Erffmeyer pointed out that the open letter about Nehemiah was "filled with lies, rumors, and insinuation." Immediately, he added, "Nehemiah was falsely accused too." The strong letter Karen and I had sent to the elders had refuted certain accusations Rev. Erffmeyer had said about me. Had he connected this with his sermon? It seemed as though he did. But, did he really believe *he* had been falsely accused? And if so, why? We would never find out, because he refused to talk about it with us, just as he had preached.

Over the next few months until the January meeting of classis, and also in the years ahead, there would be many sermons on the importance of unity in the church and in the denomination. Those people within the independent churches that had finally left the denomination were said by Rev. Erffmeyer to be a "disgrace to the name of Jesus Christ" and those who had "dishonored" God (sermon, "Is This Church Healthy?" 6-6-93, p.m.).

While our pastor spoke so ardently on the unity of the body of Christ, at the same time, he impressed upon the members of the congregation the necessity of staying away from people within the church who were negative or critical. They were pictured as fanatics fighting over insignificant problems that had no bearing on one's salvation. Maybe some were, but many were not. Unless church members were willing to hear both sides to a story, and search out Scripture for themselves, they would be led by those who refused to be questioned, giving up their freedom to think for themselves.

Chapter Nine

A WARNING TO THE CHURCHES

I know your deeds, your hard work and your persever-
ance. I know that you cannot tolerate wicked men, that
you have tested those who claim to be apostles but are
not, and have found them false. You have persevered and
have endured hardships for my name, and have not grown
weary. Yet I hold this against you: You have forsaken
your first love. Remember the height from which you
have fallen! Repent and do the things you did at first.
                                                Revelation 2:2-5a

Weeks passed. Thanksgiving, Christmas, seemed somewhat of
a blur. It wasn't the same. My friend Kim and I usually played
special organ and piano duets this time of year. I missed practicing
at church and the overall thrill of the music filling my heart and
soul. I missed the smiles of friends and the warmth of fellowship
that is so enhanced at this time of year. I didn't feel at home in my
church any more. I didn't really know where I belonged. Being
brought up in the same denomination all my life, and being a member of this particular church for over 14 years, gave a sense of
belonging, of comfort and security. The roots are strong and deep.
Now I felt myself breaking apart from something I dearly wanted
to hold onto.

The other appellants and few friends who supported us after
searching out the situation at hand, became especially dear to me.
We prayed together, we searched Scripture together, we laughed
together (a greatly needed release from all the tension). We were

91

outcasts in our own church, but as lost as we all felt at times, facing it together gave us a new sense of belonging.

The classical committee, comprised of Rev. Punt, Rev. John Dykstra, and Rev. Gary Hutt, pastor of Park Lane CRC, Evergreen Park, IL, had appointed an advisory committee of four people to study the works of L'Engle. The chairman of this committee was Rev. Lester Van Essen, pastor of Immanuel CRC, Burbank, IL. The other three committee members were Mrs. Faith Triemstra, teacher at Southwest Christian School, Oak Lawn, IL, from Park Lane CRC, Mr. Clarence Fransman, a German teacher at Chicago Christian High School, Palos Heights, IL, from First Oak Lawn CRC, and Mr. Tom De Boer, member of Kedvale Ave CRC, Oak Lawn, IL.

Each of the members had been assigned to read two or more of L'Engle's works. Their conclusions would be handed out three weeks prior to the meeting so that the minister and elder delegates from each church in Classis Chicago South would have time to read and study the report. The decision of classis (whether our consistory's decision concerning L'Engle's writings should be upheld or not), would depend largely upon the advisory committee's findings.

The Report of the Advisory Committee

Whenever we felt that it was impossible or fruitless to continue in our efforts, God always opened another door, providing the strength and encouragement needed to do so. The advisory report was one of those doors (Appendix A).

The advisory committee cut through all the rhetoric given by our consistory. They identified the central issue to be "whether or not L'Engle's books ought to be classified as those of a Christian author." It was precisely because of the fact that L'Engle's books were present in many church libraries, upheld by professors and teachers as "Christian," and taught in many Christian schools, that the committee saw "the seriousness of the matter before them." They realized this was not an insignificant, meaningless, unChristian task unmerited by fanatic, fear-induced, negative people with a political agenda in mind, though this is how we were being portrayed.

Their report was precise and to the point: "The Elders' response claims that, 'Many of the statements in the appeal are taken out of context or are interpreted differently by different Christians.' However, *the response by the elders has not demonstrated that any of the quotations cited below are taken out of context or can be legitimately interpreted differently*" (emphasis mine).

In big, bold letters, the report unequivocally declared:

1. L' ENGLE DENIES THAT THE ATONEMENT, THE SUFFERING AND DEATH OF JESUS CHRIST, WAS A SUBSTITUTIONARY SACRIFICIAL PAYMENT FOR THE SINS OF GOD'S PEOPLE.

2. L' ENGLE DENIES THAT JESUS' INCARNATION IS QUALITATIVELY UNIQUE, UNIQUELY "GOD WITH US" IMMANUEL.

3. L' ENGLE DENIES THAT THERE WILL BE A FINAL SEPARATION BETWEEN GOD AND SOME PERSONS AS PROCLAIMED IN 2 THESSALONIANS 1:9, "THEY WILL BE PUNISHED WITH EVERLASTING DESTRUCTION AND SHUT OUT FROM THE PRESENCE OF THE LORD AND FROM THE MAJESTY OF THIS POWER."

4. L' ENGLE DENIES THE UNIQUE AUTHORITY OF THE BIBLE AS THE FINAL ARBITER IN ALL MATTERS OF FAITH AND PRACTICE.

This confirmed the four doctrinal errors we had pointed out in our appeal. Because there was not enough time to thoroughly research all our allegations before the classical meeting, the committee did not address the occult aspect of L'Engle's works. However, the committee did suggest:

In the light of the above denials of essential Biblical truths the reference to occult teachings and practices found in the appeal may also be valid . . . we think it would be part of wisdom for the Christian community to ferret out these allegations.

The committee concluded "that her books do not conform to the policies established for books to be placed in the Orland Park CRC library." Their grounds were:

1. They do not conform to the purpose of their library which is stated to be:

    a. "Its purpose is to provide a wide variety of materials for use by the members of the congregation as an aid in developing a consciousness towards Christian faith and growth."

    b. "Items selected for this library will generally reflect our denomination's theological perspective, and provide resources not normally found in the public system."

2. They do not conform to their selection criteria listed in 2.B, namely: "Is the book true to Biblical teachings and the doctrinal position of our church?"

3. They do not conform to their process used in book selection found in 3.G, namely: "Reformed perspective of God's world."

The closing paragraph of the advisory report was a warning to all the churches of Classis Chicago South:

> This does not mean to say or imply that Christians ought not to read the works of Madeleine L'Engle. *It is intended to alert all the churches of Classis that to simply place her works in a church library may give her works a cloak of Christian orthodoxy that the books do not deserve* (emphasis mine).

Unbelievably, many would cling to the first sentence of this paragraph, using it to make a case against censorship, and ignoring the most significant message in the report. They saw only what they wanted to see. In the appellants' eyes, the report firmly supported our appeal because we had *never* said Christians couldn't read her works.

Meeting of Classis Chicago South, January 16, 1991

Archer Avenue CRC, Chicago, Illinois. Rev. William Lenters, Hope CRC, Oak Forest, Illinois, chairman.

The day of the classical meeting, Howard and Jo, Dean & Karen,

Si and I and a few deacons and friends who diligently supported us, drove to Archer Avenue CRC to witness the events of the day. With the roaring engines of planes flying overhead, both Howard and I presented a very short speech (a few minutes long) before discussion on the floor took place. After this, we would not be allowed to speak. To prevent any misunderstanding, the issue was sharply put into focus and I urged classis to adopt the advisory report written by their committee.

Following my short plea with the delegates of classis, I sat down and took out my tape recorder. Classical meetings were open to the public, and legally, public meetings can be taped. A few minutes into the meeting, Rev. Cal Hoogendoorn saw I was taping and asked openly for my recorder to be shut off. It was decided tape-recorders weren't to be used since we were all brothers and sisters in the Lord and should be able to trust everyone. Well, my trust had been slowly melting away for a long time already. I pondered for a minute if Matthew 10:16 which says we should be cunning like serpents, but innocent as doves, would include this type of scenario. I wasn't sure, so I obediently put my tape recorder away. I should have been more insistent, because in the months and years to come, a tape would have come in mighty handy.

Much to our surprise, Hoogendoorn pulled out a "response to the appeal" *that was "Done in Council" on the very day of classis*, and was allowed to present it, even though it was not on the agenda nor handed out to the classical delegates three weeks in advance for study, as was required. It was an overture to Classis Chicago South to "appoint a committee to study the purpose and function of a Reformed, Church library; and to provide the Churches of Classis with helpful criteria and guidelines in determining what kind of books should be placed in such libraries" (Response submitted to CCS by Palos CRC–January 16, 1991).

The overture seemed a diversionary tactic to forego or at least delay dealing with our appeal. It didn't acknowledge Orland Park CRC already had a library criteria, and the books in question should agree with that criteria. Rather, the response implied Orland's criteria was too restrictive and needed to be changed:

> If the books are removed from the library, does such ac-
> tion mean Classis and local Churches are encouraging
> members to not read such material? And if they can be

read by discerning Christians, what is the acceptable rationale to censor them from Church Library shelves?. . . .
Are Madeleine L'Engle's works the only ones in our
Church libraries that do not meet the standards of Reformed and Christian orthodoxy?

Some of these questions were legitimate, but our concern was
not whether Christians should read these books. The overture
sprinkled a cloud of dust over the true issue at hand.

Attempts were now being made to nullify our appeal on incon-
sequential, technical difficulties. I was expecting another attempt
at this when surprisingly, Rev. Hellinga (Calvin CRC, Oak Lawn,
IL), spoke in our defense. He commended the appellants for reading and opening the eyes of consistories as to how New Age, universalism, and another false view of the atonement were creeping
into the church. It couldn't have been very easy for him to speak
up so candidly, but I was terribly grateful he had.

An elder delegate from Hope CRC, Michael Vander Weele, (professor of English at Trinity Christian College, Palos Heights, IL),
brought up an interesting suggestion. He asked if Donald Hettinga,
an English professor at Calvin College, could present a paper he
had written on L'Engle. He had traveled all the way from Michigan to present his "defense" (and our consistory's).

Thanks to a motion made by Rev. Punt, and supported by other
delegates, this was not allowed. I wanted to hear Hettinga's public
endorsement of L'Engle's writings, but since I wouldn't be allowed
to respond, it was a good thing he was refused. At this point, anyone with their eyes wide open could see we were in the midst of a
spiritual battle, and not in a crisis over a case of censorship.

Somehow, after more futile talk, Hoogendoorn managed to table
our appeal. "Done," I thought, "finished." Rev. Punt stood up, ar-
guing that it wouldn't be right for classis to do such a thing to the
appellants. Discussion continued. For some reason, (I can't imagine why), several pastors couldn't decide on what our appeal was
actually saying. I was sitting right there, as were Si, Dean, and
Karen. We were the appellants, why didn't they just ask us? It
seemed a bit ridiculous.

Rev. Hutt noticed I would be more than willing to answer this
question and made a motion that I be granted permission to clarify
the appeal. I was allowed to do so, but by this time I was distraught.

Before I stood up to speak, Karen tried to calm me down. I don't remember everything I said at that time. But I do remember making it a point to say having the books in the library was not the problem. The last page of our appeal had indicated this: "Taking her books out of the library will not solve the problem if they [the elders and pastors] still consider her writings to be Christian, regardless of whether or not they agree with every last word she says." I pleaded with classis to see, "If our elders think L'Engle's works are Christian, and if they think that her works meet our church library criteria, our church is in trouble."

I sat down, tears now streaming down my cheeks. The casual way in which so many delegates treated a subject which could have such tragic consequences was infuriating and disheartening.

All of a sudden, Hoogendoorn placed a motion to take the appeal off the table (continue discussion). It was supported and brought back up on the floor. We were asked if we would accept the advisory report in place of the appeal, since everything in the appeal had not been addressed by the report. I excitedly answered, "Yes!" Emotions were running high. Things were very tense, on both sides. Our appeal was fast becoming the longest and most debated issue at this classis. The only trouble was, for two and a half hours, the debate was over the wrong thing.

I don't remember exactly when Rev. Lester Van Essen stood up to take his turn in the center ring, but he spoke firmly against L'Engle's works. Then suddenly, Rev. Erffmeyer stood up, shot back in self-defense and claimed the appellants were "fundamentalists." His voice was intense and his anger plainly visible. I wondered what his definition of a fundamentalist was. He continued to let everyone there know that the appellants were determined to get other books out of the library as well, even though we had *never* given the slightest indication this was the case. How terribly difficult it was to sit still and listen to these absurd accusations without being able to answer them.

Erffmeyer now confronted Rev. Van Essen, "Are you saying that we shouldn't have any of her books in our library?"

The suspense was mounting. What would Van Essen say? As chairman of the advisory committee, his response would be of utmost significance.

"If it were up to me and it was *my* church, there wouldn't be *one* book of hers in my church library. Her books are shot through with

New Age thought , and she *is* New Age if you ask me!" Van Essen's voice was raised, but controlled.

Silence pentrated the auditorium for a moment, then debate continued until, at last, a vote was taken to adopt the advisory report. We waited nervously, while trying to take in what had all just happened. Unbelievably, the spoken majority vote was so overwhelming there was no need for hands to be raised (contrary to what was later reported by our elders). After a three-hour-long, exasperating session, the advisory report was adopted as classis' "answer to our appeal."

Reactions varied. A few people attending the meeting congratulated us and thanked us for not giving up on such an important issue. Others had a very different opinion. Disgusted, Dave Larsen, our elder and chairman of the education committee, marched up to Howard. "Do you know how much damage you have caused?" he asked accusingly. What he meant, we could only guess.

Rev. Van Essen's strong stand and Rev. Punt's persistence not to let "parliamentary maneuvers (tricks of the trade)" as he put it, rule the decision of classis, were greatly appreciated. We, as appellants, and all those who supported us felt the issue was over.

That night we celebrated together over cake and coffee. We thanked God for providing two such ministers and for the adoption of the advisory report, which seemed a miracle in itself. We hoped the report would open many eyes to the deception of L'Engle's writings and felt the deep burden of responsibility to share what we knew with other Christians had been lifted off our heads. Maybe, finally, our families could rest.

Chapter Ten

THE WARNING IGNORED

If you hold to my teaching, you are really my disciples.
Then you will know the truth, and the truth will set you
free.

John 8:31

While preparing the appeal to classis, I had seen many disturbing patterns which compelled the appellants to get to the bottom of why L'Engle was being so fiercely protected. For instance, on October 26, 1991, the Grand Rapids Press released the following announcement by Ed Golder:

DIFFERENT "TAKE" ON SAME REALITY

A Zen Buddhist in Japan meditates on a koan, a contradictory statement that jars his mind out of rational processes and into sudden enlightenment.

A Pentecostal Christian in America stands in his church singing hymns and waving his hands in ecstatic prayer, feeling the touch of Divine love.

A Russian Jew steps out of a plane at an Israeli airport and sees the land he has read about but never touched, feeling he knows fully, for the first time, what it means to be one of God's chosen people.

Three different people and cultures, three very different religions, but something very similar at work.

In Huston Smith's words, they are different "takes" on the same reality . . . Smith . . . author of "The World Religions," will come to West Michigan to speak at a day-long conference next Saturday . . . and a conference at the I.V. Eberhard Center on Sunday.

Three Colleges are the co-sponsors of event

Sunday's event–co-sponsored by the Interfaith Dialogue Association, Aquinas College, Calvin College and Grand Valley State University–begins at 1:45 p.m. Cost is $5 in advance, $7 at the door. Students admission is free.

I read the co-sponsors again. Calvin College was co-sponsoring Huston Smith, a person well-known on the New Age circuit. The last paragraph of the advertisement stated:

In The World's Religions, Smith quotes from Rama-krishna, a Hindu saint of the 19th century:

> *"God has made different religions to suit different aspirants, times, and countries. All doctrines are only so many paths; but a path is by no means God Himself. Indeed, one can reach God if one follows any of the paths with whole-hearted devotion. One may eat a cake with icing either straight or side-ways. It will taste sweet either way"* (emphasis mine).

Trying to find out some additional information on the conference, I called the Inter-Faith Dialogue Association. Swami ----? answered the phone. I hung up–too timid to ask any questions and knowing I wouldn't understand a thing he'd say anyway.

I remember sitting down, perplexed as to the enormity of what was taking place. I thought of the warning, "If anyone comes to you and does not bring this teaching, do not take him into your house or welcome him. Anyone who welcomes him shares in his wicked work" (2 John 10-11). Had some of our professors been so duped that they couldn't see anything wrong with bringing in these gurus whose only focus was to further their cause for world unity at the expense of Christianity? Did they believe their students should decide for themselves if the message was true or false? Would Smith be debated?

I doubted it, from what I had already witnessed coming into the schools and churches. A film promoting Calvin College's physical education department suggested Herbert Benson's book, *Beyond the Relaxation Response,* to relieve stress. Benson is well-known among New Age clientele and involved in Transcendental Meditation. His book teaches the occult techniques of meditation (deep breathing, chanting, etc.), visualization and guided imagery. Benson asserts: "The purpose of eliciting the Relaxation Response by such techniques is to reach 'attunement' with the person being healed so that the healing powers, forces, energies will pass through the subject" (Berkley Books, New York, 1984, pg. 151).

Around the same time, self-professed New Age M.D. Larry Dossey had been upheld as an authority on "prayer" by CRC pastor, James Kok (*The Banner*, "Making Your Garden Grow," 2-18-91).

At a women's conference held on the campus of Trinity Christian College, (organized by our church librarian), one of the workshops led by a member of Hope CRC was called, "Prayer and the Imagination." Women were led through relaxing each part of their body, a form of self-hypnosis, and to picture themselves in a Bible story. Whatever came out of their imagination was to be considered "true." (See Appendix D to read in more detail how this related to a women's conference held at Perkins School of Theology [Southern Methodist] in Dallas, Texas, where a self-professed witch led a workshop entitled, "Returning to the Goddess through Dianic Witchcraft.")

New Age proponents such as Matthew Fox, who promotes nature worship, witchcraft, and claims we're all Christs, along with Brother David Steindal-Rast, a New Age teacher at Easlen Institute (Big Sur, CA), and Morton Kelsey, who believes Christ is the ultimate shaman (witchdoctor), were embraced in a book entitled *Space for God*, by CRC pastor, Don Postema. Mystic Thomas Merton, who combined Zen Buddhism with Christianity, and Madeleine L'Engle were also among Postema's favorite authors. (See Appendices B and C.)

There were several other clear indications that New Age thought was slowly but surely penetrating Christian churches in the CRC as well as in various other "sister" denominations. Those I didn't have time to write about, I'd try and mention in the lectures I was now presenting on the New Age Movement. It was taking time, but thankfully, there were those pastors and members of various CRC churches who had their eyes wide open and were more than willing to listen. Sadly, others did not.

Classis' Declaration Mocked

The outcomes of classical meetings were usually reported in *The Banner*. However, the editor, Galen Meyer, didn't see fit to report our three-hour debate. The only matter mentioned was that a study committee had been appointed to look into guidelines for church libraries. Imagine that! Not one sentence was printed to explain what really happened that day. Not one word was used to warn readers that *The Banner* had promoted as Christian, a writer who forthrightly and enthusiastically denied four *essential* Biblical truths!

Upset that classis' pronouncement was not revealed in *The Banner*, Rev. Punt wrote a very short, concise letter to be placed in the "Voices" section (response of readers). He pointed out the four doctrines denied by L'Engle, then stated:

> The declaration was debated for three hours; addressed a problem that had festered for more than a year in one of the churches; was the focal point of interest for that meeting of Classis; is unique in the all the annals of actions taken by classis. Classis' assessment (whether valid or not) is of interest to the many avid readers of her works throughout the entire denomination. This significant declaration was omitted from the "highlights" (*The Banner*, 3/25/91) of this meeting of Classis (Letter from Rev. Punt to Meyer dated 4-5-91).

The response he received, dated April 19, 1991, was hardly what he had expected from a fellow pastor and editor of the magazine:

> Dear Neal:
>
> Thanks for your letter in which you spell out the declarations of Classis Chicago South regarding Madeleine L'Engle. What did you folks have over there anyway–a

heresy trial? Was Ms. L'Engle present? Did she have a chance to defend herself? Which writers will you examine next? . . .

And precisely what do the lofty declarations of Classis Chicago South actually mean? That Ms. L'Engle is barred from communion in the CRC? That I should not read her books? Must I eliminate them from my shelves? Or will I be sufficiently responsive to the classis' declarations if I only offer grave warnings to anyone who wishes to read them?

One minister who was in the audience the night Classis Chicago South discussed Ms. L'Engle told me that when the meeting was over, he went to his car, turned on the radio, and learned the country was at war. "I felt," he said, "as if I had gone from Mickey Mouse to the apocalypse."

Our summary of the action Classis Chicago South took is adequate.

I see no purpose in publishing your letter in Voices.

Sincerely,

The Banner

Galen H. Meyer

Editor

What a shame it was that one could only see what happened at the meeting of classis as a silly, "Mickey Mouse" heresy trial. Just as the word "sin" and the phrase "the wrath of God" have been eliminated from many pulpits, "heresy" is also on the verge of extinction.

Realizing how crucial classis' decision was, Rev. Punt persistently tried to get his short letter into "Voices" published. He wrote Meyer once again and received another negative response, so he wrote a letter to the Executive Committee of CRC Publications Board, twice. His letter was never printed. (Will the *real* censor please stand up?)

Half-Truths Deceive

As of yet, there hadn't been an announcement concerning classis' decision in our church bulletin. On Thursday, January 24, 1991, eight days after the classical meeting, Sharon Tiggelaar called me. Her grandfather, who helped assemble our monthly church newsletter, *The Outlook*, had called to let her know he had read the conclusion of the meeting and conveyed the message that she and the appellants had "lost." Sharon couldn't provide me with the actual report, and since we were both quite upset, she went to church to get us each a copy.

The brief report written by Rev. Erffmeyer stated:

> Classis gave advice on the appeal concerning the works of Madeleline L'Engle in the Orland Park Christian Reformed Church library, but Classis did not sustain the appeal of Si & Claris Van Kuiken and Dean & Karen Leensvaart.

At church, Sharon saw Rev. Erffmeyer in his office and confronted him. "I'm really upset about this,"

"About what in particular?"

"You know what I'm talking about."

"Oh, you mean about the appeal."

"Don't you think this statement is very misleading?"

"No, I don't. The statement there is correct."

"I disagree with you there."

"Tell me what your interpretation is of what happened at classis."

"No, you tell me what you think went on at classis because there seems to be a lot of confusion here."

"Classis gave their advice in the advisory report and that is what they voted on–not to sustain the appeal–so my statement is correct."

"I dare say if you asked all the other ministers who voted by an overwhelming majority if they thought your statement was misleading, they would agree with me. The people need to know what you *didn't* say. It's important and they need to know. This was a 3-hour issue at classis and I think it warranted more than a one-sentence comment."

"There were a lot of things discussed that day."

"Not for three hours."

"Time did not permit me to go into detail on every subject presented. Though it's certainly very important to you, it does not bear the same level of importance to everyone."

"Let me ask you, do you agree that the pre-advice report was adopted by an overwhelming majority?"

"Yes, and perhaps I should have gone into more detail. I would have been wise to do so, and I'm sorry now that I didn't."

"Unfortunately, you telling me here standing in your office doesn't do any good. It's too late, and the damage is already done. What do you think people who don't know what is going on are going to think when they take this out of their mail bin on Sunday and read your statement?"

Erffmeyer was silent. Finally, Sharon asked if the advisory report could be copied and placed into everyone's mail bin at church. Rev. Erffmeyer didn't feel it would be a good idea because the council would be acting on the advice given at their meeting and would probably decide to place a copy of the report in the library for "all those who care to read it." He felt it would "accomplish the same purpose."

Not satisfied, Sharon pursued, "You know that someone walking into the library is not going to take the time to sit down and read a 7-page report in a minute, so it accomplishes nothing."

"Classis did not say that we shouldn't read her books."

"I know, but they need to be put in a separate section or labeled. . . . I have a problem with the statement made that we cannot judge a person Christian or not. You said in your sermon Sunday 'do not be unequally yoked.' If you are going to marry someone, we are called upon to make a decision as to whether they are a believer or not. I would never judge a person as to whether they are going to heaven or not, that's not my place, but I can certainly tell by the beliefs a person professes to know if they are a Christian or not."

Erffmeyer nodded slowly. "Well, what about Schuller? [Robert Schuller–CVK] His interpretation of sin is certainly different from what we interpret sin to be. Would you call him a Christian?"

"I know absolutely nothing about that man–nothing–and I have nothing to say about him. My problem is with Madeleine L'Engle's writings and her denial of our very basic Christian beliefs that our church is founded on."

"We have said all along that we don't believe in everything she says. But when she says Jesus Christ is her Savior. . . ."

"Rev. Erffmeyer," Sharon broke in, "I can show you all kinds of New Age books that say the same thing. That doesn't mean anything. Our church holds a neighborhood Coffee Break every week for women, trying to show them the way to salvation through the study of the Scriptures. When a woman can walk out of that 1-hour classroom and walk into our library and pick up one of L'Engle's books and read that Satan, too, will be in heaven, I have a problem with that, because we are promoting her writings as being O.K. and they're dangerous. Would you say L'Engle is a Christian?

"I would say she is a confused person in her beliefs."

"Never in my life, did I think I would be in the middle of such a sad, sad situation. . . . I have to go grocery shopping."

Displeased with Erffmeyer's reaction to her concern, Sharon walked out the room and sometime later brought over a copy of *The Outlook*. As I read the report, a bombshell exploded–fragments hitting me full force from every direction. I felt betrayed, I felt the members of the congregation had been betrayed. And, most importantly, I felt Jesus Christ had been betrayed.

I called Howard to let him know about the report. I didn't know it yet, but a couple nights before at an elders' meeting, the consensus had been that nobody had won, the elders or the appellants. They, along with Howard, had voted to put the advisory report in the library along with a note in her books saying,

> If there is concern regarding this author's theology, please refer to a report adopted on January 16, 1991 by Classis Chicago South which is on file in the library.

Howard had voted with the elders believing it was the best thing for the moment. When he read the account given by Effmeyer, he was completely devastated. To him, it was a pure and simple lie, a half-truth at best. No doubt it would lead the congregation to think a certain way. Because the appeal had been replaced with the advisory report, a vote to sustain or not sustain the appeal was never taken. Howard wrote up a one-page report for the congregation of what took place at classis and decided to talk with Erffmeyer himself. Erffmeyer simply pushed his letter away, refusing to read it. The meeting proved futile, but not willing to give up easily, Howard set up a second meeting with Rev. Erffmeyer and asked another elder to come along as a witness. To this day, Howard will not tell me the conversation that took place because Erffmeyer swore him to secrecy. Whatever was said, it surely wasn't good.

In the meantime, two deacons who had attended classis also confronted Erffmeyer to find out why he had not given a more accurate description of the meeting. They talked with him for a while, felt he was sorry and believed he would amend the situation by printing more of what happened. From what he had said, they were convinced he would, at the least, be acknowledging the four denials and the conclusion that some of her books did not meet the church library criteria in the March issue of our church newsletter.

Around the same time, Sharon and Karen placed several calls to different elders to find out what they had thought of the advisory report. We were surprised to learn that some hadn't even read it. Others said they disagreed with the report, but refused to spell out why they disagreed with it. Still other elders reaffirmed their position that L'Engle's writings were Christian because "the experts" said so.

Considering all the rumors that had been spread, considering the fact that so many members held high the works of L'Engle, and because we felt an obligation to the congregation, with the help of our friends, Karen and I sent out a letter (dated 1-29-91), to each member with a detailed report of what classis had adopted. We stressed the fact that the report did indeed support our appeal; listed the four denials found in L'Engle's works by the advisory committee, and quoted the main conclusions concerning their appropriateness in the church library. We also let it be known that we regretted the tensions and divisions within the congregation our concern had caused and hoped these would be healed.

We weren't sure if this was an appropriate action to take, and it may be we acted in haste. But there was nothing in the church order that covered this sort of dilemma. Was there anything wrong with letting fellow members know what really happened? We were positive the subject would not be allowed to be discussed at a congregational meeting. There was no other choice, as far as we were concerned.

An Elder Resigns His Office

At a subsequent elders' meeting in early February, Erffmeyer requested the elders to get off their chairs, turn them around, and kneel to pray for healing. A few prayers were offered to let the issue drop, when Howard prayed an earnest prayer for the elders to repent. He didn't believe their decisions had been guided by the Holy Spirit. Whatever Rev. Erffmeyer said to Howard after that prayer, I will never know. All Howard would ever tell me, is that "It was a terribly heated meeting with him as the roastee." Afraid he would resign his position over the remarks that were made, three of the elders asked to meet with him.

The meeting proved to be Howard's last as elder in Orland Park CRC, but it wasn't because he was hurt by the awful remarks made to him at the elders' meeting. During his conversation with the three elders, he asked if they still held to their position that L'Engle was a Christian author. It was their absolute, positive affirmation which caused Howard to say, "On that basis, I resign."

Over the next few weeks, Howard prepared his letter of resignation for the upcoming council meeting (council includes pastors, elders and deacons). It would be the first time the deacons would be a part of the issue. On March 5, 1991, Howard sadly made his way into the room with two resignations in hand, one written for the congregation, the other to the council. Tired and discouraged, but unwavering in his stand, he began reading his letter to the council:

> What we are going through has been, and continues to be, a spiritual warfare of titanic proportions. . . . If we don't see this spiritual battle from the throne perspective, then this is a squabble that has no meaning at all. This can be dismissed with the same degree of indifference with such issues as: should we have Christmas trees in front of church, or do drums enhance the worship service. Issues come in different sizes; small, medium, large, and absolutely essential. My point of departure with the other elders has to do with essential Biblical truths.

Howard continued with a look from the throne, reading from Revelation the war Satan rages against the light (the church); how he comes disguised as a lamb (the name Christian) and deceives many, but alas, is doomed to drink of God's fury (Rev. 1:4, 12:9, 17, 13:11-18, Rev. 20:7-10, Rev. 14:9-11a).

He gently reminded his fellow elders,

> Two of the seven churches put up with false teachers and

had to repent of that. The church of Pergamum was first commended "you are true to my name" (Rev. 2:13). But you have people there who hold to the teaching of Balaam, likewise those who hold to the teaching of the Nicolaitans. Repent therefore! (Rev. 2:15,16). The church at Thyatira was commended for faithful loving service, but they tolerated a Jezebel who called herself a prophetess. By her teaching, she misled the people (Rev. 2:20). Those who went along with her were told to repent (Rev. 2:22).

Unabashedly, Howard examined the "wall" between the elders and himself–their response to tl e appeal– nd "found nothing precious or permanent in it." The elders' proclamation, "the whole concept of judging L'Engle as to whether she is a Christian or not, is abhorrent to the Reformed Christian," tore at the heart of the issue. Once again, our concerns were brought back into clear focus. "Before the elders knew they had this abhorrency problem," Howard assessed, "they had worked through it. They made the strong judgments . . . that divided us and formed very distinct sides." It was the "ragtag appellant crew" saying, "not Christian and deadly," against the ruling elders of the church, saying, "definitely Christian and a blessing."

Disagreeing with the elders' unwillingness to make judgments, Howard admonished:

The only persons who cannot make a judgment are those without beliefs. If you have beliefs you have a basis on which to make judgments. If you have no beliefs then someone else will tell you what to believe. If the Bible is the foundation of our faith, then we must make judgments according to what it says. *The church of the living Lord Jesus says repent and believe. Believe what? Who is to judge? Who is willing to make a judgment as to what fits the body of Christ or what doesn't fit? Why do you make me go on addressing such foolishness? The sheep hear their master's voice. They know their master's voice. They will never follow a stranger. In fact, they will run away from him because they do not recognize the stranger's voice. Even sheep make a judgment who to follow"* (emphasis mine).

The heartbreaking struggle and concern Howard was feeling could be seen in his concluding statements:

> Does this mean, brothers, that I don't love you? God knows I do! This is tough love, intervention love. Look where you are headed. Look at the wall of testimony you built, and the foundation on which it stands. . . . The Holy Spirit will not bless that testimony, but the fires of judgment may fall on it, and it will be utterly consumed including the foundation. Repentance will take down the wall, or judgment will take down the wall . . . I resign as elder because of this wall between us. The oneness is broken. I will not lead the flock in the direction of the optional gospel. It is abhorrent to the other elders to make judgments on what Classis determined was essential–Biblical truths. But they have made a judgment, and I have made a judgment, and a wall stands between.

Once more, Howard looked to Revelation with the hope that the wall would crumble and they would be together again and be one as the bride of Christ, victorious and "given a dazzlingly pure white gown" with which to meet the bridegroom.

I had never read such a joyous, beautiful, yet heart-breaking letter in my life.

[Note: One can appreciate Howard's struggle better knowing that in the *Manual of Christian Reformed Church Government*, it states (quoting the *Acts of Synod*, 1977, pg. 71), "Resignation implies a deliberate forsaking of office. Assemblies should deal with this person in the way of discipline" (Article 14, Brink, William P., De Ridder, Richard R., CRC Pub., 1987, MI, pg. 94). This applies to ministers, who are considered elders in the church. In Article 14, resignation is stated to be a "sinful act" (*Acts of Synod*, 1951, pg. 17). Yet, there is no Biblical evidence for this provided in Article 14, nor have I found a precedent set in Scripture. Though Howard was not a minister, the office of elder is taken very seriously. Imagine the guilt and fear that is placed upon an officebearer for resigning in a case such as Howard Stob's, or in the case of those ministers who have since left the CRC for similar reasons.]

The Elders' Compromise

Howard left the council meeting soon after he read his resignation. The deacons were upset the elders had judged L'Engle to be a good Christian author and that this had caused a fellow elder to resign a position in the church he took so seriously. Discussion continued. A compromise was made. The books in question would be removed from the library shelves, if the deacons would promise never to bring up the issue again.

Included in that basement bargain, however, the deacons insisted that the following announcement be placed in the bulletin for all members to read:

> In the spirit of unity the Council of the OPCRC acts to remove the books of Madeleine L'Engle from the Church library and does not wish to judge the Christianity of Madeline L'Engle. This decision supersedes all prior decisions.

Frank Voss, one of the deacons who had talked with Erffmeyer and attended the meeting of classis, explained this meant the previous judgment concerning L'Engle's works was null and void. I had warned him taking the books out of the library was not the problem and that the books should stay there as long as the elders felt they met the library criteria. But the elders convinced him the above announcement and taking the books out would end the matter and hopefully bring Howard back to his position as elder. The elders, therefore, decided not to accept his resignation.

The Compromise is Broken

When the March issue of *The Outlook* came out with the retraction Erffmeyer had promised, Frank and the other deacon who had confronted him were somewhat bewildered. While there was an apology for not writing more, the only part of the advisory report he had printed was, "This report does not mean to say or imply that Christians ought not to read the works of Madeleine L'Engle. It is intended. . . ." You know the rest.

The very next sentence read: "Classis also appointed a committee to draw up guidelines for the policy for church libraries. This new committee will be reporting to a later meeting of Classis."

[Well, what does one do when something doesn't fit? You change it to meet your needs. And, that's exactly what happened–the church library criteria would be changed].

At the bottom of the newsletter, library books sitting on a shelf had been drawn with the following saying printed underneath it in bold letters:

A good thing to remember
A better thing to do
Work with the construction gang,
Not with the wrecking crew.

Two other short sayings were included for extra measure. "Life is short and we have not much time for gladdening the hearts of those who travel the way with us. Oh, be swift to love! Make haste to be kind–Henri Amiel." The other read: "Be not angry that you cannot make others as you wish them to be . . . since you cannot make yourself as you wish to be–Thomas a Kempis."

What would you think if you knew what had been said to you in private and then saw and read the above? Whether it was done purposefully or not, we knew what people would read into it.

Howard, the deacons, and the rest of the appellants were thoroughly disappointed with the retraction by Erffmeyer. More disturbing was the fact that while the elders had promised the deacons their prior judgment concerning L'Engle's works was to be considered null and void, it had been said in no uncertain terms to Howard that they still held firm to their previous judgment. Now the elders felt since they had removed the books, and added in a special bonus, that they no longer wished to judge, Howard should reconsider his resignation, and he did.

For the next two weeks, Howard sought advice from several pastors as he agonized over what he should do. His struggle was seen in his second letter of resignation. He debated: "Should I offend the appellants by abandoning them? Should I offend the council after they made quite clear to me that this is their ultimate concession: That if I come back now my reputation and influence will soar, but if I keep the resignation the congregation will know without a doubt who heads the 'wrecking crew?' On the other hand, what about principle, conviction, compromise, mercy, judgments of right and wrong? On what grounds can we reach our goal of unity?" (Letter of Resignation, dated March 25, 1991).

He prayed and asked God to "shed His light on it." He began to analyze what he was doing and realized with great relief, that his decision didn't rest upon pleasing the elders, the appellants, or even himself. Instead, he wrote, "you take a big red stamp with the words LORD JESUS CHRIST written on it. You stamp that across the list, canceling out every name on it leaving only one all important name to consider." Howard's decision would rest on whatever honored Him, nothing else.

Looking at the goal of unity for which the books were removed, he noted the elders gave up "strongly held and fought for principles without reason." Howard reminded them that "No attempt was made on the part of the elders to explain their decision, nor was there any personal communication indicating a full restoration of fellowship with them" [the appellants–CVK].

Strengthening his position, he added:

> What about those who wanted to keep the books in the library, and even add to the collection? They are all deeply offended, and no reason is given for it. We lost unity here. How about Classis? They gave reasons why some of Madeleine L'Engle's books should be removed. They said she denies essential Biblical truths. Six pages of their seven-page report were used to explain this. The elders do not agree with that report. Disagreement here means no unity with Classis.

His letter made obvious the goal of unity would not be achieved by the removal of L'Engle's works. Howard also advised:

> If the elders, or maybe now the whole Council, feels it would be a good idea to give direction and leadership in this Babel of confusion, then I suggest you give Biblical grounds for the decision to take the books of Madeleine L'Engle out of the church library. Why are you offending those who want to keep them in? Why don't you give them a reason? A good beginning toward your reason is to ask and answer this hypothetical question:
>
> If *any* author denies:
>
> A. That the atonement is a sacrificial payment for sin.

B. The unique divinity of Jesus Christ.

C. That some persons will be lost.

D. That the Bible is the final rule for matters of faith and practice.

Do you as Council have a right and even a duty to point out that he or she is not a Christian author, even though they *claim* to be a Christian author? . . .

As elders or Council of the church of Jesus Christ, if foundational doctrines are on the line, I suggest you give an answer. If you disagree with the answer given by Classis, then you should . . . make your own appeal to Classis. . . . I'm urging you to give a strong declaration to all looking for direction–a declaration, a reason, that will exalt the Lord Jesus, and bring glory to God. My resignation stands in light of the dangers of the present compromise, for I see this as the mind and the will of the One who owns me.

How thankful I was that despite personal attacks, Howard stood firm, not willing to compromise the "sound doctrine" on which our faith rests.

His second and final resignation was not read at the next elders' meeting, but was available only to those who asked for a copy. I wondered how many elders asked for one. [Note: His first resignation, written for the congregation, but given to the elders on March 5, 1991, was never read or made available to the congregation, which should have been the natural thing to do.]

On April 17, Len Kamp, Rich Jousma, and Ken Mels, the three elders who had met with Howard just before his first resignation, came to his house pleading for him to return as elder. As they walked in the door, one elder remarked, "The issue is dead. We talked about it, but we're not putting anything in writing." Once again, they tried to see the situation as a personal battle, apologizing for certain mistakes they had made which had nothing to do with the doctrinal aspect of the issue. Upset at the utter lack of caring shown for the Word of God, Howard raised his voice and spoke forthrightly: "Your ungodly defense bothered me. That's what I based my resignation on. Something is terribly wrong, and unbecoming to the Church of Jesus Christ!"

"Don't be on *that* side, don't destroy the church!" Kamp warned in a last futile attempt to achieve reconciliation.

The elders ignored classis' warning. It meant nothing to them. They couldn't see past the superficial covering our issue had been given, to the reality of an affliction which would eventually tear us apart from the church we loved.

Chapter Eleven

VIOLATION OF AN OATH

> Since an overseer is entrusted with God's work, he must
> be blameless. . . . He must hold firmly to the trustworthy
> message as it has been taught, so that he can encourage
> others by sound doctrine and refute those who oppose it.
> Titus 1:7a, 9

The varying accounts of what took place at the January 16, 1991
meeting of Classis Chicago South signaled an underlying division
among the pastors; a division that had to do with doctrine, with the
nature of "Truth."

In Palos CRC's newsletter, *Grapevine,* Rev. Hoogendoorn wrote:

> . . . After three hours of debate, Classis adopted an
> amended report from a Committee of Pre-Advice as her
> response to the appeal. There are two basic parts to
> Classis' decision. (1) Classis refused to declare L'Engle
> as either heretic or non-Christian, recognizing that is not
> the role of the Church and her assemblies. Furthermore,
> Classis considered it outside of her jurisdiction to deter-
> mine what kind of books may or may not be in the OPCRC
> library. In this respect, Classis did not sustain the ap-
> peal. (2) Classis did affirm there were some elements (4
> were identified) in L'Engle's writings that do not appear
> to meet the standards of orthodoxy. Yet, Classis also af-
> firmed that such does not mean her books cannot be read.
> Rather, the believer must read with discernment.

Reading the newsletter, I surmised either there had been a great misunderstanding about what classis had declared, or what I believed to be heretical was different than what Hoogendoorn considered heretical. At the same time, I remembered his use of Matthew 7 in the letter we had received from him as church visitor which warned about making judgments.

Maybe I had taken for granted that all the delegates at classis believed those four essential Biblical truths were paramount to Christianity, and writings which denied those truths would be considered heretical. The opposite of "orthodox" in Webster's dictionary is "heretical." We had asked classis to declare L'Engle's writings to be heretical. Hadn't the advisory report claimed "to simply place her works in a church library may give her works a cloak of Christian orthodoxy the books do not deserve?" Now I wondered what he meant by four "elements that do not appear to meet the standard of orthodoxy." Were those four doctrines of such little value that one could deny them and still be considered a Christian?

Hoogendoorn's one-sided view also made it sound as though classis had just said "read with discernment." The advisory report concluded that "some [this had been changed from "all" by protest of Mike Vander Weele at classis–CVK], of her books do not conform to the policies established for books to be placed in the Orland Park CRC library." He had neglected to mentioned this. Besides, classis hadn't demanded the elders remove the books because we hadn't asked them to. We had asked them "to suggest" this to the elders. By saying her books did not conform to the library's policies, hadn't they suggested they should be removed? More importantly, wouldn't a consistory, knowing the deception of such works and the consequences possible, want to remove them, or at the least, label them?

The issue was turning into a word game. We sent out a short letter to the congregation of Palos CRC clarifying classis' proclamation–to the dislike of many, I'm sure, but to the thanks of some.

Since the meeting of classis, not one member of our consistory had contacted me. Perturbed by the events that had followed: *The Outlook* announcement, Howard's resignation, the obvious disgust displayed against those who were out "to destroy the church," Hoogendoorn's announcement, and various other things that had happened, I got up enough courage to call Rev. Erffmeyer to ask for a meeting with the consistory. I needed to know why they still disagreed with the advisory report. Howard's "hypothetical question" to the elders in his resignation had to be answered.

Twice I called Erffmeyer, and twice he was given the message by his secretary, but my call was never returned. I then decided to call the clerk of the elders to ask for a meeting. His response was that he doubted whether the consistory would meet with the appellants.

On April 22, I was surprised to receive a phone call from my district elder, Bob Hoekstra. He asked why I hadn't been coming to church so I, in turn, asked if he'd be willing to come over to discuss my reasons for not attending. He refused. The next day I called him back and asked if he would relay to the consistory that the appellants wanted to meet with them. He agreed to do so, but said it would take a couple of weeks (after the next elders' meeting).

On May 14, Mr. Hoekstra called to inform me there wouldn't be a meeting. The conversation was tense, to say the least. He let me know quite adamantly that the pastors weren't going to waste any more time on the L'Engle issue, and that it was the elders' job "to protect the pastors" from us. Those were his words–protect, as if we were the enemy. And I guess we were. He also claimed it was not the elders' responsibility to judge. "Satan just smiled when you said that," I answered sadly.

A few days later a member from church called me, upset that M. Scott Peck's book, *The Road Less Traveled*, had been placed on a table in the narthex of church as one available resource for "The Stephen Series," a study on evangelism and caring. Because the co-pastor had used Peck's book so glowingly from the pulpit, and because he was head of this series at church, I called him. I wanted answers, and I wasn't going to quit until I got them.

I first asked Rev. De Boer what he thought of the advisory report. He told me he didn't agree with it, but would not elaborate. I also asked him to have Rev. Erffmeyer call me and relay to him that I would appreciate a meeting between the appellants and the consistory (pastors and elders). He agreed to do so, but didn't think another meeting would take place. As our strained conversation continued, I asked him why *The Road Less Traveled* was on display in connection with evangelism.

"I know many churches that use his book as a study guide. . . . Peck has brought many people to God."

"But which God has he brought them to?" I asked, stunned by

his defense of Peck.

"What God says, and what we think God says are two different things, and we can't know for sure. . . ."

"We've got the Bible, Corky," I scolded, dismayed by what his answer meant. (I couldn't believe what I was hearing, yet I was hearing it.)

"It's not my job to judge," De Boer declared, convinced of his position.

"You're violating the oath you took when you signed The Form of Subscription."

"Then maybe you should press charges," De Boer dared.

As our conversation ended, I sank down in my chair thoroughly bewildered. His defense of the "Billy Graham of the New Age Movement," disturbed me greatly. (Peck is called this by his friend, New Age author Michael D. Antonio, in his book, *Heaven on Earth*, Crown Publishers, Inc., New York, 1992, pg. 342.)

The Form of Subscription, which must be signed before taking office, is an oath by which the office-bearers promise "to teach and faithfully defend" the doctrines our church believes and to "reject all errors that militate against it." It also requires the pastors and elders to "refute and contradict these" and "to exert" themselves "in keeping the Church free from such errors. The more I thought and prayed about it, the more I was convinced the appellants should press charges.

More Requests To Meet With Our Consistory Denied

I had had enough. Another letter was in order. I asked Karen to help me once more. Writing to the elders of OPCRC, we quoted from the Form of Subscription reminding the consistory of the oath they took before taking office. We also stated we felt that, according to the Church Order, if the consistory didn't agree with classis' declaration, they should have appealed the matter to synod—an assembly representing the churches of all the classes in the CRC denomination. So far, they hadn't done so, and the required amount of time to appeal was already past.

The main emphasis of our letter was the concern that our consistory refused to make judgments. We sincerely needed to know why they insisted blasphemous teachings were consistent with Christianity and so we requested a meeting with them. (Letter dated

May 21, 1991, from Dean & Karen Leensvaart and Si and Claris Van Kuiken written at the request of my district elder.)

A couple of days later, we received this one-sentence letter, dated May 22:

> We, as Elders of Orland Park Christian Reformed Church have read your letter dated May 21, 1991 and do not feel any further meetings on these issues will be beneficial.

A meeting wouldn't be beneficial? For whom? Certainly it would benefit us.

Around five days later, I received a copy of a letter protesting classis' decision to adopt the advisory report from the council of Hessel Park CRC (Champaign, IL). The protest was, as Rev. Punt wrote in response, like a "handful of dust intentionally thrown in the air so that, as a result of it, every one must say, 'Nothing is clear.' "

I was thrilled Rev. Punt felt the need to write a six-page letter clearly spelling out why it was "completely appropriate" for classis "to make a judgment about the orthodoxy of the writings of an author who has not signed the Form of Subscription" (Appendix E). He sent it as an open letter to Revs. Jack Reiffer and Cliff Christians and to about 50 others–pastors, teachers, and acquaintances. I thanked God for his help, support, and constant concern.

Having our consistory refuse to meet with us once again, Howard and Jo, Sharon and her husband John, and now Ken and Ruth Evenhouse, who had supported us and had also been considered "on that side," decided to join in as "appellants" and sign a letter to the pastors asking for a meeting with them. We didn't like having to constantly hound these men in such a way, but we felt there was no other alternative. We desperately wanted to be a part of our church, but as long as our questions remained unanswered and unresolved, it was impossible to continue worshipping there.

In our letter, dated June 4, 1991, we asked the pastors to meet with us to discuss their refusal to make judgments, why they disagreed with the advisory report, and Erffmeyer's sermons on Nehemiah which still bothered us. We advised in our letter if they denied us a meeting, we would be contacting the church visitors.

We never received a reply from the pastors. Instead, the elders wrote us back saying:

Pastor Erffmeyer and DeBoer forwarded your letter to the elders for review. The following is the elders' response:

It is with some disappointment that we received yet another letter regarding the interpretation of the writings of the author Madeleine L'Engle. It was our hope that this controversy was behind us. It is our opinion that further discussions regarding these books either with the pastors or the elders would not lead to agreement or further unity on this issue. . . . You have raised some new questions regarding the preaching of our senior pastor. It should be made very clear that the elders fully support the ministry of the word as preached by both of our pastors. We thank God for their gifts and will continue to encourage them in their work.

We have instructed both of our pastors to refrain from further meetings with you regarding interpretation of the writings of Madeleine L'Engle. The pastors as well as the council are certainly available for any other spiritual matters. It is our hope that we can move forward from here in the spirit of Christian love.

Our letter had said nothing about the interpretation of L'Engle's writings. That had been decided, or so we thought. According to Article 29 of the Church Order, decisions made by ecclesiastical assemblies were to be considered "settled and binding." Likewise, the Form of Subscription states they should "always cheerfully . . . submit to the judgment of . . . Classis." I wondered how these two important documents could be so easily disregarded.

As we had promised the pastors, we contacted the church visitors (now Rev. Henry Lamsma, Kedvale CRC, Oak Lawn, IL, and Rev. Rick Williams, Pullman CRC, Roseland, IL.) We sent copies of our letters and the elders' responses for their review and asked if they could meet with us to discuss the "seriousness of the issues raised" (Letter to CV dated 6-24-91.) They granted our request. The meeting seemed to go well and we believed our concerns were taken seriously.

In the beginning of August, I received a letter from the church visitors letting us know they had met with our pastors and were formulating their response to both our meetings. A month later, a notice came from them telling us they had not only met with the pastors, but had also talked with several elders. The church visitors wrote:

> It appears to us that the position of the leadership remains unchanged. They are not willing to discuss the issues that you have raised. They believe that the issues have been discussed on various levels (committee, council, and classis) and the books have been removed from the church library. Consequently, they judge that further discussion will not be beneficial and will not change anything.
>
> As church visitors we judge that we are at an impasse. We do hope that each party will, by God's grace, given some time and effort, be able to be reconciled so that the work of ministry and personal spiritual growth will continue (Letter, September, 1991).

The letter didn't make any sense. How could the issues have been discussed when the issues we had raised in our letters *after* classis were different than those raised *before* classis?

I discussed the letter with Rev. Rick Williams over the phone. He admitted our concerns were serious and suggested we write another letter to the consistory as "succinctly" as possible and ask for a written response, or bring formal charges to classis. I called the other appellants and we met to discuss what we should do next. Not wanting to bring formal charges against them, we decided one last time to write, hoping to avoid something neither side would relish. On October 17, we received a very short notice from "The Elders" that they were considering the matter we raised. In late November, a letter finally came with their answer:

> After discussing our concerns with the church visitors and having considered their observations, we feel that we have acted in good faith in dealing with the L'Engle issue and with you as individuals as well.

The rest of the letter was nauseating:

> It grieves us that there is a feeling among you that we do not care for you, that we have been ignoring you, or that we even have been trying to set people against you (cf. Howard Stob's letter 11-12-91). We have repeatedly tried to send the message to you that you are important at OPCRC and can continue to be nurtured in the faith as well as share your gifts as we minister together in sharing the good news of our Lord Jesus Christ. We are thankful that some of you have continued to be actively involved in a variety of ministries here. It saddens us when anyone withdraws from worshipping with us and from participating in ministry here.
>
> Our concern for you is that you continue to grow spiritually so that our Lord may be praised. We believe that continued discussion regarding L'Engle will not bring this about. . . .

What was this, something to be used in case we pressed charges against the consistory–something to look good? Rev. Erffmeyer had told me to leave our church if we didn't like what was going on there. An elder had said the very same thing to Jo Stob. If they meant what they said, why wouldn't anybody talk with us about what really concerned us? Why had we been treated the way that we had? They could keep their concern about our spiritual growth and worry more about their own. How did they expect us to share in the good news of our Lord when we knew they were defending teachings that spat in His face?

Yes, I was angry. I was furious. Because something had happened between the time we sent our last letter in early October to their reply of November 20th. Madeleine L'Engle had been invited to speak at Bill and Gloria Gaither's "Praise Gathering," held in Indianapolis, Indiana. Sharon Tiggelaar and Rev. Lester Van Essen had attended her speeches as did Rev. Erffmeyer, Len Kamp and a few of the other elders.

Purposefully, in the presence of Erffmeyer and the elders, Rev. Van Essen asked L'Engle if she believed Satan would be saved. She replied, to the applause of most everyone there, that some people are uncomfortable with that, but "my God is bigger than theirs." Hearing L'Engle's boastful words and seeing the positive response from his fellow colleague and elders in my church made Van Essen sick at heart. While the elders continuously claimed we were taking what L'Engle said out-of-context, they had heard for themselves what she taught and continued to defend her blatant anti-Christian teachings anyway. After "Praise Gathering," both Erffmeyer and the elders who had attended defended L'Engle's "Christianity" to members of our church and Van Essen as well.

The letter from the elders indicated they had received advice from the church visitors. Wondering what that advice was, I contacted the church visitors and found out they had sent the elders a letter, but hadn't supplied us with a copy. They suggested we contact our elders and have them send us one since they didn't feel at liberty to do so.

When I finally received and read the church visitors' letter, I was somewhat confused by their statement, ". . . in none of the material supplied to us by the consistory is there a decision made that is "contrary to Classis." Maybe that was because the consistory refused to put anything more in writing after classis. However, the church visitors had noted, ". . . it might be helpful in the consistory's response to the appellants to recognize that the interpretation by Classis of L'Engle's writings is valid, even though many Christian and respected authorities have a more favorable opinion of L'Engle . . . " (Letter to elders dated, 11-14-91).

It was a shame the elders hadn't heeded their advice. Giving them yet one last chance, we wrote another brief letter (dated 11-22) stating:

> 1) We must hear from the council whether you accept the determination of Classis that L'Engle denies the four essential doctrines listed in the Advisory Report.
>
> 2) Secondly, do you believe that a person who denies these teachings may be regarded as a Christian author?

We informed the elders that without this matter being cleared up, we would be sending formal charges to Classis Chicago South in time for the next meeting, observing the deadline to send in material was December 11.

On December 6, I received their reply:

> We want to inform you that our next Elders' meeting is

12/17/91. At that time, the Elders will be discussing as a group how we feel led by the Lord to respond to this communication. You will be informed of our response shortly thereafter.

Shortly thereafter would be too late. December 11 was the deadline for material to be received by classis in order to be placed on the agenda for its meeting in January. They knew this.

For the past few weeks, Karen and I, along with help from Howard and suggestions from the other appellants, had been writing up our "charges" along with the evidence for such as best we knew how. They were sent out the day we received the elders' letter. No longer was this about the works of L'Engle, Peck, or any other author. This had to do with what our pastors and elders believed and what they had done to so vigorously defend false teachings.

[Note: In the January, 1992 issue of the Calvin Theological Seminary's issue of the Kerux, it was stated that the Assistant Professor of Moral Theology, Dr. Calvin Van Reken, recommended *The Road Less Traveled* when asked to suggest a book he had read recently which he found helpful "to understand, experience, and teach what it means to live as a Christian today" (pg. 5). This was yet another indication of the trend in thinking being accepted into our churches and schools. More information I gathered on M. Scott Peck can be found in *Trojan Horse*.]

Chapter Twelve

CHARGES FILED,
A TRIAL DELAYED

The classical committee reviewed the charges we filed against our consistory and decided they would be passed out to the delegates at the evening meeting of classis on Tuesday, January 14, 1992. The next day, classis would "make a determination whether the charges ought to be dealt with according to the provisions of the Judicial Code"–a trial within the church (Letter from Chicago South Classical Committee, 12-17-91).

Upon receiving a copy of our charges, the elders of OPCRC wrote to the Stated Clerk of Classis Chicago South, Rev. Richard Hartwell, requesting that "Classis dismiss these charges at its January, 1992 meeting. While they "discussed the serious nature" of the charges, the elders claimed, "these charges are *not* substantial and do *not* merit formal adjudication" (Letter dated 12-27-91). For support, they used Article 10 of the Judicial Code of Rights and Procedures of the Church Order which states:

> The assembly shall in its judicial capacity determine whether the written charges are substantial, requiring formal adjudication.

I thought it odd that the elders should ask for the charges to be dismissed without providing any kind of response to them. Sometime later, I found out the elders had also tried to keep our charges off the agenda for classis. In a "compromise," the classical committee decided to hand them out at the Tuesday night meeting in-

stead of passing them out the usual three weeks beforehand so everyone would have plenty of time to study our document.

According to a letter from the classical committee, the *only*
matter to be determined at the next meeting of classis was whether
the charges required a formal hearing and whether or not all spiritual means or informal efforts had been exhausted before we filed
charges. It also stated: "Delegates should understand that at this
time you do not have to try to determine whether these charges are
valid or whether they have been substantiated" (Letter dated 1-14-
92).

We were told the only reason the elders and appellants needed
to attend this meeting of classis was to answer any factual questions that might arise. With the exception of Howard Stob, the
appellants didn't feel it necessary to prepare for the meeting. In the
event he was given the opportunity to speak, Howard decided to
write down his thoughts concerning the importance of defending
"Truth," and seeking out the "truth" of what had all transpired for
us to bring formal charges against our consistory.

Meeting of Classis Chicago South, January 15, 1992

On January 15, we discreetly made our way into the back row
of Immanuel CRC in Burbank, IL. Before we knew what was happening, Rev. Cal Hoogendoorn, the chairman for the day, instructed
us to present our "case" within twenty minutes. He then informed
the elders they would be allowed the same amount of time to present
"their case."

Startled, I turned around, looked at Howard and whispered,
"Does he mean we are to back up our charges? Does he think this
is the hearing?" When Hoogendoorn requested the appellants to
speak, I advised Howard not to say anything, but he hadn't understood what I was whispering and went up to read the speech he had
prepared. While what he said was meaningful, it was not our support for the charges we had filed. Dick De Jong, one of the newer
elders elected to office (elders get re-elected every 2-3 years), now
stood up to read the elders' side of the story–their "case" against
us. We hadn't prepared to have our witnesses called or other
documentation supporting our charges heard. The appellants
glanced at one another, completely baffled as to what was going
on.

I was hoping Rev. Punt or one of the other classical committee members would stand up and object—but nothing happened. In all the confusion, I don't quite remember what happened next. But I quite vividly recall Hoogendoorn announcing the charges we had filed against our consistory were "not substantial," therefore, there would not be a judicial hearing.

A discussion on the meaning of the word "substantial" as to "substantiated" now took place. As far as I was concerned, substantial meant serious or of substance. Our charges were very serious, as the elders themselves recognized. Substantiated meant proven, in which case, we would have to supply our witnesses and evidence before the delegates. We hadn't done so. This was not supposed to be the judicial hearing, and only "an assembly acting in judicial capacity" could decide whether our charges were substantiated. In either case, the reasoning behind Hoogendoorn's announcement was incorrect.

The next thing we knew, both the elders and the appellants were sent into separate rooms while the delegates went into strict "executive session." Whatever happened during that session upset Rev. Punt and Rev. Van Essen terribly—the whole meeting did. We didn't realize it, but both of them were so taken aback at what was taking place they just didn't know what to do.

It was time to join the rest of the delegates once again so we sat back down and waited for something else that didn't make any sense to happen. And, sure enough, it did. Hoogendoorn now announced a judicial hearing wouldn't take place because all spiritual means had not been exhausted, negating their first decision that the charges weren't substantial. The verdict had been changed, the outcome remained the same with a little addition. We were instructed to meet with the elders and a "reconciliation committee" of five people appointed by classis for a period of one year.

As the meeting ended, a few of the elders came up to shake our hands. Of course, for the elders reconciliation meant not ever having to deal with the issue again, just reconcile "personal hurts." And basically, that's what the reconciliation committee's job was. They stated: "We are not to be expected to judge the merits or demerits of the case that the appellants have brought to Classis. Our reconciliation committee will not 'judge the issues' " (Letter dated March 4, 1992). But one cannot be reconciled to another if the issue separating them is not addressed. What foolishness it was to think it could be!

The next morning, Rev. Punt called to let me know how utterly disappointed he was the way things were handled. He felt so badly, he promised to help us in any way he could with an appeal to synod for a judicial hearing. I had never heard a pastor so upset nor seen one so willing, despite what others thought, to take such a strong stand against his own peers.

Part of the reason Punt was so thoroughly disgusted was that Hoogendoorn had called him just a few days prior to the meeting of classis. He had wanted to make sure he understood what the classical committee had in mind for that day since he would be acting as chairman, and so they had agreed upon what was to take place.

In a letter to the head of the reconciliation committee appointed by classis, Punt pointed out:

> Hoogendoorn had "agreed with the suggestions of the classical committee as expressed in the cover letter." The cover letter states that, "It would not be possible for this session of classis to adjudicate these charges because neither the supporting evidence nor the response to these charges is before us."

> On the day of classis, the chairman (Hoogendoorn), without previously informing the appellants or the classical committee, announced that both the appellants and the respondents would be given 20 minutes "to present their case." This was a violation of the procedures agreed upon in the cover letter.

> The appellant's spokesman (Howard Stob), *in accordance with the cover letter* he had received a week before, did not try to substantiate the charges. . . . He gave a speech dealing with generalities about the importance of searching out the truth and doing what is right and just.

> The elders' spokesman (Richard De Jong), *in contradiction to the cover letter* the elders received a week earlier, presented a formal response to the charges. . . .

> Hoogendoorn had informed the elders to be so prepared. Why had the elders been informed of their opportunity

to speak and the length of such a presentation and not the appellants? The answer given by Hoogendoorn was that the elders had called to ask him about that; the appellants had not asked that of him.

Hoogendoorn appointed the advisory committee of the day. He selected Rev. John Ouwinga (a life-long friend of the Rev. Erffmeyer) and two elders. Contrary to the intent and the expressed statement of the cover letter, this committee recommended that all the charges be dismissed because they were not "substantial." Without seeing the appellants' evidence or hearing them, classis should dismiss the charges! I may be wrong but I view that as the "buddy/buddy" system at work. *It was infuriating for any decent person who was aware of what was happening, whether it was done intentionally or unintentionally* (Letter dated 5-8-92 to Dirk Vander Steen, chairman of the classical appointed reconciliation committee, emphasis mine).

An Appeal to Synod

On February 3, the appellants sent out a letter to the 1992 Synod of the Christian Reformed Church appealing the decision of Classis Chicago South. We asked synod "to restore our access to the provisions of the Judicial Code by setting a time and date to consider our charges against the consistory of the Orland Park Christian Reformed Church."

We explained why we believed a reconciliation committee would not benefit the situation, but just delay a hearing which in one day "would bring to light the facts without which reconciliation would hardly be possible." If we followed the time table suggested by classis, most of the original elders who defended L'Engle's basic orthodoxy *after* classis' declaration would possibly be retired from office.

We also wanted the judicial code committee to understand if the "decision to refuse us a judicial hearing is allowed to stand as an acceptable precedent on the ground that 'the spiritual means have not been exhausted,' then no appellant would ever be able to conclude that he or she has 'exhausted' all other 'informal efforts.' Every 'spiritual means' available to us *was exhausted*. If left to stand, this decision would give every council and classis a tool with which they can deprive members of the church access to a judicial hearing even after written charges have been filed. An assembly can always appoint a committee to try mediation. This would become a popular device because no one, including ourselves, relishes 'formal adjudication.' If we had not been forced to, we would not have asked for a judicial hearing."

Classis had decided that all spiritual means had not been exhausted "without providing us the opportunity to present our witnesses or evidence that the consistory rebuffed every effort we made to use 'spiritual' or 'informal' means."

Without just cause, classis had taken from us the right to use the provisions of the judicial code which states: "written charges brought by a complainant against a respondent alleging an offense in profession or practice against the Word of God, the doctrinal standards of the church, or the Church Order shall, upon the request of either the complainant or the respondent for a judicial hearing, be deemed to required formal adjudication" (A. Scope, Article 1). Every delegate at the January 1992 meeting of Classis Chicago South had in his hands charges that met the requirements specified by the judicial code.

At the end of April, we received a response from Donald F. Oosterhouse, chairman of the judicial code committee of the CRC. We were to meet with them on June 8, 1992, at which time the reasons for our appeal would be heard. The narrow question of "whether or not Classis made the proper determination when it said that the matter does not require formal adjudication because spiritual means have not yet been exhausted" would then be determined by the judicial code comittee (Letter dated May 5, 1992 from D. Oosterhouse).

Synodical Judicial Code Committee Meeting, June, 1992

Dr. Nelson D. Kloosterman, Professor of Ethics and New Testament at Mid-America Reformed Seminary (now located in Dyer, IN), and an ordained minister in the CRC, graciously accepted the most unpopular position of being our representative. We were also grateful that Rev. Neal Punt and Rev. Lester Van Essen, were both fully committed to testifying in our behalf.

As we walked slowly into the room at Calvin College, we gazed upon familiar faces. A few elder representatives from our church were there, along with Rev. Alexander De Jong (father of our elder Dick De Jong), Rev. William Lenters from Hope CRC (Oak Forest, IL), Rev. Cal Hoogendoorn, and Rev. Tony Van Zanten from Roseland Christian Ministries. Hoogendoorn and Van Zanten had been our first set of church visitors. Van Zanten was the spokesperson for our elders.

We were introduced to the seven synodical judicial code committee members who belonged to various Christian Reformed Churches, three of whom were attorneys. The proceedings began.

In his opening statement, Dr. Kloosterman very briefly explained that the appellants believed Classis Chicago South inadequately handled the very simple question of whether or not we had exhausted all available spiritual means before requesting a judicial hearing. He noted that we had not been given the opportunity to produce our evidence and argument on that question. Therefore, he concluded, ". . . when we present the evidence and when we ask the witnesses to testify, we are going to ask you to judge if Classis Chicago South ought to hold a judicial hearing–that all the spiritual means have indeed been exhausted. We want to . . . demonstrate and argue that . . . single point."

Speaking for the elders, Tony Van Zanten's opening remarks were based on "how we all share a common goal." That "the end . . . we all have in mind is similar. . . . Namely, that there be reconciliation, there be unity, that the truth be spoken of in love, and that the ministry of that local congregation proceed." He defended classis' decision to "*create a new spiritual means*" by which we could supposedly reach reconciliation.

While his words sounded sweet, I knew deep down that "the truth" would not be heard, therefore, any hope for unity and reconciliation looked pretty bleak. The only solutions left would be for the "appellants" to leave their church and/or just give up out of pure frustration and exhaustion (which is what most hoped for, I believe, in our case) and just be satisfied with the "agree to disagree" compromise.

Dr. Kloosterman asked Rev. Van Essen if the appellants had been asked to give their opinions on why they thought all means were exhausted. He replied that we had not, but instead, we were given an opportunity to present our case against the Orland Park Church. Van Essen informed the judicial code committee that we had not expected to present our case against the consistory at that meeting of classis. We had been told by the classical interim committee the only question before classis was "whether or not a judicial hearing should be held."

Rev. Punt testified that the elders had not wanted the charges printed in the agenda for that classis. In a compromise, the classical committee had decided to distribute the charges the night before the meeting so the delegates could see whether or not they were totally frivolous charges or if there was some substance to them.

He also apprised the judicial code committee members that all spiritual means had certainly been exhausted before presenting our charges before classis. "The elders refused to use the informal, spiritual means," he added. Another case in point, Punt suggested, was that one of our charges against our consistory was the fact that they would not meet with us. "And so to appoint a committee and say now meet with this committee, is to dismiss that charge."

The proceedings continued as Howard Stob gave his testimony concerning the number of times we had tried to discuss our concerns with the consistory, and that the reconciliation committee appointed by classis had no intention of addressing the issues that divided us. He stressed reconciliation could not possibly take place if the facts of the case were not going to be presented.

It was the elders' turn to present their side of the story.

Dick De Jong, as representative for the elders, indicated that we had met several times with the pastors and elders (however, this was before classis had adopted the advisory report). He quickly and consistently pointed out, "the elders were, after Classis, 1992, willing to meet under an agenda of reconciliation," though "not necessarily to further discuss the ins and outs of this author." He claimed the agenda around which we wanted to meet after classis' declaration was the interpretation of L'Engle's writings, and, since "no new information on this subject had been given to warrant a further meeting on discussion of the books," the elders saw no reason to meet with us.

He knew what our letters had said and had asked. For him to use such an excuse was not only inappropriate, it was downright false. Classis had made its determination concerning L'Engle's works–the interpretation was answered–the elders had been wrong. However, they were not willing to admit this at any time. His reasoning that no new information was available on the subject was also misleading. I was gathering new information all the time, but none of the elders ever asked if we had new information, nor would they have wanted to see more information. That was the one thing they had made very plain to us from the very beginning.

Frustrated at the misinformation being fed to the committee, I began to feel like a little girl who raises her hand, frantically waving at the teacher in order to give the right answer.

Finally, it was Kloosterman's turn to cross-examine De Jong.

NDK: "Could you tell me, did the elders communicate to the appellants whether or not they agreed or disagreed with the judgment of Classis Chicago South regarding the heretical teachings of Madeleine L'Engle? Did they agree with that classical decision?

DDJ: "The elders have made no formal statement one way or another regarding that decision."

NDK: "That's correct. Isn't it true that the appellants wanted the elders to make a formal statement signifying their agreement with classis' judgment on this?"

DDJ: "You would have to ask the appellants that. . . . "

NDK: "Have the appellants ever asked you to make a judgment?"

DDJ: "They have asked us. Yes, they have asked us to make a judgment regarding the Christianity of this author. Yes."

NDK: "Have they ever asked you whether you agreed with the judgment of classis pertaining in this matter?"

DDJ: (Turns pages of letters or notes . . . um. . . .) "I would have to go through the documents to see whether that is indeed correct. I–I–believe–I believe that is the case; that they have asked us to make a statement regarding that."

NDK: "Have you answered their request of you to state your formal agreement with the classis' decision?"

DDJ: "We have not–we have not answered that in terms of whether we agree or disagree. We have not made any statements at all regarding that classical decision."

(They hadn't put anything in writing, but they had made plenty of verbal statements).

NDK: "Do you view their question as illegitimate?"

DDJ: "Define 'illegitimate.' "

NDK: "That it ought not to be answered. That you don't have to answer it. That it's for some reason a waste of time for you to answer it?"

DDJ: "No, I wouldn't think it was a waste of time. We did make some statements regarding this author and that was made to classis . . . in response to their appeal. After classis made the decision regarding the works of this author, we did not feel it necessary to do anything more with it."

De Jong was more than willing to point out that the elders had placed a copy of the advisory report adopted by classis in the library and notes in each of the books. He carried on about the burden Howard's resignation had laid on them, and how, for the sake of unity, they had even removed the books from the library contrary to the advice of the church visitors. "We felt that unity was a higher priority in this matter than continue fighting. . . . "

I had to admit this sounded pretty good if you didn't know all the circumstances.

Kloosterman pressed on.

NDK: "From June '91 to January '92, where the frustration of the appellants continues to grow, how many meetings and how many communications were there between the elders and the appellants?"

DDJ: "Well, we had met as an elder body.."

NDK: "I'm asking between the *appellants* and the elders."

DDJ: "I believe there were no direct meetings with the appellants during that time period."

NDK: ". . . there were five requests and you did not honor any of those requests."

DDJ: "Well, I want to point out one thing. Those requests were meeting around an agenda of declaring the author a heretic."

That did it. "No, they weren't," I cut in.

"No, they weren't," Karen echoed.

The chairman scolded: "We don't need any comments from the gallery." (Nothing like a good old put down to get your act together.)

The letters we had written to the elders were introduced as evidence. It was time for questions.

Rev. Al Hoksbergen, a member of the judicial code committee, showed keen insight when he observed:

"It seems to me that the real, at least the way I read it, the real situation is the appellants have a conviction about the books of L'Engle and Peck. They believe they are un-Christian books. For whatever reason, the classis decided that that was so; that these are un-Christian books. Now, the way it sounds to me, the appellants are saying that the very fact you removed the books from the library really doesn't satisfy them. They want you to say, 'Yes, indeed those are un-Christian books.' And you refuse to say that. Now, it seems to me that that's the issue. . . . *I don't see what kind of reconciliation there can be made if you have the classis ruling, the appellants' concurrence with that classical ruling, the church saying we don't agree with that ruling, but we will take the books out"* (emphasis mine).

"But may I just say, we did not say that," De Jong broke in (funny, he didn't get scolded). "We did not make any official declarations regarding the classis decision."

"I see," Hoksbergen remarked quietly.

De Jong's next statement is one you will need to remember. He admitted, *"Classis . . . found four areas that this author was theologically a heretic."*

Remember those words, because over the next year and at the trial we were finally granted, our pastors and elders insisted classis never declared L'Engle's writings were heretical. It was obvious from his statement, that classis' judgment, declaration, decision, whatever one wanted to call it, was recognized by the elders, yet they chose to remain oblivious to it. As far as I could tell, in their eyes, the word "heretic" had no meaning at all.

De Jong finished his answer by quoting the elders' favorite paragraph of the advisory report: "This does not mean to say or imply that these books should not be read, but to place them on a library shelf in a church may give them a cloak of orthodoxy that they do not deserve." He explained "the elders took that and acted in good faith and placed that report in the library for all to see."

Questions continued. "Mr. Chairman," Kloosterman began, "if I may, the issue sharply put is: Do the elders concur, yes or no, with the judgment of classis rendered in January, 1991, regarding some of the writings of Madeleine L'Engle. If they do not concur, why not? If they do concur, why don't they say so? I'd like to ask over what issue, Howard Stob resigned as elder?"

Oosterhouse decided not to get into "the substance" of the appeal, but to stay with the procedural question of whether classis was right in its judgment that there was still an opening for further spiritual means to be used in resolving our differences, or if classis should have gone ahead with a judicial hearing.

"But he continues to insist that there was an agenda behind the requests of the appellants, which requests were denied. The agenda that he speculates about is not true, Mr. Chairman," Kloosterman objected.

Rev. Punt asked if he could respond. Suddenly, without being called, Rev. Lenters, a delegate representing Classis Chicago South, interrupted: "Let's number one, admit that classis made not a judgment, they gave advice regarding L'Engle's books. I think that's the key point. They gave advice. Not a judgment, and that judgment–that advice, was based on an ad hoc committee report that was quickly decided upon in order to get through the business of the day. It was not a studied matter. Nobody came to. . . . "

I couldn't believe what I had just heard. I could see Rev. Punt and Van Essen squirming in their seats.

Kloosterman cut Lenters off objecting to his line of argumentation, but Lenters kept right on speaking, "We say L'Engle's books are not all that bad, maybe they are, that's no longer the issue. The issue is, we got to get on with the business of the church. Thus, the committee was appointed. That committee has not yet met with both sides."

Again, Rev. Punt asked permission to speak but was denied the privilege. Yet Lenters had been given the opportunity without permission. (At this rate, I'd have to be given a sedative to calm down.)

Howard Stob was now called by Kloosterman as a rebuttal witness. Discouraged and tired from the proceedings, Howard exasperatedly explained as best he could what had taken place very briefly, before and after classis, from January '91 to January '92. "We wanted them to tell us why they disagreed with classis," Howard repeatedly said.

NDK: "Okay. Were the elders willing to talk to you about that question?"

HS: "No, they never were willing to talk to me, even while I was still an elder. I was the lone elder for a year and a half to say–well, look at what this author is saying and you're accepting these as Christian. And you're telling others that a Christian makes these declarations–these kinds of declarations!"

NDK: ". . . do you believe that reconciliation . . . is possible without addressing that question you wish to have answered?"

HS: "There is no possibility of reconciliation without addressing the questions that divide us. . . . "

"Is this an accurate assessment?" Rev. Hoksbergen asked. "The

classis said, in some of her works she denies these four things. . . .
And am I correct in hearing the elder from the church say, and we
agree with that in some of her works?"

Howard answered quickly. "They didn't agree with that with
me to the point. . . ."

"I thought I just heard him [De Jong] say that," Hoksbergen
broke in.

De Jong was allowed to read what the elders had said concerning L'Engle. He emphasized they "did not agree with every last
word that Madeleine L'Engle has written." But it was their judgment, "that taken as a whole and in context, the works of L'Engle
can be understood and appreciated in a positive light."

Continuing, De Jong read, "We acknowledge that there are many
problematic passages in L'Engle's writings. There are many things
that she says in a way that we would not say them. L'Engle is clearly
not a Christian Reformed writer. The issue is whether as a whole
her writings are written from a Christian perspective and whether
they are useful for Christian readers. This is where we disagree
with the appellants. As the church visitors have reminded all of us,
we must read all literature with an eye to testing it against the Scriptures and agree with literature in so far as it is in harmony with
Scriptures. . . . The whole concept of judging L'Engle as to whether
she is personally Christian or not is abhorrent to the Reformed
Christian."

Confusion, anyone????

Whatever happened to Hoksbergen's question on whether or not
the elders agreed with classis' findings? Vanished. It was never
answered. I wondered if the judicial code committee understood
what was going on.

Howard Stob now argued that what De Jong had just read was
not at all the complete response of the elders, but the chairman
asked for final summations and things were left somewhat tossed
up in the air.

Kloosterman and Van Zanten gave their closing summations.
Then one last question posed by Hoksbergen sparked a heated debate. "If there is a judicial hearing conducted by the classis, what
would that be around? Would that hearing be around whether
L'Engle is a Christian author?"

"Oh, no. Absolutely not!" Kloosterman stated emphatically. He
explained that the hearing would be centered on the charges that

had been placed against the elders for performance of office and not agreeing with classis. "And. . . ."

"But that has to do with whether L'Engle is a Christian author or not," Hoksbergen interrupted.

"No, it does not," Kloosterman replied.

"That has been decided by classis!" Rev. Punt contended.

"No, it has not. Well, then I'm lost." said Hoksbergen.

"Yes, it has!" Punt responded emphatically.

"It's been reported wrong," claimed Van Essen.

"Who reported it wrong?" asked Hoksbergen.

"Lenters," replied Van Essen.

Things were getting interesting! Exasperated, Rev. Punt corrected, "Lenters said that it wasn't a deliberate and a studied question, and it was!! A committee was appointed and worked on that and formulated it. And classis made the definite declaration that she denies the atonement. . . ."

"In some of her works," Hoksbergen cut in.

"Well, yes!" cried Punt (as if that made any difference). I could imagine his heart was pounding by now. "And, she denies the unique divinity of Jesus Christ . . . those questions have been decided. . . . That was a studied document that was sent out with the agenda and all the consistories had it long before classis met!"

Now Lenters raised his voice. "I object to that . . . it was not a study committee appointed by classis!"

"It was too!" Punt exclaimed, thoroughly beside himself.

Lenters complained a study committee had been appointed and a report had appeared out of nowhere. He hadn't been able to vote on whether a study committee should be appointed. Secondly, he felt that the decision of classis was just an advisory statement.

One of the lawyers on the judicial code committee suggested they look at the minutes of the January, 1991 Classis.

In the meantime, Hoksbergen asked who made the study and who wrote the report. Van Essen replied that a committee appointed by the classical interim committee made the study, reported it to classis, discussed it at classis and adopted it at classis.

Oosterhouse now read the last paragraph of the advisory report. Once again we heard it:

> This report does not mean to say or imply that Christians ought not to read the works of Madeleine L'Engle. It is

intended to alert all the churches of Classis that to simply place her works in a church library may give her works a cloak of Christian orthodoxy that the books do not deserve.

". . . I think it does become fairly critical that we know precisely what classis said about this," Oosterhouse surmised.

Finally, someone saw the importance of the statement. I believe it was Jo Stob who found the minutes of classis. You could always count on Jo to have things in good order.

Oosterhouse reported, "In response to the appeal of four members of Orland Park CRC, against the elders' decision to retain the books of Madeleine L'Engle, Classis adopts the report of its Advisory Committee as its answer to them."

Another judicial code committee member spoke up:

There seems to be some confusion as to whether Classis rendered a verdict or advice. But in either case, the contention is made that the Orland Park consistory has disagreed with the decision of Classis, even though they have removed the books from the library. I'm wondering if the evidence of that disagreement is in writing . . . the only writing I've heard concerning their opinion about her works was written before this decision of Classis by a month or so. Is there any written evidence that they disagree, or is that just a verbal report that some of the elders said that in the consistory meeting?

Just when I felt like we were making some headway, a quick decision was made to end the meeting, much to the appellants' dismay. The discussion had gotten off the "narrow" question of whether or not all spiritual means had been exhausted and into documents that were "not part of the record" for the judicial code committee. The committee would meet alone and render its decision.

The appellants were disappointed that the judicial code committee decided reconciliation could best be realized with the aid of a "new objective committee" appointed by synod. This time, however, the aim was to "work out an amiable agreement on the issues that divide them" (Report of JCC, dated June 11, 1992). We would comply with synod's recommendation and meet for one year.

The grounds for their decision rested on the fact that both parties expressed an interest in reconciliation, "but the different approaches to reconciliation resulted in frustration." The reconciliation committee was asked to report to the judicial code committee by April 1, 1993 "so that, if necessary, the judicial code committee may make further recommendation to Synod, 1993."

Chapter Thirteen

UNITY VS. DOCTRINE

You must teach what is in accordance with sound doctrine.
Titus 2:1

Our fixation on right doctrine is a rampant, destructive disease. . . .
Nicholas Wolterstorff, The Banner, 6-8-92

Over the summer, the appellants drew up a "position paper" which listed ten concerns and questions we felt must be addressed and answered by our pastors and elders. We hoped this would enable the reconciliation committee to grasp, in some small way, what had taken place over the past two years and keep our discussions focused. At the same time, we were also very aware our position would be a very unpopular one to take, since unity and denominational loyalty seemed to quickly be taking precedence over sound doctrine in the Christian Reformed denomination.

I had heard Donald Hettinga, one of the professors of English at Calvin College, was given a Sabbatical leave as well as financial aid from the Calvin College Alumni to write a book defending L'Engle's brand of "Christianity." As soon as it was available through local bookstores, I would no doubt be ordering one. I guessed it was partially written because of our particular battle since Hettinga had come to the very first classical meeting to defend the elders' position. What he had to say would be of extreme significance for his words would hopefully reveal where many pastors and teachers stood on essential Biblical truths.

During the past several months, I had been contributing research and helping to write *Trojan Horse, How The New Age Movement Infiltrates the Church.* I had also been writing articles for *Christian Renewal*, a conservative magazine covering issues in the CRC and other closely-related denominations. Each of the articles I wrote (some of which appear in the appendices to this book) was written in response to the embracing of New Age authors and occult beliefs and practices by leaders in the CRC, as well as other mainline denominations.

The more research I did, the more translucent it became, that, as a whole, the denomination I had loved for so many years was compromising sound doctrine, defending false teachings, and scorning and discrediting those who stood up to expose it. There was a reason L'Engle's teachings were being so uniformly defended by CRC pastors, teachers and myriads of others. There was a reason professors were allowed to say the first eleven chapters of Genesis were myth. There was a reason feminists in certain CRC churches wanted to call God, Mother. There was a reason evolution was increasingly being defended. There was a reason certain pastors and teachers were invoked with anger when anyone dared question them or the professors at Calvin College.

All the appellants knew there was much more underneath the battle with our church than what most realized. But trying to discuss these issues even with family members could ignite a major battle. A division was taking place; a division warned of long ago by Jesus Himself who said:

> Whoever acknowledges me before men, I will also acknowledge him before my Father in heaven. But whoever disowns me before men, I will disown him before my Father in heaven. Do not suppose that I have come to bring peace to the earth. I did not come to bring peace, but a sword. For I have come to turn "a man against his father, a daughter against her mother, a daughter-in-law against her mother-in-law—a man's enemies will be the members of his own household" (Matthew 10:32-36).

Thankfully, there were those who wrote letters of encouragement and support and made it a priority to become fully aware of various disputes within the denomination. I received letters from people I didn't know, but who had heard of our struggle and had fought L'Engle's teachings in Christian schools and churches. Letters and phone calls came from around the country, which confirmed what we already knew—that ours was not an isolated, insignificant issue, but that this author, and others like her, had already had a tremendous amount of influence everywhere they traveled and spoke.

Calvin College Students Applaud L'Engle

An audio tape I received of Madeleine L'Engle speaking at Calvin College on September 23, 1987, was one more example to add to the already long list. As I listened to L'Engle captivating her student audience, the urgency of the matter seemed overwhelming. The first thing she did was to dispel the many accusations Christians had made against her works, making these parents who stood firm on essential Biblical truths look totally ridiculous. They were depicted as a growing minority group of holier-than-thou censors and compared to Hitler who "began by burning books and ended by burning people." The students clapped with intense enthusiasm as L'Engle threw out her beliefs in little spurts, hoping the students would catch them. [Note: Granted, there may be some people out there who say far-fetched things without any proof whatsoever. If so, they are destroying the work of researchers who know exactly what they are talking about.]

L'Engle described the theory of the "butterfly effect" which speculates if a butterfly is hurt, it will be felt across the galaxies. This, she said, meant that the "universe is totally interrelated." Criticizing German theologians for giving answers to her "theological questions," and putting God in "nice little boxes," L'Engle claimed, "the only valid use of German theologians is insomnia." As a matter of fact, *A Wrinkle in Time* was her "rebuttal to the German theologians" (*Walking on Water*, pg. 118).

Did those students realize the *Heidelberg Catechism,* to which the CRC subscribed, was written by German theologians? I doubted it. Oh, how "dangerous, dangerous" those "dirty-minded" people were who questioned her works. *Story* was the way to truth! (L'Engle never mentioned the Bible or Jesus as the only way to Truth.)

And what was that wonderful truth she enlightened her student audience with?

> We are not yet human beings. We're only potentially
> human. I don't think we've gone much farther than those
> first humanoids who got off their fours and were able to
> raise their forepaws and hold something and then chip
> rock and make tools. And I can imagine them saying,
> "We are man who makes tools, God has done it at last!"
> We probably have equally far to go in the journey to-
> wards being human.

L'Engle managed to endorse evolution, and went on to scorn a
"God of judgment and terror" seemingly without the least bit of
resistance from her audience. "I don't want to live in that kind of
world and I suspect you don't either," she enticed.

Please remember this next comment made in her speech at
Calvin, for it is a very relevant one: *"Great scientists say this is
how it seems to us now. If new insights are revealed, it may be
something else but this is what it looks like now. . . ."* Since famed
scientist Albert Einstein happens to be L'Engle's favorite "theologian," her comment was also religious in nature. When applied to
essential Biblical truths, it means one thing–truth is what one perceives it to be. In other words, all paths lead to God. (You'll see
how her teachings are being followed in the rest of this book.)

Those who have researched New Age thought extensively would
quickly recognize what L'Engle was teaching her listeners: All is
One, All is God, evolution into godhood, or "the potential human,"
as New Age transpersonal psychologist Jean Houston calls it. It's
no coincidence Houston endorses L'Engle and vice-versa. (See
Kything, The Art of Spiritual Presence by self-professed New Age
authors Louis M. Savory and Patricia Berne, Paulist Press, New
York, 1988, pg.18.)

College students can be easy prey to such speakers. Many are at
a time in their life when they rebel against authority (namely, parents), and are prone to listen to and believe anybody who helps
them in their rebellion. Discernment is often thrown out the win-
dow. Yet we are told by college educators today that every student
needs to make his own choices and is fully equipped with the discernment necessary to see error. Not so, especially when the "Christian" educators themselves have been duped into believing a "dif-

ferent gospel."

In the December, 1991 issue of the Focus on the Family news-letter, president Dr. James Dobson warned: "Alas, the tide of relativism has invaded the classroom, from the university down to the elementary school experience. We must stop it, at least, at the front door of the Church!" It seemed unbelievable that our church and denomination were battling over that very issue. But then, didn't pastors often preach what they were taught in the schools they attended?

The Substitutionary Atonement Denied

What came to my attention in April, 1992 while we were in the process of appealing to synod for a judicial hearing, proved L'Engle's writings, and others like hers, could have devastating effects on our children.

A recent Calvin College graduate and daughter of a CRC minister had written a letter in Park Lane CRC's church paper. She had been "Director" of an outreach program for the church for three months when her letter was printed. Here is what she wrote:

> One phrase I heard countless times as I grew up follows: "Jesus paid the penalty for our sin." Since I was young I have been confused by this rather simple explanation of Christ's influence on my life.

> Recently, I learned that I was taught the substitution theory of atonement, which means that Christ's death substituted for our own deserved death. In this theory, the thing that we are saved from is the punishment for our sins. God was going to damn us for our sins, but since he damned the innocent Christ instead, he doesn't need to damn us anymore. The impression of this idea I have from when I was little is that God's hammer was headed for humankind but since Christ stepped in the way and took the blow himself, I escaped the hammer. Through Christ's substitution on the cross for me, God's justice is satisfied for all time and God is thus able to love me instead of punish me.

> *I have a hard time with this theory because I can't trust a*

*God who would damn all of humankind but who decides
to kill his own son instead and achieve "justice" that
way.* In the following paragraph, I describe the God I see
in scripture whom I trust. This is the God I tell others
about in the hopes that they will trust him too (emphasis
mine).

In the Bible, I read that God has loved humankind
throughout all of history. God tells us it is our own attitude toward God that needs to be changed. The Bible
repeatedly proclaims that humans' hearts which will be
changed by God promises, "I will give them an undi-
vided heart and put a new spirit in them; I will remove
from them their heart of stone and give them a heart of
flesh" (Ezekiel 11:19).

Throughout Christ's life of unconditional love, he re-
verses the human ideas of justice. He says such unusual
things as, "You have heard it was said, 'Eye for eye, tooth
for tooth.' But I tell you, do not resist one who is evil.
But if anyone strikes you on the cheek, turn to him the
other also. . . ." (Matthew 5:38,39).

If Christ's words will not change our views of justice,
his actions further persuade us. Christ's loving, submis-
sive life and death is the ultimate revelation of his love
for us. Christ was born as a vulnerable babe and grew to
eat dinners with the tax collectors and sinners. Through
his life of unconditional love which ignored the religious
rules of the day, he became a man wanted for death. Christ
could have avoided that humiliating death, or he could
have retaliated with force against those who would kill
him. But Christ never ceases to love those who finally
crucify him and jeer at him. He even says on the cross,
"Father, forgive them, for they know not what they do"
(Luke 23:34).

Christ turns to me his other cheek and loves me. This is
how he turns my heart of stone into a heart of flesh. This
is how I love him.

During an interview with her pastor, Rev. Gary Hutt, the director insisted on the right to teach this view of the meaning of Christ's death. When (thankfully) he told her that would not be permitted, the director resigned.

After reading her letter, I paged through my Bible and cringed when I came upon Hebrews 10:26-31:

> If we deliberately keep on sinning after we have received the knowledge of the truth, no sacrifice for sins is left, but only a fearful expectation of judgment and of raging fire that will consume the enemies of God. Anyone who rejected the law of Moses died without mercy on the testimony of two or three witnesses. How much more severely do you think a man deserves to be punished who has trampled the Son of God under foot, who has treated as an unholy thing the blood of the covenant that sanctified him, and who has insulted the Spirit of grace? For we know him who said, "It is mine to avenge; I will repay," and again, "The Lord will judge his people." It is a dreadful thing to fall into the hands of the living God.

Talk of unconditional love and justice can be so enticing to the undiscerning reader. What a shame it is that both L'Engle and this college graduate don't seem to understand Jesus' willingness to suffer and pay the ultimate price for us, reflects the purest, true love there can ever be. Nor can they fathom the love it had to take for God to give up His only begotten Son, for "This is love; not that we loved God, but that he loved us and sent his Son as an atoning sacrifice for our sins" (1 John 4:10).

I wondered what they did with texts such as this: "God presented him as a sacrifice of atonement, through faith in his blood." He did this "to demonstrate his justice, because in his forbearance he had left the sins committed beforehand unpunished–he did it to demonstrate his justice at the present time, so as to be just and the one who justifies those who have faith in Jesus" (Romans 3:25-26). He did this "in order that sin might be recognized as sin" (Romans 7:13). If there was no fear of God or recognition of guilt, what need would there be for anyone to turn to a Savior?

My friend who had been brought up in a Presbyterian home and converted to New Age thought demonstrated the outcome of this type of thinking all too well. She rejected Jesus Christ as Savior from sin and came to believe in the goodness of man–a goodness that would turn into "godness" for every person. She never felt accountable to anyone, as long as she felt comfortable with herself, that was all that mattered. New Age is a religion of self-love, not love for God, no matter how much New Agers claim to love "Jesus." Because "this is love: that we walk in obedience to his commands" (2 John:6). And, "walking in the truth," is what "the Father commanded" (2 John:4).

Instead of taking God's Word and seeing if what they have read or heard fits into it, many "Christians" today are taking concepts from other sources and trying to fit them into Scripture, sort of molding God's Word to meet theirs. It's a backwards approach.

I was determined now more than ever to find out how our consistory would answer the question: "Can you deny the substitutionary atonement, the unique divinity of Christ, the unique authority of Scripture . . . and still be classified as a Christian author?" And I wanted that answer in writing.

Meetings with Synodical Reconciliation Committee, October-December, 1992

Things weren't getting any better. We had now been accused by an elder for the resignation of the church librarian. This particular elder was terribly concerned she might leave the church and made it known to Howard that the appellants were to blame. Yet we had been told to leave our church if we didn't like it there. While the elders continually insisted they had said and done everything out of love and concern for us, the only concern we had seen was for us to either be silent or go away. Reconciliation seemed farther away than ever.

In August, 1992, we received a letter from Leonard J. Hofman, General Secretary of the Christian Reformed Church of North America. Rev. Lugene A. Bazuin, Dr. Harry G. Arnold, and Mrs. Rose Van Reken had been appointed as the new synodically appointed "pastoral committee."

Howard Stob wrote a paper entitled, "The Issue As I See It," and sent it to the committee. Its purpose was to clearly define the "central issue" of the matter and what he felt was at stake. The appellants were tired of seeing ploys like "censorship," "what may we read as Reformed Christians," and "there are many different interpretations," being used to hide the real issue. This way it would be out in the open before our meetings began. The advisory report had defined the "central issue" as "whether or not L'Engle's books ought to be classified as those of a Christian writer." They "sought to determine if her views of the Scriptures as well as her view of eschatology could in *any way* fall into the category of being Christian." Classis had adopted the report and its declaration was unmistakable for anyone willing to see it.

I hoped Howard's words would sink into the minds of the committee and touch their hearts:

> When we allow a false gospel to stand so that people become confused as to which is the path of life or the path of death, then darkness descends. That darkness will be like the darkness of Egypt, a darkness you can feel. There will be no hope. . . . Scripture defines the substantial nature of the issue and Scripture sets forth the terms of reconciliation. . . . Repentance leads to restoration. Restoration brings unity. . . .

This was not a power struggle, the conservative Christian right, over the liberal Christian left. We weren't out to say, "See, I told you so, you'd better apologize or we won't come back!" But we desperately needed an affirmation that our leaders would no longer defend such hideous false teachings as "Christian." Only repentance would take down the wall that separated us–a wall that was filled with pride–a wall that would not be very easy to break down. While Erffmeyer's series of sermons on Nehemiah and building the walls divided the church, we were now asking him to take those walls down, difficult as it might be.

In early October, we had a preliminary "get to know you" type meeting with the pastoral committee at our church. The meeting was cordial enough, though a couple of appellants got grilled for attending a church of a different denomination. What difference that made, we weren't quite sure. It had become almost impossible to worship at Orland and just about every other CRC church that was close enough to attend. Most of us had come to the point where we could no longer in good conscience worship there, except to come occasionally to visit. We didn't want to become bitter, which is what we were afraid might happen had we remained there. We needed rest, spiritual rest and spiritual nourishing. We weren't getting either.

A week or two after our first meeting, we received a letter from the pastoral committee thanking us for our cooperation and suggesting there be face to face meetings between the appellants and representatives of the elders. We had hoped to meet with the entire consistory, but only four (out of 17) elders were commissioned to meet with us.

At our next meeting, scheduled for December 5, the elders were to give their response to our "position paper." This was what we had been waiting for. No longer could the pastors and elders remain silent. The committee seemed to realize reconciliation would be impossible without resolving the ten concerns we had listed.

The meeting was set up so that after each concern was addressed by the elders, Rev. Bazuin would ask us if their answer was satisfactory. We would then be given the opportunity to ask questions. Based on the outcome of this, the committee would determine its future course of action (Letter dated 10-15-92 from synodical reconciliation committee).

A Confidential Response

It wasn't going to be easy to face our elders. We had come to expect the worst of all scenarios, and sometimes even then we'd been caught totally off-guard at the outcome. What would happen next?

We stood anxiously waiting in the narthex of our church to be called into the room where we were to meet. This was it! My legs didn't want to move. I prayed a short prayer for calmness and clarity of mind. Then, along with all the other nervous appellants, we entered the room smelling the rich aroma of brewing coffee.

We greeted each other and took our seats. Pete Schipma and Dick Molenhouse, two of the four elders representing the consistory, were elected to office in June of '93 and had not been involved in the issue at all. It would be interesting to see what they had to say. Elder representatives Dick De Jong and Rich Jousma had served in consistory some of the time, but not during the full four years of our struggle. Rev. Erffmeyer and Rev. De Boer were not present.

After opening with prayer, Rev. Bazuin announced, "The elders have prepared their answers in this packet which we will distribute now, but they must be handed back at the end of the meeting."

His instruction startled us. The fact that the elders had put something in writing startled us. It was obvious the elders had discussed this action with the committee. Why hadn't they sent us copies to study before the meeting? Their lengthy document looked to be unanswerable with a quick response of acceptance or non-acceptance. There wasn't much choice but to continue on and make the best of the situation. The elders' packets were handed out to each of us. They were stamped in red ink, "CONFIDENTIAL." Pete Schipma, the newly designated spokesperson for the elders, read their introductory comments.

> The Consistory does not wish to see this matter proceed to a Judicial Hearing. This is not out of fear, for we are totally confident that we have done all things in good order and have the two separate teams of Church Visitors, on three different occasions to back up that statement. Nor do we fear reversal of our position in an ecclesiastical court. On the contrary, we are secure in our belief that such a hearing would sanction our position (Letter to Synodical Reconciliation Committee from Consistory of OPCRC, dated 11-18-92).

I wondered if they realized the appellants expected a hearing to sanction their position. We weren't doing this for the glory, obviously, but so the truth of the matter was out in the open. We had learned the hard way that we could not convict anyone, the Holy Spirit would do that. Our only duty was to present what we knew to the best of our ability. Confidently, he continued, "A hearing is an antagonistic situation and we have no hostility toward the appellants. A hearing is divisive and harms the body of Christ; it is a counterproductive activity that impedes the ministry of the Word, which is the mission of the OPCRC. It is our sincere desire that reconciliation with the appellants be achieved with the help of the Synodical Reconciliation Committee."

Well, that opening statement sure made us look good. A hearing is harmful, divisive and counterproductive to the mission of the church? If that were the case, why was it provided for in the book of Church Order? A hearing would provide a place for church members, whether laypersons or office-bearers, to present any "injustice . . . done" or "a decision that conflicts with the Word of God or Church Order." Those who wrote the Church Order wisely saw, "The Judicial Code provides a procedural pattern within which the law of love may be fulfilled (Cf. James 2:1,8,9)" (Article 30 of the Church Order, Manual of Christian Reformed Church Government, CRC Pub., Grand Rapids, MI, 1987).

The introduction got better. "In the most charitable and tactful phrase we can use," read Schipma, the appellants have "become carried away with this issue. We plead for them to return to objectivity in this final discussion, and avoidance of polemics such as those in Howard's missive."

I'd have to look polemics up, but I had a good idea of what he was talking about. And I guessed returning to objectivity meant returning to sanity. I could tell we weren't going to get very far at this meeting.

"Enough of the intros, let's get to the meat of the issue," I thought. Finally, Schipma reached the elders' position. "We believe her [L'Engle's] books can be read with profit in a generally positive Christian light. We believe that retaining her books in the OPCRC library is in keeping with our library's guidelines and with the selection criteria of the 'Report of the Classical Committee on Church Libraries' which was adopted by Classis Chicago South." [This was the new library criteria that had been adopted after Classis' decision of January '91, not the original criteria which the books didn't meet.]

He proceeded, "out of a spirit of reconciliation and concern for unity in the OPCRC, the consistory has taken the books out of the library." [Where was the concern for unity when all this began? More of L'Engle's works were added to the church library *after* we had appealed to Classis.] So far, the elders were looking mighty good. I wished the committee knew the elders had removed the books only after one organist resigned her position, certain deacons were ready to resign from office, and Howard had already resigned. This was not some loving gesture on the part of the elders, it was a forced reaction, a "cave-in." They hadn't seen the danger of her works and with God-filled wisdom removed them out of concern for members of their church.

My mind was spinning as the elder read on. "Our position does mean that we disagree with the adoption by Classis Chicago South, at its January 1991 meeting, of the book review by its Advisory

Committee. . . . The Elders of the OPCRC have articulated their position on MLE in their statement to Classis of 4 December 1990."

I couldn't believe it. Though I was somewhat perturbed they had demeaningly called the advisory report a "book review," finally, in writing, the elders formally admitted they disagreed with classis. There had to be a catch, and there was. The next paragraph Schipma read threw all the appellants into a tailspin:

> It should be noted that, at the January 1991 Classis meeting, a motion was made and supported to sustain the appeal of the appellants. This motion was defeated. The appeal was NOT sustained. Because of an arcane procedural rule of Classis, that defeated motions not be reported in the Minutes of Classis, this fact cannot be documented from the Minutes. However, the Chairman of that Classis meeting, Rev. William Lenters of Hope Christian Reformed Church, deposes that such a motion was made and defeated. Only subsequent to that defeated motion was the adoption of the Advisory Report approved, with many recorded dissenting votes, by Classis.

A motion to sustain the appeal had never been voted on. We had been asked by Lenters himself if the appellants would accept the advisory report in place of the appeal. We had gladly given our permission to do so because the report essentially said the same thing as our appeal. Hessel Park's protest after classis had stated: *"Instead of taking the ordinary vote, to sustain or not to sustain the appeal,* Classis adopted the findings of its advisory committee as a form of advice to the consistory and the appellants" (emphasis mine). In addition, there was no record of such a vote being taken in the minutes of classis. And what was this–that there were many dissenting votes? A hand vote had not even been taken because the majority was so in favor of adopting the report.

Schipma continued to read their response to our first concern which asked:

> Why were the elders unwilling to show us how we were quoting L'Engle "out of context," as they claimed we were doing? Did they just say this parroting the Education Committee, without requiring any proof whatsoever that

we were misquoting L'Engle? Why, with the exception of Howard Stob, were neither of our pastors nor any of our elders willing to examine her books together with us as we pleaded with them to do?

Their explanation was:

Rev. Erffmeyer "has sat down for many hours with Claris (and Karen) and gone over the writings of Madeleine L'Engle page by page, listening to the objections." He found "no passages with New Age teachings in these writings," and stated that "many times Claris and Karen do not understand the statements in their context."

This was a very misleading statement, since all I read to him were a few passages out of one book, a book he had refused to read because he was "too busy." Not only that, he had defended statements that were not Biblical.

The elders' answer went on and on about how many meetings we had with the pastors, elders, the consistory, the council . . . leaving the false impression that countless meetings had been used to examine L'Engle's writings with us. Most of the meetings spoken of were confrontations, not willing pastors and elders reading through books deciphering L'Engle's teachings. As for meeting with the whole council (both elders and deacons), we were never granted permission to do so. Howard was the only one who met with the full council when he read his resignation as elder.

Schipma read fluently: "The amount of time spent by our Pastors on this issue became so disrupting to their conduct of other duties that the Elders, at their meeting of June 19, 1990 directed that Rev. Erffmeyer and his staff decline to participate further in discussions with the appellants regarding the orthodoxy of MLE."

Why was it then, that in the minutes of the elders found in their response to our appeal to classis, already back on January 23, 1990, *before* our first meeting with the elders, "the elders went on record to endorse the *pastors'* good judgment on when to call a halt in going over the same material with the same persons time after time on the occult and New Age movement"? (emphasis mine). It was the pastor who directed the elders to direct him to decline further discussion.

The reason we asked this question was to openly discuss the note Rev. Erffmeyer had written about me before our very first meeting with the elders. (If you don't recall it, turn back to the end of chapter 4.) Howard and I knew the elders had been biased from the very beginning and unwilling to hear anything we had to say. I couldn't comprehend how we were ever going to sort through all this.

In an effort once again to defend L'Engle, the elders' response stated they had contacted Professor Don Hettinga at Calvin College. Hettinga had told them, "Madeleine L'Engle has brought many people to the Lord Jesus Christ."

The elders also claimed Mary Beth Bootsma, the church librarian, did extensive research on L'Engle. I read the one page of research she had comprised of her own opinions, which basically said there was nothing wrong with calling the Bible myth. It was all just a matter of opinion, of what colored glasses you read with. I had files filled with information. Where was hers? If there was any, I wanted to see it.

When Schipma read that even the Library of Congress didn't list her books under "New Age," I had all I could do to keep my mouth shut. Did the elders really think all literary works containing New Age thought were labeled New Age? They can be found under just about every category there is: Psychology, Environment, Education, Religion, Medicine, Occult, Parapsychology, Science, Feminism, etc. Another suggestion made was, "If L'Engle was 'New Age,' she would say so." Now there was real insight.

De Jong remarked they had consulted literary experts and Rev. Erffmeyer saw no New Age teachings in her works. But their literary experts weren't "experts" in theology or New Age and the occult, and Erffmeyer wasn't an expert on New Age or L'Engle's writings. Rev. John De Vries had written a book on the New Age movement, yet what had Erffmeyer and elder Mels done with his letter and opinion? Thrown it out. They "sought out opinions that were more charitable in their interpretations."

Our concern that Mels had stated Rev. De Vries disclaimed his letter, thereby misleading the elders, was answered with the new excuse that the letter had been summarized to the elders, not read in its entirety. At this, Howard Stob boldly protested, "It was not!" It was his word and mine (from my previous conversations with Erffmeyer and Mels) against the elders. But I was never allowed to read from my journal and Howard's question as to who summarized it was never answered.

It wasn't until Schipma answered our concern #9 that we really understood what was meant by church politics. "The Elders of OPCRC do indeed have the right to speak against the decision of Classis that adopted the Advisory Report as its answer to the initial appeal of the appellants. In accordance with Christian Reformed church polity, the delegates of OPCRC recorded their negative vote upon this occasion; in so doing they retained the right to speak against the decision."

This was news to us. Where in the Church Order did it say if you registered your negative vote you didn't have to abide by a decision of classis? If there was such a clause, why didn't the elders provide us with it? It was very clear in Article 29 of the Church Order that once a decision is made, it was to be considered "settled and binding." The only way the elders could "privately or publicly" disagree with a classical decision was to appeal to synod within 30 days. They hadn't done so.

In defense of the elders, De Jong asserted there was nothing to appeal since classis hadn't provided a "directive." But nowhere in the Church Order or in the Form of Subscription did it say classis had to give a direct order. Sometimes (as Rev. Punt pointed out in a previous case) the "directives" are implied and those of good will know what is meant and act accordingly.

The appellants were flabbergasted. We had tried to conceive what the elders might say before we met with the committee, but we had no idea they would come up with this. They had already informed the congregation in a bulletin announcement after classis that they no longer wished to judge the Christianity of Madeleine L'Engle and that decision superseded all prior decisions.

The elders had made it clear to the deacons their decision meant they took back their original judgment that her works were "Christian" in nature and simply weren't going to judge at all. Now, to the reconciliation committee, the elders were confidently saying they were holding firm to their first decision. This meant they judged L'Engle to be a Christian author and her works a blessing and that they had every right to disagree with classis' declaration concerning the four denials of essential Biblical truths.

Howard Stob tried to clarify this to the committee: "The elders made a judgment that her works are Christian and a blessing. . . . "

"Oh no, they didn't!" Bazuin burst in. How he could say such a thing, we could only guess; he had no proof of his declaration.

De Jong now wrongly surmised, "Hurt feelings, pain and hurts. That's why we're here. Your perceptions are misplaced. You want us to agree with you. We feel we have made decisions for the good of the church. People have different views, but so what. . . . " SO WHAT?? Were the four cardinal truths pointed out by classis and ourselves so unimportant? Later in the course of conversation, he added, "We do not believe that God is an angry God. We believe God is a loving God. L'Engle's writings aren't dangerous." I wondered if he was mimicking what he had heard, or if he had read her works thoroughly and come to that conclusion himself.

While the elders insisted in their response that they affirmed the four essential doctrines pointed out in our appeal, they asserted:

> As to whether God is capable of redeeming all creation, of course He is; He is God. Will He do so? *We do not believe He will, in light of our current understanding of His revelation.* This we hold as a doctrine of the Reformed faith to which we subscribe. *But note, and note carefully, that no doctrine formulated by man can ever be regarded as a comprehensive understanding of God and His purposes. We cannot constrain God. In the history of the church we have many times misconstrued what He has said to us. He does not change; our doctrines sometimes must.* There are mysteries in the Christian faith, such as the relationship between God's love and His justice, that we cannot hope to fathom and must accept as mysteries. We can try to understand and we can develop doctrines and catechisms that put our understanding, such as it is, into words. But we cannot comprehend the mind of God, and we can never put our doctrines above Him ("Who has known the mind of the Lord? Or who has been His counselor? Romans 11:34") (emphasis mine).

We had come to the heart of the issue. Unfortunately, because of the time it took to discuss the elders' introductory statement and concern # 1, Schipma was instructed to read the remaining answers to our position paper and discussion was limited. As he read the above statement, I could see the appellants all knew what this meant. I wondered if the elders realized what their own statement was saying.

God is not capable of redeeming all people, including Satan, because He is not capable of going against His own Word. For the elders to even pose the possibility placed doubt upon our doctrines. Though man cannot comprehend all the mysteries of God, God's Word was written so that man would *know* the way to salvation. Didn't Jesus say, "I tell you the truth, we speak of what we *know*, and we testify to what we have seen, but still you people do not accept our testimony"? (John 3:11). Was the apostle Paul wrong when he said, ". . . continue in what you have learned and have become convinced of, because you *know* those from whom you learned it and how from infancy you have *known* the holy Scriptures, which are able to make you wise for salvation through faith in Christ Jesus"? (II Timothy 3:14-15, emphasis mine).

God doesn't play games. If the elders believed that different interpretations might arise concerning essential doctrines, how could they believe the Holy Spirit guides you into knowing the Truth, not man–as Reformed faith holds? How could they ever know anything for certain? They couldn't. (Remember L'Engle's quote about great scientists?)

Our elders felt the only time they could judge someone's beliefs was when a person came to our church to make profession of faith. Well then, what can one do if he finds New Age teachings in catechism material, adult education material, or anything else that might be used for instruction, whether it be films, speakers, etc. . . . ??? Keep his mouth shut? With sermons on unity being constantly bombarded into the minds of people in the pew; with sermons that condemned "negativity" and the questioning of leaders in high positions, not many would dare open their mouths. If they did, more than likely, they'd go through exactly what we were.

The elders' answers were far from satisfactory. In fact, many of the questions we had raised were not even addressed. During a coffee break, we asked why we couldn't have a copy of the elders' response for study. "Then you'll come back with another lengthy document. Don't want to kill any more trees!" elder De Jong smirked.

At the close of the meeting, Dr. Harry Arnold, secretary of the reconciliation committee, collected the "confidential" packets, making sure all of them were returned. The appellants were rather offended to find out each of us had been assigned a particular number that coordinated with the confidential packet we received (they were not given out randomly). Why each of us was assigned a different number was anybody's guess.

Before we left, we asked if our pastors would be at the next meeting. Dick Molenhouse, an elder representative who had hardly spoken during our meeting answered sharply, "No way will the pastors come!" Rev. Bazuin gave him a startled look. "Well, maybe later on in the meetings . . ." Molenhouse conceded.

Too late–his outburst spoke volumes. The attitude displayed by Molenhouse and others was one which whispered, "You are the enemy."

Chapter Fourteen

RECONCILIATION
WITHOUT REPENTANCE?

To the Church in Laodicea . . . I know your deeds, that
you are neither cold nor hot. I wish you were either one
or the other! So, because you are lukewarm–neither hot
nor cold–I am about to spit you out of my mouth. . . .
Those whom I love I rebuke and discipline. So be earnest, and repent."

Revelation 3:14,15,19

Our next meeting with the reconciliation committee was scheduled for January 15, 1993. Feeling our elders had given us the run
around with newly devised arguments, we wrote the committee,
reminding them that the interpretation of L'Engle's writings had
already been settled by classis.

In addition, we brought to their attention that at *no time* during
the classical meeting in January, 1992, or at the judicial code committee meeting in June of '92 did *anyone* say our charges were not
valid because our elders had registered their negative vote, therefore, they had a right to speak against the decision of classis. We
also expressed our disappointment in the secrecy of the "confidential" packets which were not handed out until the day of the meeting, leaving us unable to consult anyone about the elders' answers
(Letter to Committee for Reconciliation, appointed by Synod, 1992,
dated 12-18-92).

In the meantime, we received a copy of the concept minutes of

163

the January, 1991 meeting of classis from Rev. Richard Hartwell, the Stated Clerk. Because the elders had asked for a copy, he felt the appellants were entitled to one as well. The last page of Hartwell's notes read:

> In response to the appeal of four members of OPCRC against the elders' decision to retain the books of M. L'Engle, Classis adopts the report of its advisory committee as its answer to them [and this sustains the appeal].

By the words, "and this sustains the appeal" was a note which read, "Removed by amendment." Not knowing who to turn to for advice, I called Rev. Punt. He suggested we write the committee and ask for the "stricture of confidentiality" to be removed so that we could discuss procedural matters with him. We were not experts on church order and the help was needed.

Rev. Punt sent us a copy of Classis' Rules of Procedure which aided us with an answer to the committee and elders (dated January 15, 1993):

> It is impossible for an amendment to change a motion from saying, "We sustain the appeal," to say "we do not sustain the appeal." "A motion to amend is not a proper amendment if it nullifies the main motion" (Classis' Rules of Procedure, pg. 24). To nullify a motion, the main motion must be voted up or down.

> If the motion with the phrase "and this sustains the appeal" would have been adopted, classis would have said that "everything mentioned in the appeal" had been evaluated and "sustained." This would have contradicted the very report classis adopted. To avoid this self-contradictory claim, the phrase 'and this sustains the appeal' *had to be removed.*

> Classis *never voted* to "not sustain the appeal." Classis voted to remove the phrase "and this sustains the appeal," that is to say, classis did not put its stamp of approval *on every jot and tittle* in our appeal."

If, when voting the delegates of Orland Park believed

that the amended action meant that "classis *did not* sustain the appeal," they would not have registered their negative vote! They wanted classis to "*not sustain* the appeal."

. . . Classis said *nothing* negative about *anything* in our appeal. Classis sustained "the central issue" of our appeal . . . .

I guess I had broken confidentiality, but then, the appellants *never* agreed to the elders' stricture of confidentiality. We didn't want any part of it. Besides which, we found out Schipma had consulted many people in an attempt to find out what had happened with our appeal at the January, 1991 meeting of classis. The elders weren't even sticking to their own rules. Politics was playing a more important role in this issue than Jesus' unique divinity and sacrificial death on the cross. It was demeaning to the One whom they were elected to defend.

The committee asked the elders to reconsider their "stricture of confidentiality" and also informed them that "the pastors will have to become involved in the discussions at some point, and we think the sooner the better" (Letter to Consistory from Dr. Harry Arnold, dated 12-28-92).

Much to the disappointment of the elders, I'm sure, the appellants killed a few more trees and decided to write a response to each of the elders' statements. Documentation was added so the reconciliation committee could see we weren't just talking out of our hats.

Meeting with Reconciliation Committee, January 15, 1993

PRESENT

Reconciliation Committee: Rev. Bazuin, Rev. Arnold, Rose Van Reken

Elders: Dr. Richard De Jong, Dick Molenhouse, Pete Schipma, Rich Jousma

Appellants: Karen Leensvaart, Ruth Evenhouse, Howard and Jo Stob, John and Sharon Tiggelaar, Claris Van Kuiken

Here we were again, about to embark on an adventure of, well, who knew. This time, however, all of us were determined to keep on the issues and not be detoured in so many different directions.

Once again our pastors did not show up, even after the committee had requested they do so "the sooner the better." Frankly, we couldn't understand how the elders or the committee expected reconciliation to take place when our own pastors wouldn't be taking part in our discussions.

Though Karen, as spokesperson for the appellants, was allowed to read our answers to the elders' response to our position paper, the meeting proved to be more disastrous than the first.

Beginning with our question #2 concerning Ken Mels' statement that Rev. John De Vries had disclaimed his letter, elder representative Dick De Jong objected, "I can't say who said what when. . . . It is known generally that De Vries is against Madeleine L'Engle's writings. I have no answer to his disclaiming his letter." [It was known generally now by the elders because De Vries' articles in *The Outlook* magazine had been printed two years ago.]

De Jong asserted, "You know, the whole response has an undertone of some sort of conspiracy which I object to–a conspiracy from the leadership."

I began reading my conversation with Ken Mels from my journal, when De Jong complained, "Are we going to have to read journals for every question? You're just re-dredging up things." (Wasn't that what we were supposed to do?)

"Who summarized De Vries' letter to the elders?" Howard asked.

"I was told," Schipma answered without naming anyone. "I don't know if we can even know who said what. . . . Are you trying to drag people into court? I called Ken Mels, and he said he respected John De Vries' opinion."

"We have to deal with truth and fact. We want to give the committee the facts and the truth," I argued.

"I think we've heard enough," Rev. Bazuin said abruptly, "Let's go to concern #3."

Concern #3 in our position paper dealt with the sermons Erffmeyer had preached while we were appealing to Classis Chicago South in September of '91. We felt he had used them to divide the congregation against us–and it had. Even if he hadn't done so intentionally, if he knew the results, why wouldn't he at least apologize to the congregation for having misled them? We couldn't understand why any minister would encourage people not to talk to other members within their own congregation. We believed this to be a terrible abuse of the pulpit.

De Jong was the first to speak: "This is very interesting. Did you as committee listen to those tapes; all three of you? You be the judge. The elders never questioned the preaching. There is strong language used here. This is *slandering* the pastor."

Rev. Bazuin tried to smooth things over: "I know myself being a pastor that points sometimes are taken differently by different people. I will have it after a particular sermon that someone will come up to me afterwards and comment that I must have been speaking to them. And I wasn't even aware of it."

Sharon spoke for the first time: "But you have to understand that we have had people unaware of everything that was going on come up to us after a service and comment that he [Pastor Erffmeyer] hit our group hard today. People other than us were perceiving this to be the case." (This didn't make an impression. The elders' point of view was, "If the shoe fits, wear it.")

"The elders are *not* going to let the pastors get involved," De Jong retorted.

Dr. Arnold suggested there wasn't enough time to listen to the tapes and that we would have to limit ourselves to the ten points of the position paper. I shrugged my shoulders. This *was* one of our ten points.

Molenhouse piped in, "We have a committee that meets to critique the sermons. Rich Jousma, I believe you're on that committee. There has never been a problem."

"We have never had any [formal] complaints from anyone about his sermons," De Jong assured the committee.

I could see Sharon was getting upset. Her father had walked out during a couple of sermons and had requested a meeting with the elders. He had met with Molenhouse and Schipma, but the conversation was to remain "confidential."

Hoping De Jong would acknowledge the truth, Sharon asked, "Richard, you said you have never had anyone approach the elders. . . . But isn't it true that you have had meetings with someone from the congregation who kept walking out during the service because of the sermons?"

While Molenhouse shook his head mumbling, "No, no, no," De Jong replied, "Not to my knowledge."

Bazuin broke in, "I think we've heard enough. Elders, concern #4. . . ."

The elders' insistence that everything had been done out of love and concern for us was at the heart of #4. In our answer to them, we brought up the fact that we had been accused of dividing and destroying the church and that we were looked upon as helping the devil. One deacon I trusted was brave enough to tell me that as far as the elders were concerned, my name was at the bottom of the totem pole. Howard had also explained in our answer:

> After the article on what happened at Classis appeared in the church newsletter, the next consistory meeting resulted in a rather vicious attack on me. The elders feared I would resign because of things that were said to me at that meeting. Later, three elders asked to meet with me. At the meeting with the three elders, I specifically asked them if they disagreed with Classis' decision. They were unwavering and uncompromising in their reply. They still defended Madeleine L'Engle as a Christian author and her works a blessing. I replied, on that basis, I must resign as elder, not on the basis of things said against me. One of the elders then told me, *"If you resign you'll never be an elder again."* The implication, of course, was that I was no longer fit to be an elder because I was destroying the unity of the Orland Park Church.

Last, but not least, was the P.S. note Rev. Erffmeyer had written about me to the elders before our very first meeting with them. He wrote that note, we explained, without ever mentioning a word about it to me. We firmly stated, ". . . it was very close to pure slander. Pastor Erffmeyer had no right to convey this information to the elders and the elders had no right to hear it without asking Rev. Erffmeyer if he had talked to Claris about these matters. Even if the information had been true, according to Scripture, Rev. Erffmeyer had the duty to confront her with this before reporting it as fact to the elders."

I was glad the documented "P.S." had been given to the reconciliation committee by the elders. Howard hadn't felt very free to use it because it was said to be another confidential matter that was to be discussed only during the elders' meetings. I happened to see it by mistake in Howard's notebook as we were going through some documents needed to write one of our many letters. "What's this?"

I had asked Howard as I read the awful note which I knew not to be true. Howard tried to take the notebook away from me, realizing I shouldn't have seen it, but it was too late. I finished reading the note and then handed it back to him. He asked me questions about what had happened on the Sunday I was supposed to have talked with kids, "before, during and after" worship services. I told him what I knew to be true.

What would be the elders reply to this concern? Read carefully.

Jousma was the first to respond to the statement, "you'll never be an elder again." "I don't recall that statement being made. It wasn't said in an angry tone." (First he says he can't recall it, then defends himself by saying it wasn't said in an angry tone?)

"How can the statement, 'You'll never be an elder again' be given in love?" asked Karen. . . . Silence. . . .

"Was anything done to restore the appellants?" Howard asked.

"Don't recall anything," Jousma admitted.

"We were viewed as the enemy. There are two sides here," Howard explained.

I was glad Ruth now brought up the P.S. note about me. De Jong advised the committee "the communication is documented by Gary Meyer [the teacher with whom Erffmeyer had talked]. "He has it in his file."

"Where is it? Let's see it. I asked you to bring it to the next meeting," I reminded him. [Note: At the December 5, meeting I had asked for the elders to show me their documentation for what I had done and also to bring in the students who claimed it.]

Defensively, De Jong responded, "This is the business of the elders. I don't consider the letter slander—maybe bias. This is private information. *It's factual.* The elders discuss many things. . . ."

"What possible reason would there be for Rev. Erffmeyer to hand this out at an elders meeting before we had an opportunity to speak with them?" Sharon asked.

"Don't have to answer that," De Jong whimpered.

Karen expressed her view that Erffmeyer should have confronted me with the information, after which Ruth brought up an excellent point: "How can you allow something you won't allow us to do? . . . You take the word of Gary Meyer, Erffmeyer, the kids—and believe them without confronting Claris. Yet we can't present our view at all . . . ?" (It seemed strange having people talk around you, but I welcomed the support.)

"According to Scripture, according to Matthew 18, I *need* to confront him on this," I pleaded.

Bazuin interjected, "On to concern #5."

Concern #5 dealt with the announcement in the church newsletter placed by Rev. Erffmeyer after classis had adopted the advisory report. To illustrate why we believed it was a false statement, we provided this example:

> . . . suppose after the Gulf war with Iraq was over, a re-mote village in Iraq was awaiting news of this war. They receive a telegram from Saddam Hussain with two statements: 'We sent scud missiles to some Israeli cities and the war is over.' That village would have a victory celebration. The two true statements given, however, would lead the people of Iraq to the opposite conclusion of the actual truth, that they had an unmitigated defeat in the war.

The appellants believed "the pastors and elders did the *least* they could to inform the congregation of Classis' decision. They did their *best* to keep the congregation in the dark." It was one of the many ways in which L'Engle's writings were defended.

"And here lies the crux of the matter; the issue that divides," De Jong suggested. "If I may ask a question of Howard, was Rev. Punt consulted or involved in any way in compiling this letter? Did Rev. Punt write this letter?" [He was speaking of a letter we had recently sent the committee concerning the concept minutes and the motion to sustain our appeal.]

Howard answered quite honestly that Rev. Punt had indeed been consulted, but hadn't written our letter. Frankly, I didn't see what this had to do with anything. The elders had consulted others, so why were they trying to railroad Rev. Punt? What difference did it make as long as the truth about what happened at classis was clarified?

I realized during our discussion that it did make a difference, because if what the elders said in their response, that a motion to sustain the appeal was denied, our pastor's statement in our church newsletter would be considered true and accurate. The elders were protecting the pastor. I really couldn't blame them for that, but I did hold them responsible for not acknowledging the truth when the concept minutes and Classis' Rules of Procedure, as well as other documentation, came to light.

Defending the elders' position, De Jong switched the blame for the whole battle on the appellants: "The only reason the appellants don't want this over with is because their agenda is being vindictive. The appellants believe classis said they were right, and the elders were wrong all along. Not until proven." (Hadn't it been proven?)

"What about vindication of our Lord Jesus Christ?" Sharon interrupted. Her face and neck turned a bright red. "I'm sorry," she quickly added. She shouldn't have been. It was a question that needed to be asked.

"Do the elders stand by their original statement about Madeleine L'Engle?" Howard demanded to know.

"Yes, we do," replied De Jong.

It seemed we were going around in circles again. I reiterated the problem was not the books in the library but that the elders considered her works "Christian" and asserted they fit the library criteria. Rose Van Reken was the first person of the reconciliation committee to recognize, "The main point is a doctrine issue, not the books in the library. . . ."

De Jong now quickly admitted that the wording of the pastor's reporting could have been better.

"Would that satisfy you, if the elders admitted they could have stated things more clearly?" Rev. Bazuin asked hopefully.

Taking this one issue in and by itself wouldn't help. We were trying to show a pattern–a pattern of defending false teachings to the point of deception. Whether the deception occurred from outright lying, misplaced priorities, or unintentionally or intentionally misleading the congregation, the outcome remained the same. It had to be corrected. Everything the elders and pastors had done up to this point was done to support false teachings, not refute them.

We had given the committee ample information in our letters to them in order to evaluate for themselves why the elders' assessment of what happened at classis was wrong, and why we felt they were not abiding by it. After making such a fuss that the appeal had been voted on and not sustained and requesting the concept minutes to prove it, neither De Jong or Schipma brought up the concept minutes, and our letter to the committee was not discussed. Bazuin concluded the committee had heard enough and we went on to concern #6–the elders' defense of L'Engle's belief that Satan would be reconciled to God and that all people would be saved.

Not only had the elders backed up L'Engle's statements that all, including Satan, would be saved with Scripture *before classis*, at Gaither's "Praise Gathering" *after classis*, they heard this proclamation by L'Engle herself and *still* defended her. At the same time, they were holding to their belief that there are many different interpretations of her writings, so we must "agree to disagree." Figure that one out. Were we now to assume that they had conceded that maybe L'Engle does believe all will be saved, but the rest of her beliefs shown by us and affirmed by classis were still a matter of interpretation?

De Jong denied the elders used Scripture out-of-context to defend L'Engle's teaching, when Schipma declared, "We do not comprehend God. We have to believe any surprise from God. We do know there will be surprises yet. . . ." Surprises? Would God, in the end, surprise us and tell us he was never wrathful and that Jesus didn't have to die to take away our sins? My mind turned to what was dictated by the demon named "Jesus" in *A Course of Miracles*:

> I was not punished because you were bad. . . . God does not believe in retribution. . . . Sacrifice is a notion totally unknown to God (pg. 32-33, Volume One, Foundation for Inner Peace, 1975).

> The Apostles often misunderstood it [the crucifixion–CVK], . . . out of their own fear they spoke of the "wrath of God." . . . these are some of the examples of upside-down thinking in the New Testament, . . . the gospel is really only the message of love. . . ." (*ibid.,* pg. 87).

I was given permission to read from the elders' response to our first appeal where they had defended L'Engle's view with Scripture.

"That's *their* interpretation," De Jong contended. Again, without further explanation, we were instructed to continue on to concern #7–our consistory's continual refusal to meet with us after classis' declaration. We apprised the committee of the fact that our elders were fully aware our requests for meetings did *not* center around the interpretation of L'Engle's writings. They weren't "to rehash the same stuff." The elders insisted our meetings had "generated no progress. The same concerns were reiterated again and again, with no change in the perceptions of either group."

The meetings they spoke of, however, were *before* classis' decision, not after. We also let it be known that at our meeting with the judicial code committee, De Jong claimed there was no new information on L'Engle, therefore the elders didn't have to meet with us. But De Jong neglected to mention the elders never asked to see new information, nor were they willing to look at anything I was more than anxious to show them. Before *our very first meeting* with the elders, they had already "endorsed the pastor's good judgment on when to call a halt in going over the same material with the same persons time after time. . . ." (Elders' minutes, January 23, 1990).

Hardly any discussion had taken place over this matter, when someone announced it was time for a coffee break.

In the hallway outside the room where we met, Sharon asked Dr. Arnold whether a person denying the atonement could be a Christian. He answered, "No," without hesitation. Everything hinged upon the all-important question we had asked our consistory, "Can you deny the substitutionary atonement, the unique divinity of Jesus Christ, the unique authority of Scripture and that some will be eternally separated from God and still be classified as a Christian author?" Up till now, our consistory had refused to address that question, which was one reason in itself to be concerned.

The whole matter of judging was a very delicate area we were treading on. This was concern #8–our consistory's attitude toward making judgments, which was simply, not to make any. Their argument, of course, was a false one, because they had already *made* a judgment. It was *our* judgment they were against. The utter lack of responsibility depicted in the following statement found in the elders' confidential response added to our grievance against them:

> The appellants also seem to feel that there is some requirement, derived from the Bible or the fact the Elders are signatories of the CRC Form of Subscription, for the Consistory to take some type of action against MLE and\or her writings. There were times in which the Christian Church tortured and then barbecued those who did not agree with them. The Church does not do that any

more. There were also times in which the Church made
bonfires of books that the Church interpreted as in disagreement with official doctrine. The Church doesn't do
that any more either. . . . We did not, and do not, agree
with the appellants' interpretation, but, even so, we respected their right as Christians to hold an opinion contrary to ours. . . .

We didn't quite know what to make of this bizarre reasoning.
We hadn't asked our elders to burn L'Engle at the stake. We hadn't
even asked them to demand members of our particular church not
read her writings, let alone burn them. Did their answer mean they
recognized L'Engle disagreed with essential Biblical truths, but her
writings should still be endorsed as Christian? Did they mean no
one could tell what her writings were actually saying so we should
agree to disagree that she denies Biblical truths? Or did they believe both of these viewpoints were reasonable answers to our imperative question?

Whether the elders liked it or not, the Bible and the CRC Form
of Subscription did hold certain expectations for elders. It was precisely because of the fact that her writings were being endorsed
and promoted as "Christian" by members of the congregation and
by teachers in our Christian schools, that they had every duty and
responsibility to "refute and contradict these and to exert [them-
selves] in keeping the Church free from such errors." I was weary
of their excuses and continuing sagas of what's appropriate for a
church library. All we wanted was an answer, one way or another.

Once again, Bazuin boldly came to the elders' rescue, alleging,
"The elders never said L'Engle's works were Christian."

I asked if I could read from the April, 1990 letter from the elders and was given permission to do so. I began, "It is our conviction that she is a Christian author, and that her work is not harmful
to the faith of children or adults."

"We said her works can be read in a general positive light," De
Jong corrected.

"Are you taking back your original decision?" Howard asked.

Guarding the elders' firm declaration, De Jong retorted, "You
think you had a victory as to what classis said. Can't you acknowledge contrary opinions in *The Banner,* from learned people? Trinity Christian College, Calvin. . . . We don't share the same cru-

sade. . . . ."

At this, Sharon couldn't stand it a moment longer (none of us could). She raised her voice: ***"It's not Madeleine L'Engle!!! Where are our leaders? Richard, I have to ask you. . . . Can you deny the atonement, the unique divinity . . . can you deny the atonement and still be considered a Christian? I really need to know that."***

All of the appellants' eyes focused on De Jong. He looked up at the ceiling, hedging, looking for the right answer.

"Dick, I need to know . . . *can you deny the atonement, yes or no?"* Sharon persisted.

"Well. . . . "

"YES OR NO?"

De Jong stared at the reconciliation committee as if he was trying to read their minds for the right answer. He raised his arms, and in a somewhat frivolous manner stammered, ***"I don't know."***

Sharon's husband, John, who had warned me to keep my cool threw down his pencil on the table before him. " 'YOU DON'T KNOW?' DO YOU KNOW WHAT YOU JUST SAID? Those are the essential doctrines of the CRC. He doesn't know if you can deny the atonement. It's that simple."

"No, we can't know," echoed Schipma, coming to De Jong's aid.

"There are different interpretations," De Jong chimed in.

"What *is* your interpretation of the atonement?" Howard asked.

"No interpretation."

"Then you have nothing to teach!" exclaimed Howard.

Changing the subject, De Jong asked what it would take for reconciliation to take place and further noted not just Christian Reformed people are saved. I wondered if he really thought we believed they were.

Bazuin abruptly ended our conversation. "Now for #9."

We had already addressed the elders' belief that because they recorded their negative vote they retained their right to speak against classis' decision in our letter to the reconciliation committee. (A copy had also been sent to the elders.) "There is no answer to this. No response," De Jong said. But at this point, none of us really cared about anything other than what we had just heard.

"The ball is in the committee's court, you'll have to agree to disagree. . . . No more letters, no communications. . . ." Bazuin concluded.

As the meeting was drawing to a close, one of the elders asked to have their packets collected. As they were being handed in, Bazuin announced there would only have to be one more meeting.

"Will the pastors be there?" asked Sharon

"Will we have the opportunity to speak with our pastors?" asked Jo.

"Mr. Chairman," De Jong broke in, "we as an eldership body have made a commitment to protect our pastors and will not bring them here to face the allegations they have made. Possibly we could consider, if we would receive a detailed agenda from the committee with specific items that would be asked of them. But the pastors will *not* come here to provide their responses. The pastors will *not* be there" [at the next meeting–CVK].

"The pastors *will* be at our next meeting," Dr. Arnold directed.

Molenhouse disagreed. "The elders are the ruling body. Our position is taken. We want an agenda. The appellants can't interrogate the pastors. *We* are the ruling body of the church, and *we* will say whether the pastors will be at the next meeting."

"And *we* are a committee from synod. . . ." Arnold replied with unquestioned authority.

After the meeting, we stayed awhile to talk. Before we left, Karen walked up to Pete Schipma and quietly asked, "Can we know anything for sure–is there any absolute truth?" To which Schipma replied, "The only thing we can know for sure is God."

Upon hearing their conversation, I probed Schipma further, "Are you saying there are so many different interpretations [of the Bible] we can't know what God says?"

"Yes," he answered honestly.

No wonder our elders were unwilling and/or unable to make judgments. As far as they were concerned (and this was said) all you had to do was say, "Jesus is my Savior" and you were a Christian. They never mentioned the importance of knowing who Jesus Christ is and what he did for us.

We had gotten our answer, for the most part. I can hardly describe what it was like to hear our elders encouraging one another to step into darkness; heartache comes close. Feelings of disillusionment, distrust and an uncanny awareness that we were no longer a part of this church family destroyed all hope for reconciliation.

Chapter Fifteen

AN UNCOMPROMISING, UNPOPULAR STAND

What you have heard from me, keep as the pattern of sound teaching, with faith and love in Christ Jesus. Guard the good deposit that was entrusted to you–guard it with the help of the Holy Spirit who lives in us.

(2 Timothy 1:13-14)

In no way am I qualified to make theological pronouncements, and I make none.

(Elder, Orland Park Christian Reformed Church)

At the beginning of our final meeting with the reconciliation committee and elders on March 2, 1993, the committee handed out copies of their observations and recommendations. The appellants and elders were instructed to meet in separate rooms to examine their conclusions and hopefully sign on the dotted line in agreement; reconciliation achieved. If both parties signed, a bulletin announcement would let the congregation know the dispute over L'Engle's teachings had come to an end.

As much as we wanted to be able to say the committee did their job well, we couldn't. Many of our questions remained unanswered and/or unresolved. The question of whether or not it is the elders' duty to make sound judgments and refute false teachings was overlooked. Rather, the committee believed "this type of matter should be discussed in the general public Christian arena and not be made

an issue between members and the elders and pastors" (which gives
one reason for writing this book). They accepted the elders' statement that all was done out of love and concern and perceived the
appellants had misunderstood the elders' motives due to the stress
of the situation. (Our pastors had showed us how much they cared
by having their elders "protect" them from us by instructing them
not to attend the meetings.) Likewise, the elders were to accept
that our motive and concern was for the Truth, not a personal ven-
detta. The one question which became the dividing factor during
this struggle was not mentioned at all.

Recommendations for Agreement

The rest seemed like the old "give and take" plan. Chide the
elders here, chide the appellants there, and all will be happy again.
To sign the agreement put forth by the committee, the elders and
the appellants would have to agree to the following:

a) . . . that there are controversial statements in the writings of
Madeleine L'Engle and that the evangelical Christian community
has not come to a common mind as to whether she is or is not a
Christian author.

b) . . . that no one should be forbidden to read her books. We
know that some claim to have benefited greatly from reading her
works, even though some of her statements do not agree with our
confessional standards as Classis has affirmed.

c) . . . that Classis judged Madeleine L'Engle to be unorthodox
in her writings in four areas, namely, in her views on the substitutionary atonement, the unique divinity of Christ, the eternal separation between the saved and the lost, and the final authority of the
Bible.

d) . . . While we disagree on how to understand and interpret
Madeleine L'Engle's writings and whether or not they are deadly
or a blessing to those who read them, we all agree with the biblical
teachings and our Reformed confessions on those points which
Classis found Madeleine L'Engle to be unorthodox; and we all
hereby affirm the following truths [listed were the above doctrines–
CVK]. We therefore, affirm our desire to be united together in the
work of the Lord on the basis of our common commitment to the
Reformed faith.

e) . . . We grieve together that our disagreement has been so prolonged and has caused much hurt among some of our members. We confess together that somehow we have failed each other in many ways–misunderstanding or misinterpreting each other's words or actions and misjudging each other's motives and intentions. We ask forgiveness of each other for any failures noted by the other in these matters. We hereby resolve that we shall seek to restore trust among ourselves by putting the best motives on each other's statements and actions.

"Finally," the committee concluded, "we believe God is building His church and we are all 'fellow workers with Him' (1 Cor. 3:9). We therefore promise to 'Make every effort to keep the unity of the Spirit through the bond of peace' (Ephesians 4:3) so that this congregation may continue to be one of God's chosen instruments in extending Christ's kingdom to the glory of God's Great Name."

The appellants read the committee's documents over carefully. When we were led back into the room, the elders had smiles on their faces. "They're going to sign the agreement," I thought. I knew we weren't going to look very good to the reconciliation committee. In expectation of the compromises the committee might make, Howard had expressed all our concerns in a written statement he had comprised before the meeting. He asked if he could read it as our answer to them. The stern look on Dr. Arnold's face told me this was not going to go over very well.

Howard began by reading Acts 4:11-20 where Peter and John were haled before the court of the Sanhedrin observing, "When man's court ruling differed from God's, they already knew they must obey God rather then men" (Acts 4:19, 5:29). "Peter and John had indisputable and overwhelming evidence of the rightness of their case (verse 14). But because this matter threatened to destroy the domain of the Sanhedrin, it didn't matter at all what the evidence was. They already had reached a conclusion. The priority of the Sanhedrin in verse 17 was to stop this thing from spreading."

As Howard continued to read, I could about imagine what the elders and committee were thinking.

> We are meeting together because all of us want to stop this thing from spreading. We differ, however, on what this thing is that we want to keep from spreading. The Sanhedrin said to Peter and John, 'don't destroy the church.' Peter and John said, 'don't destroy the truth.'

These two things should never have a wall separating them, but they did then, and they do now.

His words were strong, not flowery or wishy-washy. "This is a doctrinal issue and must be tested by Scripture. From the appellant's point of view, and from classis' point of view, the consistory's arguments failed the test of Scripture. If the efforts of the reconciliation committee fail to bring about reconciliation, then this issue must be tested by synod's point of view, either by way of appeal from OPCRC consistory or a judicial hearing by the appellants."

I glanced at the disappointed faces of the reconciliation committee. How I wished they knew everything we had witnessed over the past four years. Maybe then, they would realize why we were fighting so hard. We didn't want to be considered "schismatic" or "divisive" or seen as a group who thought they were better than everyone else. We simply had no other choice. Our consciences would not allow us to "agree to disagree."

Troubled by Howard's letter, Dr. Arnold strongly suggested that an announcement be placed in the church bulletin indicating the appellants' refusal to sign the recommendations of the committee. We were thoroughly upset at his remark; their job was to report to synod, *not* to the congregation. This would make the situation that much worse, at least for the appellants, without the matter being addressed at a judicial hearing. Though I was fairly sure of how all the appellants felt, I asked if we could take some time to think and pray over the committee's recommendations. We needed time to reflect and decide for sure if this was the road God was leading us down.

In a last-ditch effort to open the eyes of the committee and our elders, I took out L'Engle's newest book, *A Rock That Is Higher,* and asked if I could read a certain passage from it. Permission granted, I read as distinctly as possible:

> A couple of summers ago I was asked to teach a two-week writers' workshop at a well-known Bible college in Canada. I was given their statement of faith to sign. I read it, found it unscriptural, and pushed it aside. There was no way I could sign it.
>
> They called me. "Where's the statement of faith?"
>
> I spoke to the dean of this Bible college. "It's unscriptural.

I'm sorry. I can't sign it."

I read him point three, which was one of the two points out of six that I could not sign. "Because of the fall we are in such a state of sin and depravity that we are justly under God's wrath and condemnation." Point four said that the only way God could forgive us for all this sin and depravity was for Jesus to come and get crucified. "What this is saying," I told the dean, "is that Jesus had to come save us from God the Father. I don't believe that Jesus had to come save us from God the Father" (Harold Shaw Pub., Wheaton, IL, 1993, pg. 72).

I thought this passage, alongside all the other statements in which L'Engle mocks Jesus' substitutionary, sacrificial death on the cross, would be enough for the committee to understand the seriousness of the matter. It wasn't.

"That's an old pagan belief," Schipma admonished.

"We don't believe that Jesus came to save us from the wrath of the Father," Dr. Arnold joined in.

"I don't see anything wrong with her statement," Rose Van Reken added.

Astounded by what had just been said, the appellants were at a loss for words.

Towards the last part of the meeting, when the elders were about ready to sign the recommendations from the committee, our pastors walked into the room. "Now they show up?" I whispered to Karen. They needn't have bothered. Discussion over the issues were finished.

The Plea: Don't Compromise the Truth!

We left the meeting drained, tired and worn. Just the thought of a judicial hearing right now was overwhelming. During the week, the appellants consulted with each other and thankfully, all of us agreed we couldn't let things stand the way they were. The comments concerning the sacrificial atonement made at our last meeting with the elders could not be forgotten or overlooked. Neither could we forget the remarks made by Schipma and De Jong after our meetings. They haunted us, compelling us to proceed with a judicial hearing.

I drafted a letter dated March 5, 1993 to the reconciliation committee appointed by synod. It began, "After much thought and prayerful consideration, it is with deep regret but in good conscience that we have decided not to sign the committee's recommendations."

We then explained our controversy was not with the Evangelical Christian community, but with our elders' continuous defense of false teachings after classis' decision had been made. The committee's notation that no one should be forbidden to read her books was irrelevant to the tensions that developed. While the elders' signature on the document meant they now affirmed classis' declaration, they were still upholding L'Engle as a Christian author to others. To us, the affirmation by the elders of these doctrines was meaningless. We would have liked to have signed Point E by the committee, if the many differences of opinion and certain facts which we knew to be true were "faced and resolved."

I was afraid the second part of our letter would cause bitter feelings against us, but we couldn't let Dr. Arnold's defense of our elders go without addressing it. We weren't sure why he had said, "We don't believe that Jesus came to save us from the wrath of the Father," so putting it in writing would clarify our thoughts for the committee (and the elders since they always received copies of our letters). Hopefully, Arnold would provide us with a sound answer as to why he was so quick to defend the elders to the point of contradicting Scripture.

The passage I had read from *A Rock That Is Higher* was printed out in full so the committee could digest L'Engle's denial of the substitutionary atonement. We asked the committee who Jesus was "crying out to when in an anguished voice, he lamented, 'My God, My God, why hast thou forsaken me?' Was it not the Father? Didn't Jesus, when he was in the garden before his crucifixion pray, 'My Father, if it is possible, may this cup be taken from me?' What cup was he talking about? Was it not the cup of God's wrath?"

We pointed out that in the *Heidelberg Catechism,* which the CRC supposedly held to, the question is asked, "What does our Mediator do to save us?" The answer is, "By bearing our punishment and by perfectly obeying God's law, our Mediator delivers us from the wrath of God and endows us with eternal life." Underneath the answer, among other verses, I Thessalonians 1:10b is quoted, "Even Jesus, who delivered us from the wrath to come." L'Engle *denies* there is a wrath to come. She *denies* Jesus' death was a payment for sin. Oh, I hoped the committee would see the consequences of her thinking. If there was nothing for Jesus to save us from, there was no need for Him to die–this was not the message of the Bible, of Jesus' own words, of the apostles' accounts in the New Testament. She *had* to believe in "a different gospel" and "another Jesus" (2 Corinthians 11:4).

The message of Romans 5:9 was so clear: "Since we have now been justified by his blood, how much more shall we be saved from God's wrath through him!" Galatians 1:4 acknowledges that it was Christ "who gave himself for our sins to rescue us from the present evil age, according to the will of our God and Father." In his book, *Systematic Theology*, Louis Berkhof defines this to mean "that His wrath was warded off by the sacrificial covering of their sin." And that "The Father made the sacrifice of His Son, and the Son willingly offered Himself" (Wm. B. Eerdmans Publishing Co., Grand Rapids, MI, 1949, pgs. 5, 372).

All this was put in writing with an uncompromising message that we would not allow ourselves, nor our consistory, nor synod's reconciliation committee to defend anyone who so blatantly and sarcastically mocked Jesus' death for us. Nor would we be able to let our elders "agree to disagree" on such a Truth. We reminded the committee that false teachers/teachings will be in among us and asked if they thought the Christian Reformed Church of North America was exempt from harboring, protecting, or defending those who sought to destroy Truth–whether it was done innocently or not.

Giving Dr. Arnold the benefit of the doubt, we asked, "If we have misrepresented in any way what the synodical committee has said, we would appreciate a reply, either individually and/or collectively." We never received a reply. Instead, in their report to synod, the committee wrote: "None of the appellants signed within the time granted. Instead they sent a letter stating reasons why they could not sign the recommendations and included additional accusations against some of our committee members" (Letter dated March 29, 1993, to Leonard J. Hofman, General Secretary of Synod of the CRC).

A Disturbing "Private" Letter

On March 10, Howard received a letter from Pete Schipma which stated he had written his letter "not on behalf of the Council nor of the Consistory, nor of the Reconciliation Committee, nor even in light of my current service as elder." He refuted our "accusation" that he had "betrayed the faith" and denied the atonement. In the same breath, he assured us, *"In no way am I qualified to make theological pronouncements, and I make none."*

One of the requirements found in I Timothy 3:9 and Titus 1:9 for office of elder and deacon is, "They must keep hold of the deep truths of the faith with a clear conscience." 2 Timothy states: "He must hold firmly to the trustworthy message as it has been taught, so that he can encourage others by sound doctrine and refute those who oppose it."

The appellants wondered how he, as elder, would be able to refute false teachings and hold to the trustworthy message if he really wasn't sure if that message was indeed the right one. In response to the meaning of the substitutionary atonement Schipma wrote: "If I misunderstood something, it is because of the very fact that I am a mere creature and a sinful one in a fallen Creation . . . God is in control, not me . . . *I don't have to be right, because He is right. My faith does not save me, my doctrines do not save me, He saves me!"* Did he mean then, that God would save all those who claimed to know God, regardless of their beliefs concerning Jesus Christ? A promise is made between two persons. If one breaks that promise, the fault cannot be attributed to the other person. God keeps his promise of salvation to all those who believe—believe what??? Didn't it matter?

Although Schipma's letter was addressed only to Howard, Howard felt an obligation to share it with all of us because it was written in answer to our letter to the reconciliation committee. All the appellants had signed the letter to the committee, therefore he felt all the appellants should read and answer Schipma's letter. We did so, and included it in our official correspondence to the chairman of the judicial code committee, much to Schipma's displeasure. He wrote back tearing into the appellants, "How can you aggrandize to yourselves the right to treat my letter to Howard in such a way? Have you no sense of common courtesy? . . . Common decency demands that you respect my personal rights with regard to a letter so explicitly defined as private. Upon receipt of your apology for such a flagrant breach of etiquette and Christian fellowship, I may consider responding to the substance of your letter."

He hadn't clearly stated the letter was private or that Howard should not show it to anyone. I could understand his anger, but we felt he had no right to single Howard out. He had come into the discussions as elder, therefore, we did not feel it was his "prerogative" to turn the matter into a private issue. We wrote a letter apologizing if we had offended him, but also explained why we couldn't accept his first letter as "private."

It may be we shouldn't have sent Schipma's letter to the judicial code committee along with a letter explaining why we couldn't sign the reconciliation committee's recommendations. We felt strongly, however, that it was time for everything to come out in the open. As leaders of our church, they were accountable to the congregation.

In our letter to him, we included a copy of Regent College's Statement of Faith which L'Engle claimed she couldn't sign because she "found it unscriptural." I had called Regent College (Canada), and received their statement of faith shortly before our last committee meeting. Howard had given me a notice of L'Engle's visit there, and I also had her schedule sent from The Cathedral of St. John The Divine. I confirmed with the dean that Regent was the college L'Engle was talking about in her book. Points 3 and 4 read a bit differently and more clearly than how L'Engle quoted them, but the statements were obviously the same ones she had chosen not to sign. They read as follows:

3. The universal sinfulness and guilt of human nature since the fall, bringing everyone under God's wrath and condemnation.

4. The substitutionary sacrifice of the incarnate Son of God as the sole ground of redemption from the guilt, penalty and power of sin.

This statement of faith was never to be mentioned again (see Appendix F). The elder had in his possession an unmistakable piece of evidence, unable to be taken out-of-context, that L'Engle denied the sacrificial atonement as payment for sin. It should have mattered, but it didn't. Had certain elders known all along that we were not taking anything out-of-context? It sure was beginning to look that way.

Attempts Made to Thwart Judicial Hearing

A few weeks after our final meeting with the reconciliation committee, Howard Stob talked with Donald Oosterhouse (chairman of the judicial code committee). He advised Howard that if we desired a judicial hearing we would have to get a letter to him by April 12. During their conversation, Howard asked Oosterhouse to send us a copy of the report the reconciliation committee had submitted to him. We had counted on the committee to send us a copy, but so far, we hadn't heard from them.

A letter was compiled very quickly and sent the next day (April 8). Reasons why we believed a judicial hearing was necessary were given in a precise, brief detailed account of what had taken place since Classis January '91, along with our letter to the reconciliation committee advising them of our reasons for declining to sign their recommendations for agreement.

A few days later, we received the report of the "pastoral committee (from which I have already quoted). I was surprised to read, "The pastors had been excused from involvement in this matter by a prior decision of the consistory." No mention was made at all that the committee had requested the pastors to be there, but they hadn't shown up until the last minute–after all discussion was ended. Following a very broad overview of our meetings, the committee recommended that synod declare:

1. That it is disappointed with the appellants' refusal to sign the Recommendations for Reconciliation proposed by the Pastoral Committee, especially in view of the consistory's agreement with them and actual signing of them.

2. That the attempt at reconciliation envisioned by Synod of 1992 under Article 26-b of the Judicial Code has been completed (Cf. Acts of Synod 1992, Art. 93, pg. 681).

3. That the matter now rests with the local consistory as it is guided by the Church Order and synodical regulations.

4. That the Pastoral Committee has fulfilled its mandate to the best of its ability and is hereby discharged.

The possibility of a judicial hearing wasn't envisioned by this committee at all, nor, was it foreseen by our consistory. Oosterhouse sent us a copy of a letter written to him by our consistory asking, "That Synod declare that these recommendations constitute our decision on this matter *making no further adjudication necessary*" (emphasis mine) (Letter dated 4-23-93).

The letter concluded, "This situation has now existed for more than four years, consuming untold hours of the time of our consistory and generating divisiveness within the congregation we serve. Now that it has been addressed and assessed in detail, by a committee of the highest denominational assembly, it is time for that assembly to declare it finis and let the consistory and congregation of Orland Park CRC return to doing the business of the King."

The appellants worked hard at killing more trees, writing responses to both letters. Three, three-inch, three-ring notebooks were now filled with letters to and from the education committee, the elders, the church visitors, Classis Chicago South, the judicial code committee, the reconciliation committee, etc. . . . We were not going to give up easily. Too much was at stake.

A Judicial Hearing Is Granted

There was nothing we could do but to wait for the judicial code committee's report to synod. In early June, just before Synod, 1993 met, we received their report. Despite all efforts by the reconciliation committee and our elders to eradicate a judicial hearing, the recommendation was:

> That Synod instruct Classis Chicago South to proceed with a judicial hearing to deal with the charges filed by appellants against Orland Park CRC Consistory (Letter dated June 2, 1993 to Leonard J. Hofman from Donald F. Oosterhouse).

Among the grounds listed for their decision was the fact that "all spiritual means have now been exhausted" and "No assembly has addressed the merits of those charges." The judicial code committee had looked past who we were and had dealt with the facts. This was seen in that their instruction was over and against the recommendations of synod's "pastoral committee," (elsewhere referred to as the reconciliation committee).

The Appellants–A "Nuisance Factor"

While the appellants were grateful for such a report, we were not looking forward to a judicial hearing. It wasn't going to be a very popular position to take and the work involved in getting all our documents together seemed an impossibility. To make matters worse, the June 29, 1993 issue of *The Banner* did a great job of misrepresenting our concerns. The reporter for *The Banner* wrote:

> The five-family appeal regarding church-library books (by author Madeleine L'Engle) that allegedly contain doctrinal errors prompted a good bit of discussion. But much of the ado wasn't about First Amendment rights or censorship or doctrinal heresy.
>
> Rather, it centered around what some delegates regarded as a "nuisance factor." Rev. George Vander Weit of Classis Lake Erie objected to the amount of time already spent on this appeal in church, classis, committee, and synod– and the recommendation to bump the matter back to Classis Chicago South for still another hearing. "We have spent a lot of time on these appeals," he said. "Isn't there a time at which we stop and say, 'Let's not invest any more time in this?' "
>
> Rev. John Ouwinga of Classis Chicago South also objected. "I hope we get a feel for the scope of this," he said, explaining how 68 formal meetings and hundreds of hours of work with the appellants had failed to satisfy them and had only succeeded in putting a number of pastors under stress.
>
> In the end, synod approved the Judicial Code Committee's recommendation to instruct Classis Chicago South to have a judicial hearing to deal with the charges of the five families. The grounds for the decision were that classis could no longer use the excuse that all spiritual means for dealing with the problem had not been exhausted. They have now been exhausted.

The appellants were dismayed by the report. Once again, the real issue had been either intentionally or unintentionally hidden, this time under sympathy pains for our consistory. This *was* a doctrinal issue, but obviously, many people didn't want to acknowledge that fact.

And where did Rev. Erffmeyer's friend, Rev. Ouwinga, come up with a total of 68 formal meetings that were held? There may have been that many, but only a small fraction of these were with the appellants. Had the elders signed their agreement with the advisory report years ago, the matter could have been over with and they could have saved themselves "hundreds of hours of work."

The Appellants–Out for Publicity?

It wasn't till after the appellants read this distorted report that Rev. Punt sent us a copy of a letter he had written to George Vander Weit. He had talked with Vander Weit at the meeting of synod and was so upset by his remarks he responded with a letter which he said could be read "by anyone."

Vander Weit hadn't realized that Rev. Punt was from Classis Chicago South when he "mentioned that a certain classis had 'difficulties' in connection with their having conducted a judicial hearing." Rev. Punt asked him what those difficulties were so that such 'difficulties' could be avoided. In his letter to Rev. Vander Weit, Punt wrote:

> ... I understood you to say, "I just want to warn you Punt, that Synod was really ticked (mad, angry or whatever word you used) that the appellants continued to press this matter, *just to get publicity*, even after their concern was met by the books having been removed from their church library" (emphasis mine).

> My response was, "I don't give a hoot how mad Synod was."

> The reason for this response (which I stand by even after having time to think about it) is that such willful or stupid misrepresentation of the facts of the situation is precisely the reason that this matter has dragged on so long and is being forced to a judicial hearing which neither the appellants, the church council nor the classis wants.
> . . .

> It is solely because of the insistence of the elders to de-
> fend L'Engle as a Christian writer that this matter con-
> tinues to fester. . . . Those who have portrayed this on
> the floor of synod as a matter of the appellants not being
> satisfied with the removal of the books in order to gain
> more publicity, have done you, the synod, and the Chris-
> tian Reformed Church a very real disservice (Letter dated
> June 22, 1993).

I couldn't help but chuckle when I read Punt's response. It was
such a relief to know someone in his position was not against us
and had the courage to so candidly defend us. The rest of his letter
skillfully laid out why we had asked for a judicial hearing. He concluded that the judicial code committee would not have used the
word *instruct* in their recommendation to synod "if they were of
the opinion that the appellants should have been satisfied with the
removal of the books in question." Punt spelled out, *"The judicial
code committee is fully aware of the shenanigans that have been
going on. This is reflected in **their** word "instruct." Seldom when
one assembly speaks to another assembly in the church is such a
strong word used. "Therefore," he added, "I say it again, I don't
give a hoot how mad synod was. It is not surprising that, with such
misrepresentation of the actual situation as was heard on the floor
of synod, the delegates were mad at the appellants"* (emphasis
mine).

As I read *The Banner* report over again, a deep sadness filled
my heart. I wanted to grab some of the leading figures within my
denomination by the scruff of their necks, shake them, and shout in
their ear, "Wake Up!" Darkness had descended upon them, blind-
ing them to the Light. Deceit and mockery had taken the place of
their will to stand up for the God in whom they professed to love
and trust.

"The coming of the lawless one will be in accordance with the
work of Satan displayed in all kinds of counterfeit miracles, signs
and wonders, and in every sort of evil that deceives those who are
perishing. They perish because they refused to love the truth and
so be saved. For this reason God sends them a powerful delusion
so that they will believe the lie and so that all will be condemned
who have not believed the truth but have delighted in wickedness"
(2 Thessalonians 2:9-11).

Chapter Sixteen

DECEIVED BY DOCTRINES OF DEMONS

The Spirit clearly says that in later times some will abandon the faith and follow deceiving spirits and things taught by demons.

1 Timothy 4:1

No barrier of religion or ideology will be able to prevent people in every nation of the world from responding to the signal of co-creative life at the dawn of the Universal Age. . . . They are those who know that God and humanity have joined together for the transformation of the world. They will know the word when they hear it in this form, which is beyond the existing belief systems of all peoples bound to Earth. Therefore, it will be unacceptable to all dogmatists and acceptable to all who have faith in things unseen.

The Book of Co-Creation, The Revelation
—"Christ" through Barbara Marx Hubbard

The reason man has come to fear Lucifer is not so much that he represents evil as because he represents experience which causes us to grow and to move beyond the levels where we have been. . . . Lucifer is literally the angel of experience. . . . Christ is the same force as Lucifer.

Reflections On the Christ
—New Age medium David Spangler

191

There was a far more significant thing that took place at the meeting of Synod June 8, 1993 than the mockery of the charges against our consistory. Before delegates met to discuss the business of the day, they were asked to go to Calvin College Chapel where they would be shown an art piece made of "rusty pipes." After some time passed, the delegates were given a paper to help them discuss what each perceived the art piece to be. This paper, written by CRC members, Reinder and Diane Klein, was entitled, "The UNDERSTANDING OPINIONS Metaphor." It wasn't hard to understand what their opinion was because opinions aren't necessarily true or right, and that was the message this little piece of paper carried. I have reprinted it below. Please read it carefully, as it tells the story of what was underneath our consistory's defense.

The UNDERSTANDING OPINIONS Metaphor
Some Initial Observations

1. The Vantage Point
I am inescapably rooted to a unique vantage point from which I view all things
* No vantage point offers a more correct perspective, although some give more information
* While my vantage point may change, I remain unalterably attached to it
* Not being God, I can never occupy all vantage points at once
* Even from my vantage point I do not always see clearly all there is to see

2. The Object
The sum of all vantage points approximates all there is to see of the object
* Being rooted to one vantage point, I cannot "see" everything there is to see of the object
* The object is what it is; it is not affected by my perception of it
* However, I tend to make the object suit my perception of it

3. The Perception
I perceive the object on four different levels; factual (objective), emotional (subjective), interpretive (meaning or value), decisional (what to do with it)
* These four are distinct, although I sometimes confuse my emo-

tional response or my interpretation with the facts
* My perception may differ from that of others on any one or several of these four levels
* Because I am often unaware of my own emotions or fail to recognize emotional responses in others, I often arrive at flawed interpretations

4. The Communication
The collective vision of a community is always greater than that of a single member
* I can broaden *my* "seeing" by listening to what others say they see
* At best I can only *approximate* what others say they see
* Without the insight of others my own vision remains one-sided
* Community results when persons accept as valid and significant the vision held and communicated by others
* To accept the vision of others I must listen to them, and trust them

5. The Potential for Conflict
Different perceptions often lead to conflicts which in turn undermine community
* The terms "right and "wrong" are not appropriate to deliberative exercises
* When I refuse to accept the validity of another's perspective, I absolutize my own (limited) perception
* Absolutized opinions are, in effect, deeply entrenched positions from which only the walls of the trench can be seen. Trenches block dialogue and destroy community

Note: When the metaphor is applied to other situations, the term object used here may be replaced with topic, issue, subject, problem, etc.

All Paths Lead to God?

Debates on women in office, evolution, homosexuality, abortion, were just a few of the symptoms of the plague hitting the denomination. "Wouldn't it be nicer," some say, "to agree to disagree–give a little, take a little, serve the cause of justice for all, and bring in a peaceful, one-world community?"

The "Understanding Metaphor" played right into New Age thought. New Agers despise doctrine, claiming there are no right or wrong beliefs–that all paths lead to God. In their eyes, those who claim Jesus Christ as the only way to salvation are holding back the world from becoming a true global community–united under a universal "spirituality." They have the mistaken notion that lack of self-esteem (not sin) is the reason there is so much heartache and division in the world. Hence, in order to protect one's self-esteem, we should all accept one another's point of view, without making judgments as to what is right or wrong.

This type of thinking has permeated hundreds of churches and many denominations. It has destroyed relationships between family members, church members, friends, etc., and more than likely, will continue to do so. Because along with those intoxicating words– love, peace, and unity–comes a price tag which some are not willing to pay.

It seems unbelievable that the same lie Satan used to deceive Eve in the Garden of Eden thousands of years ago is still deceiving those who have been brought up in "Christian" homes and churches– those who have read the Bible and keep it in their homes. That slimy serpent suckered humans into questioning God's Word then, and continues to do so now. Whispering those few little words, "Did God really say?" he does his dirty work–undermining Scripture, questioning the validity of God's Word, telling us we can decide for ourselves what is right and what is wrong, make our own choices, be God! (Please re-read Genesis 3!)

In the Old Testament, God's prophet Samuel rebukes Saul and warns, "For rebellion is like the sin of divination and arrogance the evil of idolatry" (1 Samuel 15:23–King James Version uses the word witchcraft instead of divination). Today, there are more and more books being written by mediums or "channelers"–those who claim to know God; who go deep within themselves through various techniques of stilling the mind, and listen to their Higher Self or Selves. Whatever comes out of their "imagination" is considered "true" and worthy to be added to God's Word. Consider, for a moment, what some of these "spirit guides," "guardian angels," "Higher Selves," or whatever one calls the demons they contact, say:

> Truth is all of these seemingly distinct, separate, different realities. So Ruburt is a part of the truth he perceives,

and each of you are part of the truths that you *perceive.* "Truth," reflected through Ruburt, becomes in a way new truth, for it is perceived uniquely, (as it would be for each individual who perceived it). It is not less truth or more truth in those terms. It becomes new truth (*Seth Speaks,* "Seth dictates his startling view of the universe through channeler Jane Roberts," Bantam Books, New York, 1972, pg. 454).

We must allow no doctrine or teaching to divert our awareness from the simple basic truths which we all share in common trust as the spiritual heritage of humanity. . . . We must follow Jesus fully, not in worship but in shared realization of the human heritage of divinity. As he became the way, so must we. That is a basic esoteric doctrine. . . . One does not walk the path; one is the path. . . . Jesus demonstrated the truth for us (*Reflections of the Christ,* Spangler, David, Findhorn Publications, Findhorn, Moray, Scotland, 1978, pgs. 30-31).

So, you see when you understand the Bible as God said it–not just as it's been interpreted to you by your parents, not just as some preacher's told it to you, but as it really is . . . then you'll have true freedom, the freedom to be your Real Self–And that's why I'm telling you these things–because, you see, you have to discover the Path for yourself. It's not a matter of accepting or rejecting what I say . . . or what someone else says. It's a matter of understanding what is Truth. . . . The solution to all of this is the Truth that the First Coming of Christ is in the exemplar, the son of man Jesus. . . . Christ is our original Self (*The Lost Teachings of Jesus 2, Mysteries of the Higher Self,* Prophet, Mark L. and Elizabeth Clare, Summit University Press, 1986, pgs. 278-279, 33, 57).

. . . you are one Self, united with your Creator, at-one with every aspect of creation, and limitless in power and in peace. This is the truth, and nothing else is true. Today we will affirm this truth again, and try to reach the place in you in which there is no doubt that only this is true (*A Course in Miracles,* Foundation for Inner Peace, 1975, Vol. 2, pg. 165).

I could list more examples, but they all relay in different ways the same message. Each person perceives "truth" differently, and each person has the right to do so, because the only "Truth" that is certain is that we are all "God." How different is our consistory's defense of L'Engle and "The Understanding Opinions Metaphor" from the anti-Christian message channeled through demons? Study these things well, for this may very well be what your son or daughter or you yourself have been subtly taught.

Teachings heard through the use of occult techniques of meditation (deep breathing, chanting, centering or focusing on a candle, etc. in order to come into an altered state of consciousness) have become just as authoritative as the Word of God. Since God condemns these practices (Deuteronomy 18:9-14, etc.), whatever comes out of the "imagination" in this sense, *cannot* be from Him.

The warning of the Lord spoken to Ezekiel lends credence to this fact:

> Say to them, "This is what the Sovereign Lord says. . . . For there will be no more false visions or flattering divinations among the people of Israel.". . . Son of Man, prophesy against the prophets of Israel who are now prophesying. Say to those who prophesy out of their own imagination: "Hear the word of the Lord! This is what the Sovereign Lord says: 'Woe to the foolish prophets who follow their own spirit and have seen nothing! Your prophets, O Israel, are like jackals among ruins. . . . Their visions are false and their divinations a lie. They say the Lord declares, when the Lord has not sent them' . . ." (Ezekiel 12:23a, 24, 13:2-4, 6).

Did the Apostles Misunderstand Jesus?

Equally disturbing as the Understanding Opinions metaphor was Donald Hettinga's book, *Presenting Madeleine L'Engle.* I had recently purchased a copy and found Hettinga had made fun of the "extreme Evangelical right," those who exposed L'Engle's writings for what they truly were. Rev. John De Vries and I were both named in his book and falsely targeted as being part of the fanatical few who despise fantasy and imagination. Hettinga denied the charges made by so many Christians about L'Engle's use of occult practices and her belief in universalism, in a roundabout sort of way.

It didn't come as much of a surprise that he failed to provide passages of her mockery of the substitutionary atonement in his book. Nor did he bother to mention any of the many passages where L'Engle claims all will be reconciled to God again, including Satan. Instead, he defended and preserved the occult teachings so richly held by L'Engle and her followers. The sad part of it was, I would find out very soon that he, along with many other teachers, knew all along what L'Engle taught, and they promoted her teachings regardless of the fact.

One of the most disturbing elements of Hettinga's defense was his statement, *"To L'Engle's eyes the story of much of theology has been one of reductive miscomprehension; ever since God appeared to humanity, he has been misunderstood and limited by those to whom he has appeared . . ."* (pg. 18, emphasis mine). These words discredited the "Truth" about God in the Old Testament (a God L'Engle describes as a "patriarchal," "chauvinist pig," "tribal," "cartoon god" with a "bad temper"), and jeopardized the salvation message as recorded by the apostles in the New Testament. In other words, it destroyed the whole of God's Word. It destroyed Christianity.

Though I hated what they were doing, my anger wasn't fixed on Hettinga or L'Engle, but was thoroughly directed at the one who had deceived them and continues to deceive by disguising himself as an "angel of light" (II Corinthians 11:13).

On September 13, 27, and October 11, just prior to the judicial hearing which was to take place on October 21, *Christian Renewal* printed my reactions to Hettinga's book (Appendices G, H, I).

Witchcraft in Christian Schools and Churches?

While in the midst of writing my three-part series, "Battle to Destroy Truth," for *Christian Renewal,* I received the October, 1993 issue of *The Christian Educator's Journal* (CEJ, Vol. 33, No. 1). On the front cover, was a picture of a little girl sleeping soundly in bed with her arm around a book entitled, *The Witch Herself.* Underneath the picture the caption read, "Fantasy and Imagination in Literature."

I had a feeling I would find something about L'Engle in this issue. I was wrong. There wasn't just something about L'Engle; it was pretty obvious the whole issue was dedicated to defending her writings as "Christian." The magazine was yet another sign to the appellants that God had led us to this point and confirmed the need for a judicial hearing.

Because it is terribly important for you to see the incredible influence her writings have had on Christian school teachers, and to understand the enormity of the conflict going on at the time the charges against our consistory were about to be heard, I am providing a few examples from CEJ.

Lorna Van Gilst, Professor of English at Dordt College (Sioux Center, Iowa), and managing editor of the *Christian Educator's Journal*,[1] wrote an editorial which provides a glimpse of the damage already done:

> Rarely have I met Christian school teachers who wanted to purge all magicians, hobbits, and munchkins from their classrooms. I suppose such teachers exist, but I am not aware of them.
>
> I am keenly aware, however, of fervent conflicts over these matters in Christian schools. Usually they arise in the name of Christianity. And always they seem to pit educators against parents, with the pastors of the community splitting sides on the matter, *depending on their willingness to acknowledge metaphor as essential in understanding the Word. (The Word, of course, is the prime metaphor.)* (pg. 5, emphasis mine).

I had a pretty good idea where this thinking was taking her readers and a few paragraphs later, I found I was right. With an added touch of sensitivity, Van Gilst added:

> But sometimes I am troubled about the manner in which we educators defend the value of metaphorical language. Sometimes we fail to respect those who differ with our views, and we come across pompously better informed than "those poor mistaken literalists who don't know how to read correctly."

I don't believe it was a coincidence that I had just purchased a book entitled *Metaphorical Theology, Models of God in Religious Language*, by Sallie McFague, a Carpenter Professor of Theology at Vanderbilt Divinity School in Nashville, Tennessee. She couldn't have made it any clearer as to what is meant by "The Word is the prime metaphor":

> The Bible is metaphor of the word or ways of God, but as metaphor it is a relative, open-ended, secular tensive judgment. It is . . . the premier metaphor, the classic model, of God's ways for Christians, *but as a metaphor it cannot be absolute, "divinely inspired," or final* (Fortress Press, Philadelphia, 1982, pg. 54, emphasis mine).

Like Don Hettinga, Van Gilst, and many other "evangelical Christians" today, McFague has a problem with "literalism." The problem stems from the fact, she believes, "that many people have lost the practice of religious contemplation and prayer, which alone is sufficient to keep literalism at bay . . ." (*ibid.,* pg. 5).

Experience is the vogue in style, according to McFague. It is the mystics of all religious traditions, "who feel conviction at the level of experience, at the level of worship, but great uncertainty at the level of words adequate to express the reality of God" (*ibid.,* pg.1).

Now, I don't believe for a moment that the majority of Christians take every word in the Bible literally. Jesus taught with parables at times, for instance. However, to say we cannot take the Bible literally, as L'Engle does, is to denounce all the history and facts included in it. God's sovereignty, and all that points to Jesus' first and second coming, is tossed in the air and up for grabs. The *purpose* for His coming could be fashioned to meet anyone's design, and that's exactly what is happening.

I turned the page in *The Christian Educator's Journal* and found an article entitled, "Fear Not: Selecting Fantasy Literature for the Christian Classroom," written by Karen L. Kalteissen, a 6-8th grade language arts teacher at the Mustard Seed School in Hoboken, New Jersey. Kalteissen, who uses L'Engle's works in her curriculum stated, "Failed imagination affects community health, moral decisions, and the life of faith."

I always thought sin is what ailed society, but this elementary teacher offered an alternative explanation: "Think too, how often Jesus encountered failures of the imagination; at Bethany, where no one could imagine anything better than healing a sick man; at his own empty Easter tomb where one of his closest friends couldn't imagine anything but a stolen corpse; and, of course, Thomas, the universal representative of the thoroughly failed imagination."

Now *here* was THEOLOGY! Please excuse my touch of sarcasm, but I have such a hard time believing people can actually fall for such nonsense. Kalteissen makes her point in her concluding paragraph:

> In the epilogue to George Bernard Shaw's Saint Joan, De Stogumber reflects that his faith came to life not as a result of official Church teaching but rather from witnessing Joan of Arc being burned at the stake. Cauchon asks, "Must then a Christ perish in torment in every age to save those who have no imagination?"

Is that why *a* Christ died—to save our failed imaginations??? Would more Christs have to die to save them? Could it be if all of us just imagined or visualized a perfect, healthy, sustainable world, the world would eventually be transformed? Interesting question that would fit in nicely with New Age ideology. Of course, for New Age author, Barbara Marx Hubbard, the answer is yes (re-read chapter introductory quote). Christians however, should politely say, "No way."

Unfortunately, Cathy Smith, learning resource teacher at John Knox Christian School in Wyoming, Ontario, might agree with Hubbard. In her article defending L'Engle, "A Wrinkle in Time: A Point of Contention," she wrote:

> Ideas about time travel [astral projection–CVK] and telepathy may be deserving of more serious consideration by Christians. We know that our physical bodies have changed over the past few hundred years. . . . If through God's grace, our bodies are capable of improvement, is it so improbable that our brains may develop in ways that we cannot yet fathom? Searching the Bible with respect to these questions, L'Engle raises a number of thought-provoking facts.

In *Walking on Water* she states, "God is always calling on us to do the impossible. It helps me to remember that anything Jesus did during his life here on earth is something we should be able to do, too" (pg. 19). We confess that Jesus was fully human. He walked on water, and so did Peter. In his glorified body, after his resurrection, Jesus came and went without regard for walls. Philip disappeared from the sight of the Ethiopian. These truths must cause us to ponder "What does it mean to be wholly human?"

Should we be upset with L'Engle for exploring these ideas? Today's heart transplant would have been incomprehensible to any sincere Christian five hundred years ago. If it could have been imagined, would it not have been condemned as presumptuously entering upon God's domain? If the Lord should tarry another fifty or one hundred years or longer before his return, what advances might future Christians be thankful for which we at this point can only conceive of as evil? . . .

I don't think we ought to ban all imagining or exploring ideas about telepathy or time travel as sinful. Let us not delude ourselves into thinking that we in the twentieth century now possess all available insight into what it means to be a Christian any more than did the monk in the second century who forbade shaving (pg. 21).

It wasn't until I read the following paragraph that I was certain that many teachers knew exactly what L'Engle was preaching through her "fantasy" novels and non-fiction. Smith contended:

. . . an author has the creative license to imagine a beast to be like an aunt, a witch to be good, a lion to be gentle, or an eraser to think. *While it is true that Scripture prohibits believers from engaging in occult practices,* how this admonition relates to the realm of the imagination appears to me to be a different matter entirely (emphasis mine).

I wondered if Smith had read Deuteronomy 18, Ezekiel 12 and 13, or the many other passages in Scripture which so fervently warn

against such practices. I hoped she would read Part III of my series, "Battle to Destroy Truth," which explained just what is meant
by the imagination in occult language, but I doubted she would.

It was amazing to me that those who had come to my house and
read from a book of witchcraft and compared it to L'Engle's writings saw the likeness immediately. If this learning resource teacher
would read one or two books on witchcraft or magic, she would
see what the imagination had to do with occult practices–that is, if
she didn't know already. Either way, this "Christian" school teacher
had just endorsed, defended, promoted, and secured the teaching
of occult practices and beliefs in the Christian school system.

Don Hettinga's book, *Presenting Madeleine L'Engle*, also came
in handy in "Wrinkle on Trial," written by Henry J. Baron, another
professor of English at Calvin College and chairperson of the CEJ
board. Baron told the story of a battle that took place at Heritage
Christian Middle School. He described a "blood" scene in which a
parent demanded to have L'Engle's book pulled from the shelves
(much like our issue was portrayed). "Principal Badge had beat a
hasty retreat, leaving his feisty librarian frowning fiercely while
clutching a copy of Donald Hettinga's *Presenting Madeleine
L'Engle*," Baron descriptively wrote. He candidly thanked Grace
De Vries, an elementary language arts teacher at Heritage, for coming to the principal's rescue. I was glad she wouldn't be coming to
my children's rescue. Listen to what she had to say:

> We talk about the evil forces in our own life and in the
> world beyond our walls. And we talk about the power of
> God and the love of Jesus through which, L'Engle teaches
> us, we are indeed more than conquerors. The children
> understand that, maybe more feelingly than they ever did
> in Sunday School.
>
> Sometime later they'll learn about Einstein and
> Michelangelo and Madame Curie, but right now those
> names don't mean much to them. Sometime later they'll
> learn about physics and wrinkles in time or "tesseracts,"
> and then they may want to know about all the research
> and study that went into the writing of this book [*A
> Wrinkle In Time*–CVK]. Sometime later they'll learn
> about New Age thinking and the occult and learn to cri-
> tique it from a Christian point of view. Then, they may

want to evaluate whether L'Engle's message and the messages of other authors promote or denigrate faith and spirituality. Since this is a Christian school that is confessionally Reformed, they better get to that when they're ready for it. But in my sixth grade I'm profoundly grateful when one of your children comes up to me, as one did recently after we finished *A Wrinkle in Time*, and says, "Mrs. De Vries, God is really great and good, isn't he?" (pg.13).

Will De Vries' students be able to discern New Age or occult teachings when they're older? I don't think so. Why? Because our children are not being taught discernment! They're being taught to *accept* New Age concepts. Obviously, Mrs. De Vries wasn't able to discern L'Engle's teachings. *Unless parents teach their children well and are aware of what is being taught in school, their children will be left to the mercy of teachers who let them decide for themselves what is right and wrong.*

The picture of the little girl clutching the book, *A Witch Herself*, was, ironically, a picture of what that child might just very well become.

Which book is more dangerous–*Big Red*, by Jim Kjelgaard, or *A Wrinkle in Time*, by Madeleine L'Engle? Robert W. Bruinsma, associate professor of education at The King's College in Edmonton, Alberta and CEJ regional editor for Western Canada votes for Big Red–a story about a prize Irish setter. His contribution to this October issue of CEJ was "Of Dogs and Witches; Dangerous Books in the Christian Classroom" (pg.16). Bruinsma wanted to help people see "that *Big Red* is a far more 'dangerous' book than is *A Wrinkle in Time*."

While Bruinsma may be right in his assessment that *Big Red* promotes a "humanistic, Darwinian self-sufficiency," he is dead wrong that *A Wrinkle in Time* "provides a far more realistic (i.e. truthful i.e. biblical) account of reality than does an ostensively "realistic' novel like *Big Red*." At least, *Big Red* is not considered to be a Christian book while feeding our children a theology that contradicts Scripture, and not only contradicts it, but despises and rejects it. Which book and author is more dangerous? Think again, professor of education! Does that mean you absolutely cannot teach *A Wrinkle in Time*? No. It means, if you do, teach it showing its contradictions to Scripture and use it as a tool for discernment!

While ridiculing those parents and researchers who are concerned about the influence of L'Engle's writings, little do these educators realize that they themselves demonstrate the evidence for such concern. I was about finished reading this upsetting issue of the *Christian Educator's Journal* when I discovered something that shook me down to the bone. There was a book review of another work written by Donald Hettinga, entitled *SITTING AT THE FEET OF THE PAST, Retelling the North American Folktales for Children* (pg. 33). I recognized the name of Hettinga's co-author, Gary D. Schmidt, as the name of the person who had reviewed L'Engle's works in *The Encyclopedia of Children's Literature Review*. As written up in the first chapter of *Trojan Horse*, he described the development of the children's "astonishing intuitive powers . . . their *psychic powers*" in *A Wrinkle in Time* (Gale Research Co., Detroit, MI, 1988, Volume 14, pg. 141, emphasis mine).

The review revealed Schmidt was also an English professor at Calvin College. More than likely, both he and Hettinga had known all along what L'Engle was advocating, and taught it in the classroom as Christian literature.

****

The evidence of how widely witchcraft is being accepted into many churches today can be seen in the articles in the back of this book. It is beyond comprehension for some. But it has come in, slowly, subtly, and ever so meekly disguised under dozens of masks, the worst of which is the mask of being "Christian."

Something to remember: One does not have to be a full-fledged witch, or New Age, to promote false teachings. All it takes is for a Christian to accept bits and pieces from false teachings and practices condemned by God to help blend them into "Christianity." Eventually, more and more of those bits and pieces combine to thoroughly distort God's message making one vulnerable to slowly accepting another gospel. How careful we must be to test everything against Scripture and listen to what it says.

Footnote

1. The Board of Trustees of *The Christian Educator's Journal* includes those from Calvin College, Trinity Christian College, Christian Educators Association, Christian Schools International, Ontario Christian Teachers Association, Dordt College, The King's College, Institute for Christian Studies, Redeemer College, Covenant College, British Columbia Teachers Association, Denver Christian School Association, Pacific NW Christian Teachers Association, SW Christian Teachers Association and SW Minnesota Christian Teachers Association.

   The Christian Educators Journal Association "publishes the Journal as a channel of communication for all educators committed to the idea of evangelical Christian day schools at the elementary, secondary, and college levels."

   While it is stated that "the views expressed are those of the writers and not necessarily those of the association," one has to ask, "Who finally takes responsibility for leading so many readers astray?"

Chapter Seventeen

A FINAL WARNING

**I am astonished that you are so quickly deserting the
one who called you by the grace of Christ and are turning to a different gospel–which is really no gospel at
all. Evidently some people are throwing you into confusion and are trying to pervert the gospel of Christ.
But even if we or an angel from heaven should preach
a gospel other than the one we preached to you, let
him be eternally condemned! As we have already said,
so now I say again: If anybody is preaching to you a
gospel other than what you accepted, let him be eternally condemned.**

Galatians 1:6-9

After the June, 1993 Synod instructed Classis Chicago South to
hold a hearing, our consistory prepared another "confidential" document requesting the CCS Interim Committee to have our "contempt-
ible" charges dismissed on the grounds that they were "not substantial" and were "not of sufficient merit to warrant a hearing."
Elder Pete Schipma also wrote, "To regard these charges as sub-
stantive would be to give them a cloak of lucidity and credibility of
which they are utterly unworthy" (Letter dated June 30, 1993 to
Rev. John M. Ouwinga, Rev. Henry B. Vanden Heuvel, Rev. Calvin
Hoogendoorn).

The total disregard for synod's instructions and attempt to keep
this document from the appellants displayed an attitude of arrogance which was rather hard to swallow. The pastors to whom this

207

letter had been sent would be part of "the jury." Therefore, to have these "jurors" read their confidential letter without a response from us "would be very similar to what is called 'jury tampering' in a secular trial." Whether only these pastors or all of the delegates (as the Consistory requested) were exposed to this confidential pleading, the result would be a "tainted jury" (Letter dated August 28, 1993 to Rev. Richard M. Hartwell, Stated Clerk of CCS, from Appellants).

Thankfully, Rev. Henry Vanden Heuvel (newly appointed pastor of 1st Oak Lawn CRC and member of the Classis Chicago South Interim Committee), thought it was only proper to inform us of the elders' confidential letter and sent a copy to Rev. Punt since he was our representative. Upon receiving it, I, with the help of Rev. Punt and the other appellants, wrote a letter to the delegates of Classis Chicago South to be handed out by Hartwell, the Stated Clerk, *only* if the elders' document was given to them prior to the hearing. In our cover letter sent to Hartwell, we wrote, ". . . should there be any extended or serious discussion on the floor of classis to deny us a Judicial Hearing . . . we ask you to inform the delegates that any such denial would be appealed" (*ibid.,* cover letter).

Other than the ridiculous new implication that the appellants were stealing L'Engle's books out of church libraries, our consistory's defense was very similar to their previous "confidential" response (which was finally sent to us by the chairman of the judicial code committee). Therefore I will not say much more about it.

The Judicial Hearing, October 21, 1993 Calvin CRC, Oak Lawn, IL, 9:00 A.M.

The preparation for the hearing was hardly finished by the morning of the trial. Due to meetings regarding the amount of time we would be allotted in which to present our case (at first, we were to be allowed only thirty minutes to present four years of evidence) and other procedures for the hearing, precious time needed to have all our questions and evidence in order was lost.

All the "complainants," as we were now called, were exhausted. Rev. Punt, who was in the midst of retirement and moving to Michigan was also exhausted. But there was yet another problem we had to worry about before the hearing. The elders had sent an overture to classis questioning the "role of the Rev. Mr. Neal Punt" as our representative. How I wish I could relate all that happened to try and discredit this man before the hearing, but I cannot. It is sufficient to say, and Rev. Punt would agree, he had taken on more than he had bargained for. Nevertheless, the strength to continue was given him–and all of us.

The meeting of classis opened with devotions and singing. The delegates, complainants, respondents (our pastors and elders) and visitors sang out, "Lead me, guide me, along the way; for if you lead me I will not stray. . . ." It seemed so ironic, yet appropriate to begin with such a song.

It was time. But, just before the proceedings got under way, an appeal from our consistory was presented to classis. It was an appeal against one of the rules for the judicial hearing which stated, "The delegates from the Orland Park CRC may not be present for the discussion, nor will they be allowed to vote."

Our consistory wanted to be included in the deliberations with "the jury" after all testimony was concluded and be able to vote on the verdict! They insisted this was their right. We sat stunned in our seats. This was no different than having "the accused" sit in with the jury while deciding one's fate and even being able to vote in order to sway the verdict! Would this be allowed? We couldn't imagine that it would even be considered, but it was. At the end of the trial the delegates would re-evaluate the rule the consistory appealed.

The charges against our consistory were now read by Rev. Rick Williams, the presiding "judge." To the charge of Violating the Form of Subscription and Church Order the consistory pleaded "not guilty." To the charge (which stemmed from the first) of displaying conduct unbecoming office-bearers, their plea was, of course, "not guilty."

Rev. Punt and the elders' representative, Dave Vander Ploeg, a CRC member, lawyer, and executive director for The Barnabas Foundation, were asked to give their opening statements.

Rev. Punt opened with a request for the delegates to understand that this situation started with a real-life experience. He explained the problem "arose from Christian parents who were taking a very real interest in what their children were being taught in our Christian schools. The interest was not a concern about books or a book . . . but how these books were being taught in our Christian schools."

Contrary to what *The Banner* had portrayed, Punt pointed out that "these parents didn't want to ban any books. They did the very proper thing that every Christian parent should do in that situation–they went directly to the teacher at school." The teacher and later the pastors and elders hadn't shown "empathy" towards their concerns, but quickly and defensively judged L'Engle's teachings as Christian. They did this not by pointing out paragraphs or sitting down with them to calmly and rationally discuss page by page why they believed this, but by looking to the "experts": *The Banner*, Wheaton College, Calvin College professors, etc. This didn't resolve their concern, Punt noted; it deepened it. If indeed these books denied essential Christian truths, it was "extremely important to understand her theology" that L'Engle herself claims "you can find underneath her works–if you want to." "If you want to," Punt repeated. Trouble was, nobody wanted to.

In a short twenty minutes, he outlined a brief history of what had taken place over the past four years. It wasn't an easy task, but he did well. He stressed to the delegates that they were not there to determine whether or not L'Engle does, in fact, deny the cardinal truths of Christianity. Classis had already determined that and the decision should be considered "settled and binding." We had some suspicion that the validity of the advisory report would be questioned. One of the elders' witnesses was Donald Hettinga. The only reason he would be called, we determined, was to throw doubt on what had already been decided by classis.

Knowing the many rumors that had been spread and misleading *Banner* articles that had been printed, Punt asked the delegates to disregard any preconceived notions and put them out of their minds. Quoting from Proverbs 18:13, he ended, "He who judges a matter before he hears it, to him that is a folly and a shame."

Vander Ploeg now stood to begin his opening defense for the consistory: "Today, we are going to hear a lot of things, but when it all boils down, *this is a matter of a difference of interpretation*."

We had been right; the interpretation of L'Engle's writings was going to be brought back into question and everyone there would be led on a wild goose chase. Everything was a matter of interpretation: L'Engle's writings, Scripture, the sustaining of the appeal, etc. There was one thing, however, Vander Ploeg made certain everyone understood. If the delegates found our consistory "guilty" of such "serious" charges, he warned, "That means you'll have to kick Rev. Erffmeyer and Rev. De Boer out of the ministry and that you could remove the entire body of elders from the Orland Park Christian Reformed Church." We hadn't asked for that to be done. But we had asked for them to be admonished in some way.

"You've known these people," he reasoned. "You've sat with them. . . . You've served with them on the boards of Southwest Christian Schools, Roseland Christian School, Elim, Rest Haven . . . and other Christian organizations. . . . You *know* where they stand."

We had thought we knew where they stood, too.

To depose a fellow friend and co-worker would be a frightening decision to make for any of the delegates. Finding our consistory "guilty" of violating their oath of office and the Church Order would take an awful lot of courage and love, or stupidity depending on which way you looked at it. It was a great strategy, but it wasn't the worst one.

Gaining sympathy for the consistory, Vander Ploeg described the numerous meetings the elders had during the last 4-5 years. He told the delegates of the church visitors' attempts and efforts of the pastoral committee appointed by synod–"The many, many hours devoted to various reconciliation attempts and the desire of the elders to bring about a restoration of a fractured relationship, all of which ultimately failed. . . . Each of these," he emphasized, "repeatedly gave advice which the elders embraced. The complainants critiqued the advice and in some cases, attacked the participants."

This wasn't going well. Now we looked like an angry bunch who had physically attacked the elders. But it was nothing less than we had expected, so far.

[NOTE: While I would like to continue a detailed report of all that was said and done during the many hours of the hearing, after listening to all the tapes for the first time while writing this book, I don't believe there is any way possible for me to do so without repeating much of what I have already written. I will instead provide some of the highlights of the hearing and the verdict that was rendered.]

Opening statements were now completed. Rev. Punt called Karen as the first witness to testify for the "complainants." For the first time, our side of the story, at least partially, would be heard. Throughout the trial, however, cross-examination by the elders' representative proved that politics and "winning" were more important than the truth of what had transpired. To the shame of many, it was of more importance than God's Truth. The issue at hand was purposefully obscured and the Church Order became a set of rules one could disregard at will.

Vander Ploeg's defense for the elders hung on the fact that the advisory report had not called L'Engle a heretic, in those exact words. We had asked for classis to declare L'Engle's "writings to be heresy." If denying the four cardinal truths of the gospel did not constitute her writings to be heretical, what would? It was the word game again. As elder De Jong said, "It all depends on how you define heretic."

It hadn't occurred to Rev. Van Essen, the one who had written the report, that some pastors and elders would debate whether or not someone who denies these fundamental doctrines was heretical. He took for granted all would certainly know this. In his first draft of the advisory report, he testified he had even written that "L'Engle was not a Christian." Van Essen had changed the wording, I was told, so the report would have a better chance of being adopted. He was concerned that if such a strong statement was used, the delegates would be hestitant to vote in favor of the report.

As the trial continued, it was irritating to see Vander Ploeg use all the tactics of a secular lawyer. He had Karen read a passage in the advisory report that made it sound as if L'Engle held to all the cardinal doctrines classis had said she denied. "So, it's all a matter of interpretation, isn't it?" he bullied. Vander Ploeg didn't give Karen the opportunity to read the next paragraph which clarified the first. It stated: "What L'Engle does is to attach these essential Christian truths to nearly everything, every person and every religion. She thereby, either wittingly or unwittingly, denies the uniqueness of the revelation given once for all in the Holy Scriptures" (pg. 3). Vander Ploeg used confusion to acquire the desired results.

He now began to question the process by which the report was adopted. Thankfully, Rev. Williams would not allow that line of questioning because the report had already been adopted. If there had been any questions, he pointed out, "it should have been appealed to synod."

The pastors and elders simply had no defense; so they found excuses. One example for the charge of conduct unbecoming office-bearers was the P.S. note Rev. Erffmeyer had written about me to the elders before our very first meeting with them. Rev. Punt asked Rev. Erffmeyer if he had spoken to me first before reporting it as fact to the elders. "No, I did not," he replied. Erffmeyer believed he didn't have to ask me about it because he had heard it from "a reliable source."

"Even if you had seen Claris doing such a thing with your own eyes, wouldn't concern for her as one of the parishioners of your church require that you speak to her about this offense before relating this information to the elders?" Punt inquired.

"I believe I have an obligation as the pastor to work with the consistory under whose authority I am," Erffmeyer answered, dodging the question.

"Did you ask the elders to contact Claris about this kind of conduct?"

"I did not tell them what to do, no."

"To the best of your knowledge, did you or the elders ever contact Claris about this alleged misconduct?"

"Not to the best of my knowledge."

Rev. Erffmeyer's answers revealed what little concern he and the elders had for my well-being. The elders' first and foremost concern was to keep the pastor safe *from* me, and at all costs, pledge their loyalty and trust in him.

Punt tried to show how the P.S. note had created a bias against me. This was evidenced by the unwillingness of the elders, from the very beginning of this issue, to work with us, the attitude displayed by elder Ken Mels toward Karen and me when we first visited him, and his reluctance to read Rev. De Vries' letter to the elders. Almost all crucial testimony concerning these things, however, could not be addressed because Mels didn't bother to show up at the hearing.

As I began to recall my conversation with Mels, Vander Ploeg cut in, "I'm sorry, are you testifying us to what Mels said? I'm afraid we cannot let you testify to what the substance of the conversation was when the person's not here."

Rev. Williams interjected, "My advice here is that he is a respondent as you know. . . . The respondents include the two pastors and all of the office-bearers from when this thing started to the present . . . the fact that he is not here–for whatever good reason, I would imagine, does not rule out the fact that he is a respondent and should be here."

"In our discussions, there was never any indication that it was our responsibility to produce each and every person who served as an elder in Orland Park Church since 1990," Vander Ploeg insisted.

The judge didn't budge. "I cannot accept that, attorney Vander Ploeg, because you're here as a respondent and you have to bring as many people as you can to make your case."

Upset by the events taking place, Rev. Punt called Mels at his office during a short coffee break. (He works with Vander Ploeg at the Barnabas Foundation.) Mels excused himself by saying he hadn't gotten a call to attend. His name was on our witness list given both to the elders and the classis. Rev. Punt had talked with him the day before. He knew he was supposed to be at the hearing.

The trial was a game of politics and word play. The fact that the elders had endorsed L'Engle as a Christian author both before and after classis' declaration was under review. During cross-examination, Vander Ploeg asked me, "Are you in possession of or have you ever seen any letter or any written communication that calls L'Engle a Christian author other than the April, 1990 letter?"

I directed him to the elders' response to our appeal, and their confidential response to our position paper in which they affirmed they stood by their original decision. I didn't understand why it was so vital to have me find all these passages until he asked, "Where did the elders *ever* term Madeleine L'Engle 'a *wonderful* Christian author?' "

The fact that our elders had classified someone who denies the unique divinity of Jesus Christ and the substitutionary atonement as a Christian didn't matter. The point that mattered above all else was that I had used the phrase "*wonderful* Christian author" and couldn't point to those exact words in that exact sequence in their writing. I guess I shouldn't have included the word "wonderful" in quotes, though I had heard the phrase. But why make such an issue out of something so insignificant? Wasn't the whole dividing issue over the fact that the elders had made a judgment that L'Engle was a Christian author and her works were a blessing, and we had made a judgment that her writings were not Christian and deadly? Did the word "wonderful" mean anything? Yes, it did . . . for Vander Ploeg, whose sole purpose for badgering me with this line of questioning seemed nothing more than to make me out a liar.

Vander Ploeg proceeded to ask if I thought the elders didn't believe the four Biblical truths discussed. I explained while they affirmed them now, that didn't necessarily mean they would believe them in the future. He asked where the elders said that. Surprisingly, I was given the opportunity to read their statement given in their confidential response. Quickly, he changed the subject to how often I worshipped at Orland Park Church and then ended my torture.

Rev. Punt now called elder Pete Schipma to the stand. He asked him to read from the confidential letter they had sent in June to the classical committee. Their letter stated, "We contend that it was not required for the Elders to appeal Classis' decision to Synod . . . there was no directive to the OPCRC in the decision of Classis."

Punt read from Article 29 of the Church Order: "When decisions have been reached after careful and prayerful consideration, they should be considered settled and binding." There was only one exception to that rule, Punt explained, "unless it is proved that they conflict with the Word of God or the Church Order." Now Punt slowly and pointedly asked Schipma, "Does that sentence say anything about a directive?"

"I don't think I can speak to what the Church Order doesn't say," Schipma replied flippantly.

Punt repeated his question two or three more times trying to get a direct answer from Schipma, but he wouldn't admit there didn't have to be a directive given in order to appeal a decision.

Concerning the question of whether or not our first appeal was voted on and not sustained, Punt asked, "Can't you see that if classis had sustained everything in that appeal the motion would be self-contradictory?" He reminded Schipma of the testimony Karen had given earlier that we had accepted the advisory report in place of the appeal. Again he asked, "Can't you see that if this motion was passed, classis was saying everything in both the advisory report and the appeal was sustained?

"I cannot see that. As I said before, it is a very interesting philological problem."

"Oh, you can't see that?"

"No, I do not."

"I hope the delegates can," Punt sighed.

The fact that the elders now stood by their original position and judged L'Engle to be a Christian author was made clear by

Schipma's continuing testimony. The fact they did so even after announcing to the congregation that they no longer wished to judge the Christianity of L'Engle and that that decision superseded all prior decisions was also made crystal clear.

"Have you appealed that decision to classis?" Punt asked speaking of the declaration of classis concerning her denials of the Christian faith.

"No."

"The decision was passed, wasn't it?"

"Yes."

Schipma was now instructed to read once more from the elders' letter. He began, "The Elders have not declared Mahatma Gandhi a non-Christian author, nor so declared regarding Josef Stalin, nor. . . ."

"If," Punt interrupted, "the Elders of Orland Park would officially say Gandhi and Stalin *were* Christian authors, do you think there might be some objections?"

"I should presume so."

"I would, too," Punt agreed.

The elders had contended our charge of violating the Form of Subscription by their refusal to make judgments and refute false teachings could "be regarded as substantial only if the consensus of the broad evangelical Christian community as a whole is that the writings of Madeleine L'Engle are those of a non-Christian author" (Confidential letter dated June 30, 1993, pg. 4).

Once again, the elders' unwillingness to accept the declaration of classis had come through loud and clear, and their justification for this statement revealed why:

> *If there exists reasonable doubt that the Appellants are the sole possessors of truth regarding the teachings in these books*, then this charge too evaporates. . . . We take issue with the fact that the Appellants aggrandize unto themselves the right to claim that theirs is the only correct interpretation of L'Engle's writings. *It smacks strongly of "the sin of presumption; the belief that there is but one method or formula by which we enter the kingdom, and that we alone possess the knowledge of that one way* (*ibid.,* pg.4; emphasis mine).

The elders couldn't acknowledge the fact that false teachers will be in the broader Christian community because their reasoning, when you come right down to it, was that no one has *the* "truth." I hope, my readers, by now you can see what is happening throughout this whole ordeal.

Vander Ploeg didn't take the time to cross-examine Schipma. Maybe that was because his disrespect for Rev. Punt had come through loud and clear in his pompous answers and he surely hadn't helped the elders' cause. (Punt had to ask Rev. Williams more than once to request Schipma to respond in a decent manner to various other questions as well.)

Rev. Punt now called Howard Stob to the stand.

"Did the elders ever seriously consider the request to study L'Engle's books as . . . their letter of March 21 [1990] said that they would?" Punt questioned.

"No!" Howard replied firmly. "The education committee had done that. I remember breathing a sigh of relief because I wouldn't have to get involved. We considered the matter studied and over. Never, never again was it studied," Howard insisted. "It was quite discouraged to do that!"

"Did Claris call you later?"

"Yes, she did."

"What happened when you met with her?"

"In the first place," Howard began to explain, "I was not too eager to go because I felt like a traitor to the elders to do that. If anyone would, after a unanimous decision, talk to Claris about it they indicated *strongly* that you would be caught in her web because she has a personality that is very persistent. And so, some of the weaker members would be caught in her web."

"Did she suggest you read a book by Madeleine L'Engle?"

"Yes. . . . *A Stone for a Pillow.*"

"What was your conclusion concerning that book after reading it?"

"It was deadly to the Christian faith!"

Howard continued to explain the only reason he felt it was important for him to compare L'Engle's works with the Bible instead of accepting the fact that so many leaders in the Christian community speak so highly of her, was because he had read something in it that upset him greatly–that L'Engle could not cope with the atonement if it meant Jesus had to die for our sins. He resigned his position as elder even after the books were removed because the judgment of the elders stood between them. It was "continual fooling the people about a false teacher" and "not defending doctrine that was the basis for our charge against the Form of Subscription," Howard firmly asserted.

I was moved to held-back tears when Howard humbly added, "For all eternity I'll rejoice that I took the position I did." His unwavering stand meant more to me than I think he realized.

Instead of turning to Scripture, Vander Ploeg turned to numbers. "Do you acknowledge that a fairly large part of the Christian community does regard L'Engle as a Christian author?"

"This is what brought our attention to the enormity of the issue. I'm *aware* of it. I'm *aware* of it," Howard replied sadly.

"And, it's your view that there is only one way to read the writings of Madeleine L'Engle?"

"That's why it was appealed to classis," Howard explained. ". . . Judgments have to be made of what fits the body of Christ . . . on the basis of Scripture." Vander Ploeg questioned that it was the responsibility of the elders to make those judgments. "They should," Howard maintained.

The last witness Rev. Punt called for "the defense" was deacon Frank Voss. He testified that immediately following Howard's resignation from office, there was a great deal of discussion between the elders and deacons due to the turmoil the issue had created in the church. The elders asked the four deacons who had read L'Engle's works and were also convinced of their danger, if they would be satisfied if the books in question were removed from the library. Frank said for him, that would be enough (even though I told him that wouldn't help the situation). The deacons had to promise the elders never to bring up the subject again once the books were removed. A bulletin announcement was then agreed upon by the elders and deacons. [It stated, "In the spirit of unity the Council of the OPCRC acts to remove the books of Madeleine L'Engle from the Church library and does not wish to judge the Christianity of Madeleine L'Engle. This decision supersedes all prior decisions."]

Frank explained the wording of the bulletin announcement and added the elders' response had been that "they would rather not judge *anybody* as to their Christianity."

"So why are you here today?" Punt inquired of Frank.

"Because they are back to judging her as a good Christian author."

"Did you hear him [Schipma] say that the consistory today is still holding to that?"

"Yes, I did."

"Is that in direct contradiction to the bulletin announcement?"

"Yes."

Vander Ploeg cross-examined, "In what document did they say they stand by their original position that she is a Christian author?"

Frank responded, "We heard it here today. Therefore they canned the bulletin announcement."

"No further questions," Vander Ploeg conceded.

Despite all the confusing arguments, we felt through it all, enough was said so the delegates could get a glimpse of the struggle we had gone through and why we were compelled to do so. But Vander Ploeg hadn't pulled his trump card yet. And he was about to do so.

"I'd like to call Professor Donald Hettinga," announced Vander Ploeg.

I waited for an objection from Rev. Punt. It came quickly: "I question the relevance of Hettinga's testimony. The charges are about what the elders have done. . . . I hope we're not going to get into a discussion on L'Engle. . . . I wonder if he is an authority on the conduct of the elders of the Orland Park Church."

While Rev. Williams conceded Punt was right, he allowed Hettinga to be examined. He didn't know what Hettinga had to say and thought it only fair to listen to him, at least up to a certain point.

Vander Ploeg made sure all the delegates were aware of Hettinga's position at Calvin College and literary accomplishments, including his recent work, *Presenting Madeleine L'Engle*.

"You're a Ph.D. Is that correct?" Vander Ploeg rubbed in.

"Yes, I have a Ph.D. from the University of Chicago."

After asking Hettinga to describe his background as a teacher of writing, Vander Ploeg made certain that everyone knew he had served as both deacon and elder and had signed The Form of Subscription.

"Mr. Chairman . . ." Punt broke in, agitated at where Vander Ploeg's line of questioning was going. But, once again, Hettinga was allowed to be questioned.

Holding up Hettinga's book, *Presenting Madeleine L'Engle*,

Vander Ploeg asked him to explain what research he did before he wrote it. It didn't surprise me that he claimed to have widely read many of L'Engle's own materials but Scripture and the occult were not mentioned. I wondered if anyone else saw the flaw. I mean, if you're going to research somebody's work, research! Research who they quote and why they quote them; research the concepts talked about; research and compare with Scripture to find out if L'Engle's "Word about God" comes close, etc. I was dying to cross-examine Hettinga myself.

Repeatedly, Punt objected to Hettinga's testimony, to no avail. The "courtroom" was quickly becoming a battlefield. Punt had to remind Rev. Williams continually that even if classis had made an awful error, its declaration stood as "settled and binding" unless and until it was appealed. "Maybe classis made a horrible mistake," he argued, "but even if they did, that's none of our business here today. Classis made the decision. It's binding and that's it!"

"Mr. Chairman," Vander Ploeg implored, "I began this day by saying that the matter we are going to consider here today revolve around differences of interpretation. . . ."

I began to picture children singing, "Ring around the rosy, pocket full of. . . ." We were going around in circles.

Vander Ploeg finally made his point. There were varying interpretations of what classis decided way back in January, 1991. The elders saw what happened one way and we had interpreted it another way. "We are *entitled* to have Dr. Hettinga testify here as an *expert* on how Madeleine L'Engle is viewed in the Christian community and take this into account!" he demanded.

I don't know how many times the word "expert" was used but it was definitely more times than was needed. The term "highly qualified" was also used, as if ministers couldn't possibly have any understanding into what L'Engle was teaching. It seemed a bit contradictory to me that while the elders claimed there were differing interpretations of L'Engle's writings so no one could know for sure what she was saying, they themselves pointed to their "experts" as knowing the right interpretation.

Despite all of Punt's efforts to keep Hettinga from testifying, Williams allowed Vander Ploeg to continue. Personally, I was anxious to hear what Hettinga would say, even though I knew his words would shed doubt on the credibility of the advisory report. We didn't know it yet, but Hettinga's testimony would be crucial in determining what God would have us do—stay in our denomination or leave it.

As Hettinga described how L'Engle was regarded within the larger Christian community, I couldn't help but chuckle when he declared L'Engle "a *wonderful* Christian author" after Vander Ploeg had made such a fuss about whether the elders had ever said that.

"Professor Hettinga," Vander Ploeg continued, "What is your opinion about . . . that L'Engle denies the atonement, that it was a substitutionary sacrificial payment for the sins of God's people?"

"I do not believe that in the bulk of her work or in her life that she does do that. . . . There is that pattern throughout her work in which she clearly indicates that she believes that Jesus atoned for her sins."

His testimony made my skin crawl. He knew what those books said. He had read them.

"Taking all of L'Engle's books that you've read and her writings, is it your opinion that L'Engle denies that Jesus' incarnation is qualitatively unique, God with Us, Immanuel?"

"No, I do not. I believe that she believes that Jesus' incarnation is unique. . . . She is clearly talking about a God that is outside of her. A deity that can be addressed. She is not talking about a God within her, and she is not talking about some kind of inner Christ. . . . When she is talking about that, she is talking about seeing the face of Christ in other people and ministering to them as Jesus said you ought to when you minister unto the poor and to the hungry you're ministering unto me."

Had this man *read* her books or just skimmed through them? What did he do with these passages?

> If we shed our idea of God as being someone Out There, separate from all that has been made, and begin instead to think of God within all Creation, every galaxy, every quantum, every human being, then we cannot hold ourselves "out there" either (*A Stone for a Pillow*, pg. 86).

> A young reader knowing of my love of new words, sent me a beautiful one: namaste: I salute the God within you. . . . If we accept that God is within each of us, then God will give us, within us, the courage to accept the responsibility of being co-creators (*And it Was Good*, pg. 19).

Namaste: L'Engle knew what it was–a Hindu salutation performed out of devotion to "God" in which the palms are placed
together and raised to touch that point on the forehead that is popularly known as the third eye representing the meeting of the higher
and lower aspects of one's nature. L'Engle was far from being naive and uneducated. In her book, *A House Like a Lotus*, one of her
characters says, "In the Upanishads–a series of Sanskrit works
which are part of the Veda. Here it is, Pol, listen: In this body, in
this town of Spirit, there is a little house shaped like a lotus. . . ."
Was it just a coincidence that L'Engle used the symbol of the Lotus
which represents the development of seven chakras by which one
attains psychic powers and supreme enlightenment (godhood)?–a
symbol which is also sacred among the Hindus because their god
"Brahma" was born from it? I think not.

"In your opinion, does Madeleine L'Engle deny that there will
be a final separation between God and some persons at the end of
time?"

His answer to this question would tell me exactly what I needed
to know. In his book, he made it look like those who accused L'Engle
of being a universalist just were not understanding that she was
emphasizing God's love. But my articles had also been published
and Hettinga had read them (he told me during break). What would
he say now?

Hettinga stammered,

> Uh, yes, she does, and I find it very, very troubling. I
> would say that she *is* a universalist. She even, as I be-
> lieve, has been entered into the record, she does even say
> that Satan will be saved. And I find this disturbing and I
> wish she didn't say it. I think she is clearly wrong on this
> point. But even then, as she is a universalist, and as she
> says outrageous things like that: that Satan will be saved,
> will be reunited again, because she imagines that God is
> love, and she cannot imagine a God that is love that will
> not reconcile all persons. . . .

Finally, an outright admission there was one interpretation that
was correct! I wondered if the other delegates recognized that if all
would be saved, including Satan, it necessarily followed that Jesus
didn't suffer the wrath of God for our sins–no wrath, no condem-

nation. To me it seemed so clear. To even suggest Satan would be saved would be to call God a liar and the Bible no different than any other "myth" which, of course, she does.

** [Note: It wouldn't surprise me if someday Hettinga admitted L'Engle didn't believe in a sacrificial, substitutionary atonement. Others have admitted it, such as Harold Shaw Publishers. On September 20, 1993, just before the judicial hearing, Shaw sent out a newsletter to several Christian bookstores to counteract the documentation in *Trojan Horse, How the New Age Movement Infiltrates the Church*. Steven Board, the publisher for Shaw wrote: *"If she is troubled by a doctrine of Hell, or the penal satisfaction view of the atonement, she speaks up and says so—something a faculty member at an evangelical seminary usually cannot do. This forthrightness is one thing her loyal readers like about her. But . . . some readers and some bookstores will be uneasy with this candor, it will sound concessive to them. To the authors of* Trojan Horse *it sounds 'blasphemous and heretical,' Shaw contends this is reckless language"* (emphasis mine). I believe it's much more reckless to promote the works of an author who willfully denies the purpose of Christ's coming and uphold them as "Christian." But at least Shaw had the guts to admit she does have trouble with it.]

Did these experts really think we were so naive as to believe because we weren't literary experts we couldn't possibly understand those blatant denials in her works? And why was it so very hard for them to admit she did deny fundamental doctrines? Was it because they had their own agenda to teach the "gospel of Madeleine L'Engle" to their students despite the objections of parents? Had they turned away from sound doctrine and listened to "what their itching ears wanted to hear"? Oh, how I hoped and prayed that whoever was listening to this testimony would know instantly that something was dreadfully wrong.

Again, Rev. Punt interrupted but was cut off by Williams. "Let him speak," I thought, "let the people hear what he has to say." The verdict would tell us just where our colleges and denomination were headed. Then I nudged Rev. Punt to tell him I wanted to take the stand to refute Hettinga's defense for L'Engle.

"Is it your opinion that L'Engle denies the authority of the Bible as the final arbiter in all matters of faith and practice?" Vander Ploeg asked.

"No, I do not believe that it is," Hettinga stated for the record.

"I understand that some of her statements about the Bible and myth and story are confusing to some people and understandably so. I think that she is using language in a different way and using terms in a way that people in her audience may not understand them. . . . When she is talking about the Bible as myth, she is talking about it in a way that is very similar to the way that we would talk about the Bible in the Reformed community. She is using different language."

This was too much. A different language? How about a different gospel?

"In your opinion, do you believe that L'Engle is a proponent of the New Age Movement?"

"Absolutely not . . . it seems to me characteristics of proponents of the New Age movement have some kind of recognition of the divinity within a person. Saying somehow that Christ or God is within me. L'Engle clearly worships a God that is not within her. . . ."

I had *had* it. Hettinga couldn't be this naive. He had seen all my documentation and I had good reason to believe Vander Ploeg had read a copy of *Trojan Horse, How the New Age Movement Infiltrates the Church.* During coffee break, I had told Hettinga very frankly that he knew L'Engle uses occult practices in her works and is encouraging one to develop psychic powers. His answer had been that Scripture says we will do greater things than He. I politely answered, but God *condemns* occult practices, Dr. Hettinga! We talked about having a debate sometime; maybe that time will come.

Vander Ploeg now asked, "Why such differing opinions of L'Engle in the Christian community?"

In his highly educated manner, Hettinga answered,

> She uses different language; from not reading from a Reformed perspective noting that we do learn from common grace, that God uses all sorts of avenues to bring truth. Fantasy novels—when an author creates a character who maybe engages in traveling through time or flying or seeing things in, *what we might call in reality occult ways, scrying—she uses the term in one of her novels* (emphasis mine).

But Hettinga explained, "When an author does that, she is trying to get us to think a certain way about that character in the world of that novel; so when a character uses scrying, seeing through a crystal ball, in a novel for the purposes of good, she means us to see that character as a good character within the world of that novel and to read the whole book and to then evaluate that character's actions and values at the end of it."

I was amazed Hettinga so forthrightly admitted L'Engle does use occult practices in her works, since, in his book, he tried to make myself and others look as though we were silly to think these practices were of the occult. I guessed my articles might have done more good than I realized. Hettinga was right on one point: L'Engle does intend for her readers to see that the use of occult practices is good in her novels. But, to his discredit, leaving out the fact that she also promotes them in her non-fiction works, is downright deceptive. Her goal, as she readily admits, is to put her theology in her works. Why, would one suppose she does that? So Christians can argue over whether she is using them just in the world of the novel or not? "Come on, let's get real, Dr. Hettinga," I thought.

Our education committee had denied there were occult practices in L'Engle's works. Now I wondered if they had known all along that she conveyed them as God's gift in her works. Were the elders listening closely to what Hettinga had just said? Were the delegates? Did they even care?

I listened intently as he further pointed out, "To say that such incidences are meant to, or that one should not read books, certain books, because such incidents are in them would be analogous it seems to me, to say that we ought not to read another fantasy book like *Charlotte's Web*, because the character talks to animals, and that might induce young people to have an inappropriate view of reality and start talking to animals. Those incidents and elements are in a novel for purposes of plot and characterization, not to be emulated any more than we are not to emulate characters in a movie or in some other works of art."

Here we were again, back to an issue of censorship. We had never said one could not read L'Engle's works if they so desired. In fact, I would welcome using her books in the Christian school classroom or adult education classes in the church to teach discernment by comparing them next to Scripture. Today, more than ever before, both children and adults need to be aware that New Age/occult teachings are being heralded as "true Christianity." They *must* be shown how false teachings undermine Scripture.

My mind drifted for a moment until Vander Ploeg asked Hettinga, "As an expert on L'Engle, and as a former elder in your church in Grand Rapids, if you had been a delegate to the January 1991 meeting of Classis Chicago South, would you have voted for the adoption of that advisory report?"

I glanced over at Rev. Punt waiting for him to object. How dare Vander Ploeg question the validity of an adopted report!

"OUT OF ORDER!" the presiding Rev. Williams burst in. It was about time he saw this was out of order, but the damage had already been done. Classis' declaration had been overshadowed by an "expert" of literature. Vander Ploeg had done the very thing he was not to supposed to do and had gotten away with it.

The "complainants" were flabbergasted and, at the same time, somewhat relieved after Hettinga's testimony, for he had just supported much of what we had said all along. The delegates and visitors there had heard his statements. Our job was finished; the truth had found a way to come through. I could see by the troubled looked on Rev. Punt's face that he had not expected to hear such a testimony. I begged him to put me on the stand to refute Hettinga's claims with L'Engle's own words, but for some reason, God did not intend for that to happen. Instead, Punt just reiterated that Hettinga's testimony was not valid because the advisory report had been adopted. It wasn't until he was allowed to cross-examine Dr. Arnold, the secretary of the reconciliation committee from synod, that he laid out the one question we had wanted to ask throughout the whole trial.

Rev. Punt carefully and slowly asked: *"If a writer **denies** both the qualitative unique divinity of Jesus Christ and **denies** that the atonement is the sacrificial payment for the sins of God's people, would you say that such an author should be classified as a Christian author?"*

"Mr. Chairman, I don't think I have to answer that. I don't think that's pertinent," Arnold retorted.

It wasn't pertinent? Not only was it pertinent to the case–it *was* the case! Dr. Arnold's testimony was the perfect summary for every witness that fell in line to defend Madeleine L'Engle's teachings since 1989–when it all began.

Frank Voss, the deacon who had testified concerning the elder's misleading announcement in the church bulletin was astonished.

The appellants gasped. Some of the visitors winced. Rev. Punt stammered, "Well, I think you can see it. I'll let it go if it's going to be debated—I'd have no difficulty answering it."

Punt was so floored and dismayed by Arnold's remark, he didn't see any reason to continue the cross-examination. Arnold knew that question was pertinent. It was the most important question we had demanded to have answered. The unity of the church rested upon the answer to this question. But, what was the use? The refusal to answer such a crucial question revealed the hard-heartedness we were dealing with. Unity was being held higher in priority than the fundamental doctrines of the Christian faith. How sad it was to hear Dr. Arnold answer in the way that he did. It left us limp with grief for our church and for our denomination.

All the conflicting arguments concerning the P.S. note, Rev. Erffmeyer's sermons, the bulletin announcement, the vote on the original appeal, the fact that no elders had been willing to talk to us after classis' declaration of January 1991 concerning their "interpretation" of what happened, (which was refuted by Erffmeyer after Vander Ploeg asked if he wanted to change his testimony), etc. . . . was left in a trail of dust after Hettinga's testimony. Besides, all this boiled down to a matter of who you wanted to believe. It was the pastors' and elders' word against ours.

If Hettinga hadn't made clear what our consistory was believing, maybe elder Dick De Jong would. He claimed the question, "Can you deny the atonement and still be classified as a Christian author," was a *loaded* one. He had answered, "I don't know," because he felt "trapped." De Jong testified that he had made other comments to us also, but they must have been "lost." No, they weren't lost. We had heard them perfectly clearly. He explained to the delegates that:

> There are differing understandings of the atonement in Christian thought. Different denominations articulate the atonement differently than we do, and *we do not hold everyone to articulate the atonement in the terms of the limited substitutionary atonement that we understand in the Reformed faith* (emphasis mine).

Maybe different denominations did articulate a different view of the atonement, but was it a right view? Was it a redeeming view?

Could one even say? Though all the elders and pastors who took the witness stand affirmed their belief in the four cardinal doctrines in question, it was a tongue-in-cheek affirmation, one that meant nothing if you believed these doctrines were not unchangeable truths, or if you believed one could deny them and still be acknowledged and defended as a Christian.

The trial was coming to a close. Rev. Punt pleaded with the delegates as he made his closing observations:

> Throughout this denomination there are those who are refusing more and more today to make judgments concerning sound doctrine. It's a permeation within the church. And now with a not guilty verdict, we are going to be saying, "You know, it's not the elders who have to make these kind of judgments concerning sound doctrine. . . . No, God has chosen to use a group of "experts." God has appointed all the vast Evangelical Christian community, not elders to guard the church of Jesus Christ from false teachings.

Turning to Scripture he read from 2 Peter 2:1-2:

> But there were also false prophets among the people, just as there will be false teachers among you. They will secretly introduce destructive heresies, even denying the sovereign Lord who bought them–bringing swift destruction on themselves. Many will follow their shameful ways and will bring the way of truth into disrepute.

He left the delegates with a strong warning concerning the urgent and critical need to make judgments; one that the apostle Paul himself had given to the churches in Galatia: "But even if we or an angel from heaven should preach a gospel other than the one we preached to you, let him be eternally condemned!" (Galatians 1:8).

How proud I was of this man who stood up to defend sound doctrine despite what many of his colleagues would say about him. His words should have put shame on all the elders' faces. But, right now, they were more intrigued with the "little visual" Vander Ploeg had brought along to help him "make a point." He distributed to all the delegates a picture of a woman's face which was partially shaded. Holding it up for all to see, he presented his closing argument:

> The question is, what do you see? Anybody want to hazard a guess what you see? Do you see the young woman or do you see an old woman? And if you look long enough you will see either one of them. This morning I told you that this is about differences of interpretation; how we perceive things. One of the differences has to do with the writings of Madeleine L'Engle. And we've heard a lot of testimony about that today. As you know, the elders were originally with that large part of the body of Christ who regarded her as a Christian author. The complainants have denounced her as a heretic, and they regard her as a great danger to the Christian church. And, as Professor Hettinga said today, that view is shared by some who are part of the body of Christ. He clearly set out this divergence for us. He recognizes there are two sides to this. Some of the passages that L'Engle writes in her books are troublesome. The elders have said that . . . we've never denied that. And, what we have suggested as a way we can live together is that we agree to disagree.

Not one verse from Scripture was quoted in his summary. But then, I really hadn't expected there to be.

Using the picture of the woman was the same ploy used at the June, 1993 Synod in which the delegates were instructed to gaze at the art piece made of rusty pipes. Vander Ploeg's conclusion–there are no right or wrong answers; everyone perceives "Truth" differently, so let's just agree to disagree. It was unity at the price of sound doctrine. The probable cost: one's eternal soul.

I envisioned a little girl sitting on her father's lap looking lovingly up into his face with eyes full of trust. "Daddy, did Jesus really die to save us from our sins so we could go to heaven?" she asks.

Patting her gently on the back, he pauses for a moment, raises his eyebrows and shrugs his shoulders. "I don't know, sweetheart. Some people think so, you'll just have to decide for yourself when you're older."

As his words echoed in my head, I imagined thousands of voices–

a heavenly choir, singing the beautiful hymn:

> I know not why God's wondrous grace
> To me he hath made known,
> Nor why, unworthy, Christ in love
> Redeemed me for his own.
> But "I know whom I have believed,
> And am persuaded that he is able
> To keep that which I've committed
> Unto him against that day."

Oh, what a "Blessed Assurance" it is to *know*, Jesus is mine!

EPILOGUE

It was the young people's chance to speak to the rest of the Christian Reformed Church, and their message was clear: Let's stop worrying about doctrine and be more inclusive.

The Banner, September 19, 1994

But I am afraid that just as Eve was deceived by the serpent's cunning, your minds may somehow be led astray from your sincere and pure devotion to Christ. For if someone comes to you and preaches a Jesus other than the Jesus we preached, or if you receive a different spirit from the one you received, or a different gospel from the one you accepted, you put up with it easily enough.

2 Corinthians 11:3-4

It was after 10:00 p.m. The trial had lasted over 12 hours. While being so insistent that the judicial hearing be held exactly as one in the secular courtroom, attorney Vander Ploeg now contended our elders had the right to be in the room with the delegates who were discussing the evidence, and also had the right to vote! Unbelievably, our consistory, contrary to what would ever be done in a judicial court system, was allowed to sit in on the deliberations. Thankfully, I believe they weren't allowed to vote.

Out of a jury comprised of 30 delegates, four found our consistory guilty on the first charge of violating the Form of Subscription and Church Order. As to the second charge, displaying conduct unbecoming office-bearers, six found them guilty. The majority of delegates, however, found our consistory, "not guilty" and the majority, in this case, ruled. For us, the verdict meant having to leave our church and denomination. No longer was there a doubt in our minds of what we had to do.

Rev. Williams closed this historic classical meeting with a prayer for peace and reconciliation in our church. After all that was said and done, he still hadn't seen the impossibility of such being accomplished.

The Sunday following the hearing, Rev. William Lenters was asked to preach at Orland Park CRC. His sermon had been entitled, "Circle of Reconciliation," but at the last minute, he decided to turn it into a slam session against all the appellants. Speaking of the judicial hearing, Lenters lamented that all preachers "could identify with what it's like to be under the grill." Contrary to Paul's commendation to the Bereans for faithfully testing his teachings, Lenter's continued, "And we don't need a delegation of people to ask us every once in a while, 'Are you abiding by the forms of unity that hang this church together?' " He didn't appreciate the "dudley do-rights" and their "straw gospel"–those who think they can put a "mysterious God in a bottle."

After listening to the tape of Lenter's sermon which was given to me by a member of Orland Park CRC, all the appellants were convinced reconciliation was never a top priority on our pastor's list, nor on the list of the elders. How contradictory it seemed that after Lenter's sermon, in the November issue of our church's newsletter, Schipma reported, "Rev. Williams . . . asked that God would permit all of us to see the completion of this situation as a new opportunity for healing and reconciliation, and work through us to bring that about. We ask that you pray that this might be in God's will."

The next few weeks I took time to rest, being both physically and mentally exhausted from the last four years. I picked up a copy of the Sept/Oct, 1993 issue of *The Other Side* magazine, supposedly for evangelical Christians. The first two articles were entitled, "A Thousand Trains to Heaven," and "One Way: For too Long, I misunderstood the meaning of Jesus' words."

The first article was written by contributing editor John Linscheid, who is active in the Germantown Mennonite Church in

Philadelphia. Linscheid scorned an evangelist for calling out, "I tell you, no one–the Bible says no one–cometh to the Father but by me." He maintained, "We discover God in a million places, including some where normal Christianity find only the danger of heresy. . . . My own experience of Christ is diverse. I have known Christ as straight, as gay, as man, as woman, as stranger, as friend. . . . " (pg. 8, 14).

The second article, written by the pastor of the United Christian Church in Levittown, PA., added an extra dose of poison to the first:

> We don't find the way, the truth, and the life by learning things about Jesus or about God. Rather, it is by coming into mystical union with Jesus that we enter into the divine life and become one with God's truth, one with God's life. Since Jesus is the way, we come to know God by being one with Jesus (pg. 17).

> John 14:6 is not a theological way of saying, "We're In, You're Out." Jesus wasn't speaking about a person's "religious affiliation" or "faith preference." He wasn't spouting a "party line." Instead, John 14:6 points us–and points all people, whether Christian or not–to the basic truth Jesus lived by, to the truth which Jesus was, that the way of God in the world is to empty oneself and become a lowly servant. No one comes to God except by that way. Jesus personified it. By coming into a mystical union with Jesus, by living as he lived, we come to God (pg. 18).

The words stung, bringing tears to my eyes once again. Fresh wounds from the bleeding hands, feet and side of Jesus Christ formed in my mind. He had only to die once for our salvation, but it seemed He was being crucified over and over again by those who had known the Truth, but now betrayed it. These articles were a foretaste of what we believed was seeping into our own church and denomination–the erasure of Biblical knowledge in favor of imaginative experience. How thrilled I was to read in the next issue of *The Other Side*, someone's objection to those articles and subsequent cancellation of their subscription!

A couple of months passed. It was around Christmas time when we all wrote our final letters of resignation from the membership of the Orland Park Christian Reformed Church. We had been sent a letter from Pete Schipma telling us to either come back to OPCRC or transfer our membership to another church, or, if contact wasn't made, they would lapse our membership as of January 1, 1994. No phone calls were made to us. A district team of elders was never sent to talk with us, and church discipline was never applied.

After detailing the many reasons why my family felt compelled to leave, our letter concluded, "The type of unity envisioned by the CRC, in order to create community, costs dearly. We are not willing to pay that cost or be obligated in any way to support that ideal. . . . It is with deep concern and heartfelt sorrow that we leave a denomination which we had believed would forever remain dedicated to preaching, defending and preserving the gospel."

After the new year, Howard and Jo Stob, John and Sharon Tiggelaar, Ruth and Ken Evenhouse, and my family joined Covenant Church, now officially part of the Orthodox Presbyterian denomination. Other members from Orland CRC and other CRC churches soon followed and transferred their memberships to Covenant. Dean and Karen chose to go to Grace Fellowship, a non-denominational church of Baptist background.

Over the summer months I took the time to relax and just enjoy being with my youngest daughter Hilary, now 7 years old, swimming in our back-yard pool. The tension had eased and now all the appellants felt at home once again in a church where they knew the pastor and elders were like-minded. (Howard Stob was quickly elected as one of those elders.) Though Covenant Church received some rather negative publicity from *The Banner* and Orland CRC's own newsletter, and was talked about as that "schismatic, divisive bunch," the church continually strives to be faithful to God's Word and has slowly grown to approximately 40 families.

In the winter of 1994, a letter was sent out to all members of the CRCNA from the Board of Trustees of the Christian Reformed Church in North America. The intent of the letter, dated January 10, 1994, was to put a stop to all "negative networking" and "charges . . . being leveled at the CRCNA and its various agencies." The Board of Trustees promised members of the denomination the allegation "that the CRCNA has departed from its confessional position that the Holy Scriptures are our only rule for faith and practice," was "simply not true." Yet, not one shred of evidence was provided in the letter to support their promise.

I wrote a response to the Board which was later adopted by the Committee of Concerned Members (of the CRC), Reformed Fellowship, Reformed Believers United, and *Christian Renewal*. It was printed in *Christian Renewal* and in *The Reformed Witness* as a formal response to their letter (Appendix J).

The Board of Trustees never answered me personally, nor did they bother to address the response from those concerned about the CRCNA publicly.

Just prior to receiving their letter, I had written an article entitled, "New Hermeneutic or Ancient Wisdom?" in the October 3, 1994 issue of *Christian Renewal*. It was a reply to Dr. John Boer, a missionary for Christian Reformed World Missions working in Jos, Nigeria, who had written a piece for the Calvin Theological Seminary AlumNews called, "Miracles and Healing." After witnessing the powerful work of shamans (witchdoctors) Boer ridiculed those who believed psychic healing powers came from Satan. He claimed humans could possess the same supernatural powers Jesus had (sound familiar?) and mocked Westerners for their rejection of African healing.

What was worse, Boer claimed, "The miracles of both the Old and New Testament are expressions of human powers restored by God (OT) and Christ (NT)"! Comparing the miracles performed through Moses by Almighty God, to that of the "miracles" through the Egyptian magicians, Boer alleged the only difference between them was that the miracles performed by the magicians were distorted and used with wrong intent. Those with a knowledge of the occult would readily recognize Boer's assertion as the difference between white and black magic, both of which are condemned by God. In another article he wrote, Boer forthrightly admitted that he watned to study under these African healers, and was searching for literature dealing with parapsychology (the occult study of psychic powers). Boer and I continued our discussions publicly in *Christian Renewal* and many responded positively to my answer to him. Nevertheless, he remains a missionary dedicated to setting up "holistic" hospitals in Jos, Nigeria, which may very well include African healing (use of occult techniques/psychic powers/shamanism).

In the midst of writing articles back and forth with Dr. Boer, I received a telephone call from a member of a Christian Reformed

church in Michigan. He was terribly concerned after reading a brochure for a "Diversity & Unity" conference held on October 7-8 in
the auditorium of Calvin Seminary. Its purpose was to discuss "The
Goals, Contents and Methods of Interreligious Dialogue."

He sent me a copy of the brochure, which, even after all I had
already documented and witnessed, surprised me still. The co-
sponsors were the Interfaith Dialogue Association, Aquinas College, Calvin College and Grand Valley State University—those who
had co-sponsored Huston Smith in 1991. The keynote address,
"Finding a Way/the Ways/Our Way Into a Future With Diverse
Spiritual Understandings But a Common Hope," was presented by
Dr. David Ramage, Jr. former chair of the Council for a Parliament
of the World's Religions, and president emeritus of McCormick
Theological Seminary. Dr. John Primus from the Calvin College
Religion Department gave the opening welcome.

Listed below are just a few of the workshops that were offered
which so completely dishonored our Lord and Savior:

1. Learning from God's Other Voices; the Idea of the Ineffable.
   Dr. Timothy Light, Dept. of Comparative Religion, Western
   Michigan University (Paper). Ineffability, a central concept
   in many religions, provides a link beyond which conversation with other traditions can progress with humility and understanding.
2. The Religion Beyond Religions and Unity in Diversity. Dr.
   Methuselah J. Mishear, Chimney Mission and Negro Lincoln
   Human Services, and Dr. Jitendra M. Mishear, Grand Valley
   State University (Paper). *Religion beyond religions is the
   totality of all religions and is an expression of every religion
   and absolute truth, leading to supreme peace, perfection and
   freedom* (emphasis mine).
3. Learning and Teaching "Toward a Global Ethic." Joel Bever-
   sluis, editor\publisher, *A Sourcebook for the Community of
   Religions* (Workshop). Using the declaration from the Parliament (drafted by Hans Kung with many others), this workshop will 1) study its content and challenges, and 2) explore
   a discussion method that participants may use in groups or
   classes to stimulate interfaith understanding.
4. Chi Kung as Therapeutic Exercise for Interfaith Practice. Dr.
   Douglas Change . . . presents Chinese Chi Kung as an inte-

gration of physical, psychological and mental training which can also *provide an interfaith and interdisciplinary paradigm to integrate individuals for a harmonious world community.* [Chi Kung is "Chinese Yoga, a system closely related to the more familiar Indian yoga. . . . *In its more esoteric aspects, the meditation practices of Chinese yoga concentrate on arousing a kundalini-type energy through the chokers in order to achieve enlightened states and/or magical powers" The Aquarian Guide to the New Age*, Campbell, Ellen & Brendan, J.H., The Aquarian Press, 1990, pg. 87–CVK].

Toward the latter part of 1994, Mid-America Reformed Seminary professor Dr. Nelson D. Kloosterman, our representative at the judicial code committee meeting, left the CRC and, therefore, was banned by Classis of the Heartland (Iowa) from preaching in Christian Reformed churches (though he still receives requests to do so). *The Banner* refuses to print advertisements by Mid-America Reformed Seminary (which began as a necessary alternative to Calvin Seminary in 1982), insisting those ministers and professors are "divisive."

When one takes a good, hard look at all that has transpired over the last few years, a very grim picture arises. Thousands of Christians have fallen prey to the most self-gratifying idea that it is their job to call every person to a unity based on love. For them, God already has, or will become, the Ultimate Reality of all religions. Doctrine is out, experience is in. Consequently, New Age beliefs and practices have been included into an ever-widening definition of the word, "Christian."

As the years go by, more and more "Christians" are deceived into thinking syncretism (the uniting of all religions), is the sole way of finding peace in the world. A "universal" or "global spirituality" is quickly taking precedent. In the melting process, the sacrificial death of Jesus Christ and His victory over sin will be consumed in the blazing zeal of those eager to feel good about themselves (just look at all the church-school curriculum enhancing self-esteem). World peace is a wonderful goal, but it cannot (and will not) come at the expense of betraying the One who bought us.

Even though I am no longer a member, I grieve for the denomination I loved so dearly. Knowing what is taking place, while many remain unaware that the doctrines, creeds, Form of Subscription and Church Order of the CRC are fast becoming meaningless, has been a tremendous burden to carry. To watch family members, friends, relatives, and so many others devote themselves to authors, professors, pastors, etc. who have either deliberately or unknowingly scorned, undermined and/or flippantly disregarded sound doctrine, tears at the very core of my being.

My intent in writing this book then, is not to further divide the CRC (though it may), but to call it back to a unity based on a steadfast love and devoted loyalty to the Truth; that Truth which the CRC so bravely taught and defended at first.

Some may say, "Wait a minute, the doctrinal standards in the CRC haven't officially changed. How dare you accuse the denomination of promoting false teachings!" To them, I answer, "Just because the doctrinal standards haven't changed means nothing, and to think otherwise is both foolish and detrimental to the health of the denomination. Think about it. By the time the CRC would change its doctrinal standards, it will *already be* an apostate denomination! By not applying loving discipline to those embracing, promoting or defending false teachings within its walls, synod has, without officially doing so, given its approval of those teachings, and has helped spread the disease that is raging throughout the body.

I understand and expect those leaders in churches and schools who have, with fervent desire set their hearts against those who have exposed the false teachings of L'Engle and other more blatant New Age authors, will try to discredit my story. L'Engle herself, as personable as she is, may write about it in her next work of nonfiction, dubbing researchers like myself as those who hunt for Satan. But, no matter how hard each one may try, I am convinced God has a purpose for this book and that somewhere, somehow, He will use it in ways one might never suspect. At least, that is what I pray for.

Since the judicial hearing, there has been an increasing amount of evidence tracing the fatal course which members in the CRC, as well as other mainline denominations, seem determined to follow. I cannot list them all here, but hopefully, in this book, I have provided enough information so that anyone with open eyes and a heartfelt desire to discern truth, will see and understand the crucial need for repentance throughout the Christian community.

Please, don't allow "let's stop worrying about doctrine," to be the ungodly legacy left to the children of the next generation.

Sound doctrine: Know it, believe it, defend it, preserve it! For it is the Truth about Jesus Christ; the Truth that Jesus promised by His grace will set us free!

> Therefore Jesus said again, "I tell you the truth, I am the gate for the sheep. All who ever came before me were thieves and robbers, but the sheep did not listen to them. I am the gate; whoever enters through me will be saved. . . . I am the good shepherd. The good shepherd lays down his life for the sheep."
>
> John 10:7, 8, 9a, 11

Appendix A

For those with questions or comments about this book and/or inquiries on how to obtain the official documents cited, you may write to the author. The address is:

> Claris Van Kuiken
> c/o Educational Research Group, Inc.
> P. O. Box, 1213
> Tinley Park, IL 60477

Additional copies of this book are also available from the address above.

Appendix B

A CHRIST WITHOUT A CROSS

"Can We Learn From Witches? You Bet!" was the title of an editorial in the National Catholic Reporter, *November 11, 1988. In this article, Cardinal Joseph Ratzinger was criticized for demanding that Starhawk, a practicing witch, be terminated from her teaching position at Matthew Fox's Institute in Culture and Creation Spirituality. The editor then stated: "Frankly, witchcraft is not our cup of tea. We feel more comfortable along the varied paths provided within the tradition of our Catholic faith.* Yet, we recognize that more than one path leads to God. . . . *We must resist the temptation to belittle another's spiritual path, a lesson with application both in and outside the church"* (emphasis mine).

Besides Miriam Starhawk, a Wiccan Priestess and national leader of the Neo-Pagan Movement, Fox also appointed to his faculty a Yoga instructor; an Episcopal vicar who has become a Zen Buddhist; Juisah Teish, a Voudon Priestess, and Buck Ghost Horse, a Native American Shaman.[1] Shaman is another name for witchdoctor; one who will use rhythmic drumming, dance, chanting, fasting, drugs, sweat lodges and vision quests to induce trance states (altered states of consciousness) which allows the shaman's soul to enter the spirit worlds to enlist the aid of spirits for healing, divination, and magic. (Christians know these spirits as demons, since God condemns every aspect of witchcraft in Deuteronomy 18:9-12.) Fox participates in shamanic rituals and promotes the use of these rituals in his book, *The Coming of the Cosmic Christ.*

Matthew Fox, a controversial Dominican priest, was silenced temporarily for his unorthodox views by the Vatican in 1988. He is founder of the Institute in Culture and Creation Spirituality (ICCS), an avant garde master's degree program at Holy Names College in Oakland, California. The article in the *National Catholic Reporter* reveals the effects of Fox's teachings and the imprint he is embedding in society. Incredibly, not only does Fox lecture at New Age gatherings around the country, he says, *"Many of the invitations that I accept now are from Protestant seminaries"*[2] (emphasis mine).

How is this possible? Many can be deceived when false teachings come disguised under the banner of being "Christian," and when the historical Jesus is replaced with a counterfeit Christ. Fox believes we have been too preoccupied with the historical Jesus, and that we have "to move from a 'personal Savior' Christianity–which is what an anthropocentric and antimystical Christianity gives us–to a 'cosmic Christ' Christianity.. . . ."[3] "The Cosmic Christ is not restricted to Jesus," he proclaims.[4] "The Cosmic Christ lives and breathes in Jesus and in *all* God's children, in all the prophets of religion everywhere, in all creatures on the universe."[5] "It's the 'Buddha Nature' that's in all of us, if you're a Buddhist. It's the divine light that's in all of us."[6] "We are all Cosmic Christs, 'other Christs.' "[7]

Which Christ?

Jesus of Nazareth said, "I am the light of the world, whoever follows me will never walk in darkness, but will have the light of life" (John 8:12). Acts 4:12 states: "Salvation is found in no one else, for there is no other name under heaven given to men by which we must be saved." Since Jesus is *the* Christ (1 John 5:1), and others claiming to be Christ are called "false Christs" by Jesus (Matthew 24:23-24), which Christ does Fox believe in?

In his book, *The New Age Cult,* Walter Martin, founder and director of Christian Research Institute International, Cal., describes the Cosmic Christ: "In esoteric schools of thought, the Christ is considered to be a universal spirit or a cosmic force. The primary goal of this impersonal spirit or force is to guide the spiritual evolution of mankind."[8] (French Jesuit priest and mystic, Pierre Teilhard de Chardin, called this cosmic evolution.)

In the New Age/occult section of a local bookstore, I found the *Harper's Encyclopedia of Mystical and Paranormal Experience,* which also defines Fox's Christ. It states: "In *The Coming of the Cosmic Christ,* Fox articulates his concept of a Cosmic Christ, as opposed to an historical Jesus, who embodies the aforementioned qualities. . . . The Cosmic Christ is an archetype, and must be reincarnated repeatedly in the mind and immunization before it takes hold as a force."[9]

For Fox, Jesus was an enlightened master, no different than Buddha, Krishna, etc. who incarnated the Cosmic Christ–as we all can do. This basic concept is seen in Hinduism, which teaches that God is an energy force within everyone and through techniques of Yoga, transcendental meditation, etc. we can awaken to our divinity and become God. (This is known as self-realization.) However, this may take many reincarnations. Eventually though, everyone evolves into godhood, and thus, saves themselves. (Hebrews 9:27 denies reincarnation.)

Since, according to Fox, we have to shift our quest from a "personal Savior" to a "Cosmic Christ," it naturally follows that we have to move away from a "sin and redemption" theology to a creation spirituality.[10] Perhaps one of the best illustrations of creation spirituality is the example Fox gives from his mentor Meister Eckhart–a late thirteenth century, early fourteenth century German mystic. In an interview with Michael Toms, host of the national public radio show, New Dimensions, Fox stated:

> Meister Echart, who represents so beautifully the creation tradition, says: "When I flowed out of the Creator," meaning when he was born, "all creatures stood up and shouted, and said, 'Behold here is god!' and they were correct." Now that's Creation theology, which says that we're not only not worms and guilty worms!– but that we are divine.[11]

The Creation theology Fox speaks of is exactly that–creation centered. Fox robs Jesus of His unique divinity, and exalts and likens the creation to the Creator. Romans 3:23-25 says, "For all have sinned and fall short of the glory of God, and are justified freely by his grace through the redemption that came by Christ Jesus. God presented him as a sacrifice of atonement through faith in his blood." There is no sacrificial act of atonement on the cross for our sins in Fox's theology. Faith in Christ Jesus is replaced with faith in Self.

Fox denies belief in pantheism (doctrine that teaches God is all, that all created matter is god), but rather, claims he is a panentheist–one who believes God is in everything and everything is in God.[12] However, in his book, *Meditations with Meister Eckhart*, Fox writes: "*Everything that is in God is God.*"[13] Since Fox teaches that "the Cosmic Christ" is the Western term for God being present in all things, including "stars, galaxies, whales, soil, water, trees, humans, thoughts, bodies, images . . . the sacred everything,"[14] isn't he actually advocating everything is God?

Romans 1:22,25 clearly sets God apart from the creation: "Although they claimed to be wise, they became fools, and exchanged the glory of the immortal God for images made to look like mortal man and birds and animals and reptiles. . . . They exchanged the truth of God for a lie, and worshiped and served created things rather than the Creator."

In Isaiah 48:8, God declares He will not give His glory to another or His praise to idols. And, only Jesus Christ is God! (Romans 9:5, Isaiah 9:6, etc.). Yes, we can see God's handiwork in all of creation and should marvel at His power, but that is not where Fox leaves off.

Mother Earth

Several months ago, my sister-in-law and I attended a book review of *The Coming of the Cosmic Christ* given at The Center in Palos Heights, Illinois, by Rev. Virginia Shotwell. (Her husband, also a minister, was at the meeting of the World Council of Churches in Canberra, Australia, at the time. Both are residents of Palos Heights.) Saying we were all Christs, that because we were a part of God, therefore, we were God (which she explained was pantheism) made us squirm in our seats. Then she continued to describe the earth as being part of God's belly, that Mother Earth is a living, breathing organism called Gaia. When Rev. Shotwell said we were going to do a ritual to Gaia, she passed out incense sticks and told us to form a circle and chant, "The earth, the water, the fire, the air, returns, returns, returns." Recognizing this as a ritual of witchcraft, Karen and I decided it was time to leave.

As in the Wiccan tradition (witchcraft), and in Native American spirituality, Fox *reveres* the earth as Mother–(Goddess). He is also openly supporting the feminist revival of goddess religion–as exemplified by hiring Starhawk and promoting the "Spiral Dance."[15] (Starhawk is author of *The Spiral Dance: The Rebirth of the Ancient Religion of the Great Goddess*, Harper and Row, San Francisco, 1979.)

I was, to say the least, dumbfounded after reading an article by Thomas Boogart, associate professor of Old Testament at Western Theological Seminary (Reformed Church of America), Holland, Michigan. In the January, 1991 issue of *Perspectives*, Boogart praised Fox's book, *The Coming of the Cosmic Christ,* and ended his article saying, "*Matthew Fox ends his book with a description of his vision of the second coming of Christ. He describes a great awakening. May it be so, and may his book be a means of awakening for churches in the Reformed tradition!*" (emphasis mine).

All Paths . . .

When Fox speaks of the second coming of Christ and an awakening, he is not referring to a literal return of Jesus Christ to gather up His Church. Rather, it is the awakening to our divinity–to the goddess within, our higher Christ-consciousness. And, through this awakening a union of all religions, or to use Fox's term, a "deep ecumenism."[16] "Universalism is a common characteristic to all the traditions of the Cosmic Christ," says Fox.[17] It would have to be, if you believe, as he does, that "all paths lead to God."[18]

All this is possible, he declared, because "mysticism is, like art, a common language uttering a common experience."[19] All the religions of the world can unite under a common experience perceived through an altered state of consciousness. But they will never unite under the teachings of the apostles and Jesus Christ Himself. Jesus made that plain when he said, "If the world hates you, keep in mind that it hated me first. If you belonged to the world, it would love you as its own. As it is, you do not belong to the world, but I have chosen you out of the world. That is why the world hates you" (John 15:18-19).

Salvation through Jesus Christ is a gift to the whole world as so beautifully written in John 3:16, but that doesn't mean all religions are valid! God created humankind, but not all are God's children. Only those who accept and believe that in Jesus Christ "we have redemption through His blood, the forgiveness of sins," did "he give the right to become children of God" (Ephesians 1:3-13, John 1;12, Romans 8 and 9:8).

Wayne G. Boulton, professor of religion at Hope College (RCA), Holland, Michigan, is also supportive of Matthew Fox. He did note, however, that Fox is silent about a severe judgment on this world.[20] Why shouldn't he be? How can there be a God of wrath and judgment when all paths lead to God?

I don't believe I'll ever forget a quote by H. Richard Niebuhr printed in the Chicago *Suntimes* newspaper: "A God without wrath brought men without sin into a kingdom without judgment through the ministrations of a Christ without a cross" (Lehman, Daniel J., "The Passionate Struggle of Religion for America's Soul," 4-28-91).

As author Ron Rhodes points out, "Fox's Christianity is not just a distortion of biblical faith, it bears no resemblance to it. His Christ is completely foreign to the pages of the New Testament, which is the only authentic source for knowledge of the subject."[21]

Which Christ do you believe in?

[Note: There is an increasing amount of documentation supporting the fact that Fox's teachings have gained momentum in many mainline denominations including: The United Church of Christ, Presbyterian Church USA, American Baptist, and the Reformed Church of America.]

I was deeply concerned after reading Rev. Don Postema's book, *Space for God*, in which he quoted Matthew Fox favorably (not to mention Zen Buddhists, etc.). I couldn't help but wonder if he knows what Fox teaches and has accepted the mystical Cosmic Christ as God, or if he just doesn't realize what Fox is teaching.[22]

Equally disturbing was the fact that Calvin DeWitt's name was listed along with Matthew Fox's under Bear & Company's "honor roll" for those supporting creation spirituality. Bear & Co. is a very prominent New Age publishing firm.[23.]

Are Fox's beliefs, by whatever means, also affecting the Christian Reformed Church of North America? I have been told, in so many words, that we are not to question our leaders. However, in Acts 17:11 the Bereans were commended for examining the Scriptures daily to see if what Paul said was true.

I encourage everyone to search the Scripture, the only word that is Truth.

Notes:

1. Melton, Gordon J., *New Age Almanac*, Visible Ink Press, Detroit, MI, 1991, p. 324.
2. Toms, Michael, *At the Leading Edge*, Larson Pub., Burdett, NY, 1991, p. 37.
3. Fox, Matthew, *The Coming of the Cosmic Christ*, Harper & Row Pub., San Francisco, 1988, p. 79.
4. *Ibid.*, p. 168.
5. *Ibid.*, p. 7.
6. Toms, Michael, *At the Leading Edge*, p. 52.
7. Fox, Matthew, *The Coming of the Cosmic Christ*, p. 137.
8. Martin, Walter, *The New Age Cult*, Bethany House Pub., Minneapolis, MN, 1989, p. 125.
9. Guiley, Rosemary Ellen, *Harper's Encyclopedia of Mystical & Paranormal Experience*, Harper San Francisco, 1991, p. 123.
10. Toms, Michael, *At the Leading Edge*, p. 45.
11. *Ibid.*, p. 36.
12. Fox, Matthew, "Meister Eckhart, Mystic of Deep Ecology," *Mountain Luminary*, Vol. 6: No. 3, Summer 1991, pp. 1,9.
13. Fox, Matthew, *Meditations with Meister Eckhart*, Bear & Co., Santa Fe, NM, 1983, p. 8.
14. Fox, Matthew, *The Coming of the Cosmic Christ*, p. 8.
15. *Ibid.*, p. 218.
16. *Ibid.*, p. 228.
17. *Ibid.*, p. 228.
18. Fox, Matthew, *Meditations with Meister Eckhart*, p. 64.
19. Fox, Matthew, *The Coming of the Cosmic Christ*, p. 230.
20. Boulton, Wayne G., "The Thoroughly Modern Mysticism of Matthew Fox," *The Christian Century*, April 25, 1990.
21. Rhodes, Ron, *The Counterfeit Christ of the New Age Movement*, Baker Book House, Grand Rapids, MI, 1990, p. 223.
22. Postema, Don, (Christian Reformed pastor of Campus Chapel, Ann Arbor, MI) *Space for God*, CRC Pub., Grand Rapids, MI, 1983, p. 18-19.
23. Cumbey, C., *A Planned Deception*, Pointe Pub., Inc., East Detroit, MI, 1985, p. 140. (Calvin DeWitt is co-author of Calvin College Fellows book, *Earthkeeping*.)

In addition to Ron Rhodes book, *Revealing the New Age Jesus* by Douglas Groothuis is also an excellent book which gives an in-depth look at the relationship between Gnosticism and the counterfeit Christ, and exposes the false teachings of Matthew Fox.

Appendix C

JUST WHOSE GOSPEL IS GOING TO RUSSIA?

In the October, 1992 issue of the Mission Courier, *the article "Russians make 'Space for God' in their lives" proudly announced the presentation of the Russian translated version of Rev. Don Postema's book,* Space for God *to former Russian KGB officer General Stolyrow. Stolyrow is "a leader in the Faith & Courage group" in Russia which is dedicated to "improving the moral and spiritual character of the nation's leaders." He gratefully accepted his copy of* Space for God *from Gary Mulder and John De Jager of CRC Publications and is looking forward to the donation of 5,000 more copies to university libraries. Another 5,000 of the books will be sold through both Christian and secular bookstores in Russia.*

While this may seem to be a wonderful God-led event and gesture on the part of CRC publications, it is imperative that we examine the beliefs of some of the authors Rev. Postema quotes in his book to support his message. In doing so, we can receive a glimpse of what "gospel" may emerge from this book, with the distinct possibility of leading many people to a "different gospel" and another Christ (II Cor. 11:4).

In *Space for God*, Rev. Postema writes that he is "indebted to Brother David Steindl-Rast . . ." for some of the ideas in his book (p. 55). Brother David Steindl-Rast, a Camaldolese Benedictine monk, gives workshops at Esalen Institute, a well-known New Age institute which "has been the acknowledged centre of the human potential movement" (Campbell, Eileen, & Brennan, J. H., *The Aquarian Guide to the New Age*, The Aquarian Press, Wellingborough, England, 1990, p. 120). He is also co-author with leading New Age physicist, Fritjov Capra, of the book, *Belonging to the Universe*.

Recently, there was an interview with Steindl-Rast printed in *Creation*

Spirituality magazine of which Matthew Fox is editor. In the interview, Steindl-Rast explains that in "the language of astrology" we are in a transition period of moving away from the age of Pisces into the "age of Aquarius" which "is the New Age." In New Age thought, this basically means that to think of Jesus Christ as the only way to salvation is out-of-date, narrow-minded and intolerant. The New Age is considered to be that time when all humanity will have evolved into a higher level of consciousness (godhood). All religions will become united ushering in an era of peace and guided by a new World Teacher. This, of course, eliminates true Christianity and those well-grounded in Scripture will recognize the world teacher as the Anti-Christ spoken of in Revelation 13 and 14.

Steindl-Rast continues to call himself a Christian and claims that he is expressing the "Good News in the language of a new age. . . ." He further elaborates: ". . . whether I'm teaching about Christian mysticism or Christian-Buddhism dialogue . . . everything I do somehow fits into the New Age Movement" (*Creation Spirituality*, Nov./Dec. 1992, issue, Volume VIII, Number 6, p. 26).

It is quite evident in reading pages 52-55 in *Space for God* that Rev. Postema seeks to combine Buddhism with Christianity as did his teacher, Brother David Steindl-Rast.

Morton Kelsey, "an Episcopal priest," is quoted by Postema to describe who we are in relationship to "the Other." (The Other is another name for "God" in occult literature.) Kelsey is also a Jungian therapist (one who follows the work of occultist and psychologist Carl Jung). Jung, whose works are heavily promoted in New Age literature, was deeply involved in the occult and was often in contact with discarnate entities (demons). One of these entities "was a pagan . . . with a Gnostic coloration" called Philemon (Jung, Carl, *Memories, Dreams, Reflections*, Vintage Books, a division of Random House, Inc., New York, 1961, p. 182).

Jung believed that ultimate truth was found in the "collective unconscious" into which spiritually developed beings could tap. Jung's "spirit guides" influenced his theories of the "collective unconscious" and are even credited by Jung as having forced him to write some of his works (*ibid.,* pp. 190-193).

Quoting Kelsey, Postema writes: "Each of us becomes the artist as we allow ourselves to be open to the reality of the Other and give expression to that encounter either in words or paint or stone or in the fabric of our lives. . . ." (*Space for God*, p. 19). This is supposedly accomplished through meditation. Carl Jung taught that "the modern artist, after all, seeks to create art out of the unconscious" (*Memories, Dreams, Reflections*, p. 195). Through occult techniques of meditation, one can come in contact with demons (New Agers believe they are part of your Higher Self) who will give people the ability to write, draw, do miracles, and whatever else one may wish. This is exactly what Kelsey is propagating in the quote used by Postema.

One has only to look at the literature that comes from the C. Jung Institute in Chicago to know the extent of occultism that is promoted, from witchcraft to vampirism. In view of this fact, it is not surprising that in his book *Transcend*, Kelsey writes that Christ is "the ultimate Shaman" (witchdoctor) (Kelsey, Morton, *Transcend*, 1981, Elements, Inc., Rockport, MA, p. 218). In addition to this blasphemous statement, Kelsey endorses divination, shamanism, and mediumship, as well as other occult practices. Believing these practices to be compatible with Christianity, he calls Edgar Cayce, a well-known medium, "a dedicated Christian" (*ibid.,* p. 31).

In an interview with *Common Boundary* magazine, Kelsey says "you can find most of the new-age practices in the depth of Christianity" (*Common Boundary*, Jan./Feb. issue, p. 19). New-Age practices are from the depths, but they are certainly not found in the depth of Christianity. In reference to finding God, Morton Kelsey states: ". . . I am in no position to look down upon any tradition that offers help, transformation, renewal or hope to human beings" (*ibid.,* p. 20).

Heretical Dominican priest Matthew Fox is spoken of highly in Postema's book. As you may recall from my article, "A Christ Without a Cross," in the September 21, 1991 issue of *Christian Renewal*, Fox promotes witchcraft, shamanism, earth worship and the uniting of all religions into one, which he claims can be done through mystical experience.

In the December, 1992 issue of the *New Age Journal*, Fox speaks of his "Cosmic Christ" as opposed to the historical Jesus of Nazareth as the only Christ: "You see that Christ is in all things, not just in Jesus, but in every being in the universe. Therefore every being has something to reveal about Divinity" (p. 28). In this article, Fox cleverly seduces his interviewer and readers to conclude that traditional, orthodox Christianity is "an enemy to life on this planet" (p. 28).

The *Christian Research Newsletter* relayed the message that the "Dominican Order in Rome decreed Matthew Fox's dismissal due to his New Age teachings" (July/Sept. 1992, Volume 5, Issue 4). The Dominican Order banned Fox; Postema has embraced him.

Rev. Postema repeatedly refers to the works of Thomas Merton throughout his book giving him a wholehearted endorsement. Merton, a Catholic Trappist monk and mystic, was greatly influenced by Eastern mysticism (Zen Buddhism in particular). He authored the books, *Mystics and Zen Masters*, *Zen and the Birds of Appetite*, and *The Way of Chuang Tzu*.

Merton, like Matthew Fox, believed in a mystical, cosmic "Christ." In his book, *New Seeds of Contemplation*, he writes: "You and I and all men were made to find our identity in the One Mystical Christ . . ." (p. 70). ". . . God became not only Jesus Christ but also potentially everyman and woman that ever existed. In Christ, God became not only 'this' man, but also, in a broader and more mystical sense, yet no less truly, 'every man' " (p. 294). "And indeed, if Christ became Man, it is because He wanted to be any man and every man" (p. 296). These false assumptions led to Merton's belief that we can "transform" the world. Is it any wonder that Fox credits Thomas Merton for having told him where to go for his doctorate in spirituality (Toms, Michael, *At the Leading Edge*, Larson Publications, Burdett, New York, 1991, p. 36)? Or that Brother David Steindl-Rast's works have been compared to Thomas Merton's (*New Age Source Book*, 1992, p. 85)?

In the New Age classic, *The Aquarian Conspiracy, Personal and Social Transformation in Our Time*, self-acknowledged New Age author Marilyn Ferguson writes how Thomas Merton responded positively to New Age activist Barbara Marx Hubbard's invitation to "a thousand people around the world . . . to form a 'human front' of those who shared a belief in the possibility of transcendent consciousness" (Ferguson, Marilyn, *The Aquarian Conspiracy*, St. Martin's Press, New York, 1980, p. 57). Ferguson also lists Thomas Merton as among those who were influential in promoting New Age thought (*ibid.*, p. 434).

One page in *Space for God* is a "Love Letter" to God by author Madeleine L'Engle (pg. 146). Unfortunately, L'Engle's "God" is not the same God revealed to us in Scripture, though L'Engle would argue that point. L'Engle denies the substitutionary atonement, the unique divinity of Jesus Christ and the unique authority of the Bible. She prophesies that all humanity, including Satan, will be saved. This was confirmed by Classis Chicago South with the adoption of an Advisory Report on January 16, 1991.

When you read "Word" by L'Engle on page 120 of *Space for God,* where she talks about prayer and silence, keep the following in mind. In her book, *And It Was Good*, L'Engle encourages the use of the Eastern/occult techniques of meditation (p. 135) and explains that her view of reality is compatible with that of author Lawrence le Shan in his book *Alternate Realities* (p. 84). Lawrence le Shan, whose books are appropriately labeled "New Age," also wrote *How to Meditate* and *The Medium, the Mystic and the Physicist: Toward a General Theory of the Paranormal. And It Was Good* is a book about co-creation, one of the basic elements in New Age thought. It comes from the Hindu belief that the world as we see it is just an illusion, Maya, and that through meditation we can become co-creators with "God" enabling one to create his or her own reality.

Madeleine L'Engle, a radical feminist who advocates goddess/earth worship, divination, the occult practice of astral projection, and a myriad of other occult practices and beliefs is lay-pastor/librarian at The Cathedral of St. John the Divine in New York City. St. John the Divine was noted in the *New Age Journal* as the "Miracle on 112th Street." The cathedral houses Shinto and Native American shrines; T'ai Chi rituals and earth masses (earth worship) are performed and it was noted for displaying a female figure of Christ called "Christa" (Sept./Oct. issue, 1986). The Gaia Institute (an institute founded upon New Age scientist James Lovelock's theory that the earth is a living, breathing organism and named after the Greek goddess of the earth) is located inside St. John the Divine (*New Age Journal*, Feb. 1991 issue, pg. 15).

L'Engle is also on the faculty of Omega, a New Age Institute for Holistic Studies. Omega promotes shamanism (witchcraft), astral travel, Tantric Yoga, channeled demons such as Emmanual, astrology, tarot readings, homosexuality, etc. (*Omega*, Summer 1992).

Self-proclaimed New Age authors Louis M. Savary and Patricia Berne have credited L'Engle for giving a name to "kything" in their book, *Kything: The Art of Spiritual Presence* (Paulist Press, New York, 1988). This book is both dedicated to and endorsed by Madeleine L'Engle. "Mental telepathy is the very beginning of learning to kythe" according to L'Engle. (L'Engle, Madeleine, *Wind in the Door*, Dell Publishing, New York, 1973, p. 96). She's right; it is. In *Kything*, communication with the dead, plants, animals, flowers and trees is taught, as well as the New Age concept that though meditation "humanity can raise the level of human consciousness and . . . transform the mental and spiritual climate of the planet" (p. 23).

The occult techniques of meditation–relaxation, deep breathing, chanting, guided imagery and visualization–are the means given to be able to accomplish this. Leading New Age transpersonal psychologist Jean Houston holds workshops all around the country on L'Engle's concept of "kything" (p. 18). How sad it was to be at Wheaton College and hear a student ask L'Engle how to kythe. It was sadder still that, after L'Engle talked of communicating with the dead, most of those who were in attendance that night, including ministers, teachers, students and their parents, saw nothing wrong with what she said.

In her works, L'Engle twists good for evil and evil for good. Occult practices are seen as "a gift" from God. The God of the Bible who warns us of false teachings she claims is Satan or Lucifer. A God who would sacrifice His own Son and punish those who reject Him is a "cartoon," "forensic god" according to her theology. L'Engle claims to be a Christian. She also denies knowing anything about the New Age Movement, which is ludicrous. But what is worse, many of our college professors at Calvin, Trinity, Dordt and Wheaton Colleges, and elementary school teachers are defending, teaching and promoting her works as those of "a wonderful Christian author" to our children.

Madeleine L'Engle, Brother David Steindl-Rast, Morton Kelsey, Matthew Fox and Thomas Merton all combined Eastern mysticism/occultism with Christianity, the two of which, just don't mix. The result: "a different gospel." [I think it is of importance here to mention that Brother David Steindl-Rast is also on the board of directors for the global interfaith association, The Temple of Understanding. The Temple of Understanding is located at The Cathedral of St. John the Divine (where L'Engle works), and is dedicated to the uniting of all religions into one. Thomas Merton is also listed as one of the founders (Notice from St. John the Divine)].

While on the surface *Space for God* sounds "Christian," and though there are some good points made about prayer and justice in the book, Postema leads thousands to the beliefs and practices of Eastern mysticism/occultism along with those people who are working towards bringing in a one-world religion. All this is tucked subtly in-between Scripture, hymns and teachings of John Calvin, as if they were all in agreement. How deadly this is for those not well-grounded in Scripture.

Does he know what is he doing? Unfortunately, I believe he does. In the February 10, 1992, issue of *Christian Renewal*, Elizabeth Langendoen described a missionary retreat with Postema. She wrote: "Postema quoted T. Merton to explain that the spiritual life basically means to keep awake or to pay attention. Buddha was held up as an example; his name means 'I am awake' (or 'the enlightened one'). Buddhism means to be always awake; Zen Buddhism, to watch to live now. Sin is whatever lulls us to sleep or dulls our senses. We were told that we need to pay attention and 'let your senses lead you into prayer.' "

According to Langendoen, Postema later declared that because we are images of God, we therefore, can say "I am who I am!" This title belongs exclusively to God! In so many words, it appears that Rev. Postema was teaching the missionaries that we are all God; we just forgot we were God; we've been sleeping. So let's wake up to our Divinity within and declare who we really are, God! The authors I have mentioned in this article whom Rev. Postema endorses, believe precisely that.

I would encourage those reading this article to write to CRC Publications and World Literature Ministries of the CRC and express your disapproval of further publications and distributions of *Space for God*, in any language—for the good of the church as well as for the good of those in our denomination who are promoting these beliefs.

May God grant all of us the discernment and wisdom needed to "test the spirits" in the coming years.

Appendix D

THE RE-EMERGENCE OF THE GODDESS
(Prayer, Imagination & Feminism)

"The archetype of the Cosmic Christ, like that of the goddess or the Buddha-nature, celebrates the divine image in all things. By exploring this archetype in circle dancing, imaging and discussion, we will reconnect with the wisdom stories of our mystical ancestors and with our own wisdom. We may even find a whole new way to read Western scriptures."

Matthew Fox

Our Mother, which art in heaven, hallowed be thy name . . . might very well be the new beginning of "The Lord's Prayer" in the near future. "The era of the Divine Mother is now coming into full expression. . . ." prophesies Corinne McLaughlin, co-author of the New Age book, *Builders of the Dawn*.[1]

The Divine Mother is the feminine principle, the divine presence or feminine consciousness within everyone and within nature. Our problem today, says McLaughlin, is that *"we are often afraid to lose rational control and trust our intuition* and our softer, nurturing feminine side–women as well as men. We are afraid to drop our illusion of separateness and see our *inner-connectedness*, which is the feminine perspective. The remedy to this alienation is sometimes called the '*reawakening of the Goddess.* . . .' "[2] (emphasis mine). (Note: Losing rational control and trusting our intuition refers to the practice of *occult* meditation. In Zen Buddhism, for example, "Followers of Zen are taught to empty their minds of all intellectual reasoning, thereby opening up their minds to higher levels of perception–known as intuition. . . . According to Zen teaching, real understanding is possible only through intuition and not through any logical thinking process."[3])

254

The December, 1985, issue of the feminist magazine *Ms.* featured an article by Karen Lindsay called "Spiritual Explorers." Lindsay comments: "The feminist spirituality movement began to emerge in the mid-1970's and has become one of the largest submovements within feminism. It's amorphous, blending in a surprisingly smooth amalgam radical feminism, pacifism, witchcraft, Eastern mysticism, goddess worship, animism, psychic healing, and a variety of practices normally associated with 'fortune-telling.' It exists nationwide and takes the form of large, daylong workshops, small meditation groups, and even covens that meet to work spells and do rituals under the full moon."[4] "Emily Geoghegan, a minister in the United Church of Christ and wife of an Episcopal priest, sees no conflict between her ministry and her participation in goddess-invoking ritual," she continued.[5]

In February, 1990, a woman's conference was sponsored by the woman students at Perkins School of Theology (Southern Methodist) in Dallas, Texas. The invitation announcing the conference was entitled–*Wisdomweaving: Women Embodied in Faith*. One of the main speakers was a Native American Spirituality specialist, Sr. Jose Hobday, OSF from Matthew Fox's Institute in Culture and Creation Spirituality. Among the variety of workshops offered were: "Feminine Images in Buddhism–Past & Present," "Women in Transcendence: Lessons from the Ancient Vedas of India," and "Returning to the Goddess Through Dianic Witchcraft." (I should note that the speakers of these classes were not converted to Christianity.) The closing worship service at the end of the conference was–Weaving our Sisterhood!

Radical feminist, lesbian and self-proclaimed witch Linda Finnell led the session, "Returning to the Goddess Through Dianic Witchcraft." The statue of the goddess Diana Diana was set up on a table surrounded by lit candles and other artifacts (tarot cards etc.). Finnell described how witches cast a circle, channel energy, and chant for healing. She then taught the basic techniques of occult meditation. While music played softly in the background, she instructed the participants to close their eyes and relax. After reading several relaxation exercises (deep breathing techniques), Finnell read a story that was to be "*experienced.*" Each person was to picture themselves on an uphill path reaching for a light on the horizon. Upon reaching the horizon, they were to meet and dialogue with their "spirit friend."

In her book, *The Spiral Dance, A Rebirth of the Ancient Religion of the Great Goddess*, practicing witch Miriam Starhawk writes: "Magical training varies greatly from coven to coven, but its purpose is always the same; to open up the starlight consciousness, the other-way-of-knowing that belongs to the right hemisphere and allows us to make contact with the Divine within. The beginner must develop four basic abilities: *Relaxation, Concentration, Visualization, and Projection*"[6] (emphasis mine–CVK). Why? Because, Starhawk points out, "*in trance we find revelation*. We invoke and become the Goddess and God, linked to all that is"[7] (emphasis mine CVK). "In Witchcraft, each of us must reveal our own truth."[8] Warning the reader (as many occultists do) she also explains: "Trance can be dangerous, however, for the same reason it can be valuable—because it opens the gate to the unconscious mind."[9]

Late in the spring of 1991, a women's conference held at Trinity Christian College, Palos Heights, IL, had one session similar to Linda Finnell's. Only this time, the session was not given by a self-proclaimed witch. Nor was it entitled, "Returning to the Goddess Through Dianic Witchcraft." Rather, the session was presented as "Prayer and the Imagination" by Gladys VerHulst, a member of Hope Christian Reformed Church (Oak Forest, IL) and student at McCormick Theological Seminary in Chicago, IL. She has also written articles for *Partnership*, a publication of the Committee for Women in the Christian Reformed Church.

VerHulst introduced her session telling of her experience in spirituality workshops with the Jesuits in Boston where "a lot of imaginative praying" took place. She explained, "imaginative praying . . . turned me on to prayer." Pieces of paper with her "method" for this type of prayer were then handed out. "Is it really okay to expand on the words of Scripture?" she asked. VerHulst answered her own question affirmatively and continued, "Imagination is a gift from God—and imagination is one of the ways in which we can discover truth. Through the imagination, we can hear God speaking."

In order to discover "truth" through the imagination, VerHulst instructed her class to focus and concentrate on their breathing. Playing music softly in the background, she said, "Feel the weight of your body against the chair, or the floor, wherever you're sitting. Be aware of your feet, your legs, your belly, your chest, your neck, your face, relax." (She gave a long pause between each part of the body.) "Now, I'm going to read a story to you and then I'm going to give you about fifteen minutes to enter the story . . . ," she continued. (A Bible story was used and you were suppose to visualize yourself with Jesus.) After some time passed, VerHulst would give a five-minute notice and then let each person write down in a journal what they *experienced*. She admitted to the people there that the methods they were using were dangerous, but assured them that they would know if what they had discovered through the imagination was good or evil by the fruit it bore.

Whether wittingly or unwittingly (hopefully unwittingly), VerHulst had led her class in the basic techniques used in witchcraft and sorcery. You will find these "meditation" techniques also in books dealing with communion with spirits, mediumship (or what is more popularly coined today as channeling), mysticism (as seen in the ancient books of Jewish mysticism, *The Cabala*,), Eastern religions, etc. Unfortunately, many in the church are naively using these techniques in order to have a "mystical experience," thinking they can get to know God better and virtually become one with Him. Others have asked me, "What's wrong with using occult techniques for something good?"! How can we possibly gain something "good" from what God has forbidden? (Deuteronomy 18:9-12, Leviticus 20:6, Revelation 22:14, etc.).

Maria Harris, who holds a doctorate from Union Theological Seminary in New York, writes in her New Age book, *Dance of the Spirit*, ". . . we need to develop community with other women–especially with women of spiritual insight–whom we may not have listened to up to now. Among these are women of our own and other religions whose attitudes toward God are different from our own. . . . Not only will these include women of the great world faiths (in one of my spirituality classes, for example, this means Buddhist, Muslim, Jewish, Protestant, and Catholic women coming together regularly), but those who are creating new religious forms or reinstating forgotten ones, such as *worship of the Goddess*."[10]

Harris guides the reader in steps for self-transformation. Based on "Eastern spirituality," Harris uses deep breathing exercises, mantras (repetitious chanting also used to put one in an altered state of consciousness), concentration (or centering), and visualization. This is also seen as *prayer and the imagination*. God is addressed as "the Unnameable, Father, Mother, Goddess, . . . the Other."[11] Harris believes in order "to pray to the Divinity," we need two companion disciplines, "*Breathing and Centering*." She then points to a Hindu teacher who told his students to concentrate on their breathing because the air they breathed in and out was God. Following these instructions, the Hindu's students "discovered a wisdom that held firm for a lifetime: Prayer is not a difficult, secret activity available only to chosen initiates–it is as simple as breathing."[12]

It is interesting to note that in Gnosticism (the very thing the apostles Paul and John fought to keep out of the church), the knowledge or "gnosis" (the development of intuition) is known as Wisdom or *Sophia, the World Mother*.[13] In many Gnostic systems, the Trinity consisted of God the Father, God the Mother, and God the Son. The Goddess is seen in many different aspects in other ancient cults and religions. The Babylonians had Astarte and Ishtar; the Egyptians, Isis and Hathor; Shakti and Vach by the Hindus; Tara, by the Buddhists; Diana and Venus by the Romans; Gaia, Demeter, and Sophia by the Greeks, etc.

In the past few years, the goddess of Wisdom, Sophia, has made a tremendous comeback infiltrating mainline denominations. United Methodist ministers Susan Cady and Hal Taussig teamed up with Catholic writer Marian Ronan and wrote the book, *Wisdom Feast, Sophia, in Study and Celebration*. Replacing the name of Jesus in the beloved hymn, "Fairest Lord Jesus," they wrote: "Fairest Sophia, Ruler of all nature, O Thou in whom earth and heav'n are one. . . ."[14]

The Christian Century printed a review of *Wisdom Feast*: "The authors claim that anywhere the Wisdom tradition surfaces in Scripture . . . Sophia's role may be clearly seen. Indeed, they hope that thorough study of this role will introduce the concept of goddess worship to Christian communities in a biblically grounded, and thus non-threatening, way. They assert that by studying Scripture from the perspective of contemporary feminine spirituality, which emphasizes '*experiencing*, expressing and effecting the radical *connectedness of all creation*, and the radical equality of all human beings,' one will discover that in the biblical tradition Sophia plays second only to Jesus and God. Furthermore, they argue, one can infer from a series of specific New Testament texts that Jesus is Sophia . . . *Sophia is a warm, nurturing, powerful force* . . ."[15] (emphasis mine–CVK).

Caitlin Matthews, author of the 1991 published book, *Sophia, Goddess of Wisdom*, writes: "Speaking from within Christianity, Susan Cady boldly asserts, 'We must find a way to mainstream the goddess into the universe within which women are actually living their lives. . . .' Many feminists have already made an exodus from such ground into actual Goddess spirituality, as we shall see."[16] Matthews is an ordained Priestess of the Fellowship of Isis, a world-wide confederation of Goddess Spirituality.

Unfortunately, in reading the May 17, 1991 issue of the *Calvin Seminary Kerux*, it appears that feminists in the Christian Reformed Church have embraced "goddess spirituality" perhaps without recognizing it for what it is. Karen Gritter, a student at Calvin Theological Seminary (Grand Rapids, Mich.), wrote an article about prayer and the imagination entitled: "Reflections on Spirituality." It didn't surprise me to find books by Thomas Merton as suggested reading. A firm believer in Sophia, Merton writes: "In Sophia, the highest wisdom-principle, all the greatness and majesty of the unknown that is in God and all that is rich and maternal in His creation are united inseparably, as paternal and maternal principles, the uncreated Father and created Mother-Wisdom."[17] And, where you find Sophia, you will inevitably find the idea that we have to go into our unconscious minds in order to know "God."[18]

Like Matthew Fox, Merton believes in a mystical Cosmic Christ (see: "A Christ Without a Cross," 9-23-91, *Christian Renewal*) believing that we, like Jesus, can all evolve into godhood. Merton states: "For in becoming man, God became not only Jesus Christ but also potentially every man and woman that ever existed. In Christ, God became not only 'this' man, but in a broader and more mystical sense, yet no less truly, 'every man.' "[19]

Gritter also suggested *Inviting the Mystic, Supporting the Prophet*, by Carroll and Dyckman for "an introduction to spiritual direction." Carroll and Dyckmen used Matthew Fox's work, *On Becoming a Musical Mystical Bear*, as a basis for their "own presuppositions about spirituality."[20] Using an example from George Lucas's Star War series, they portray "God" as the "Force."[21] Lucas is a firm believer in Hinduism.

In his work, *Creation Spirituality*, Matthew Fox insists that he "cannot listen to language about God as mind of the universe and the mystical experience of an 'all embracing universe' without thinking of the mystical and cosmological tradition of Sophia or Wisdom. . . . She lies at the heart of the creative process, a *co-creator* of the ongoing process of the universe. It is Sophia who teaches holy ways of living in the universe; she is the matrix for all three persons of the Trinity for she is present as Creator, as Prophet, and as Spirit making all things new. . . . The resurrection of the feminine, known both as the 'Assumption;' and the '*return of the Goddess,*' can and will happen for our salvation, our wholeness"[22] (emphasis mine–CVK). (Fox makes many references to the Cosmic Christ as Cosmic Wisdom or Sophia giving examples from Gnostic texts in this book.)

Fox believes, "Trust in self, of imagination, of others, and of all creation–here lies the basic meaning of faith in the Gospels and in our own time."[23] What happens when we try to discover truth through the imagination? In a brochure from McCormick Theological Seminary, pastor Susan Andrews, who found herself "dialoguing with Matthew Fox, . . . a variety of feminist theologians, . . . Native American spiritualists . . ." declares: "We are not called to make everybody see Jesus. Rather, we are called to see Jesus in everybody. We are called to recognize the image of God in every Buddhist and Muslim and atheist and secular humanist we meet and to discover the truth of God which they have to offer. And then we are called to invite them to view the world through our unique Presbyterian lens–not because our truth is the whole Truth–but because our truth added to their truth may lead us closer to the wholeness we all seek."[24]

Many are finding a "whole new way to read Western scriptures" through the "reawakening of the Goddess." And, in the process, have lost the Truth and turned to "doctrines of demons, "myths," and "those who prophesy out of their own imagination" (1 Timothy 1:4, 2 Timothy 4:4, Ezekiel 13:2). Paul cautions: "Timothy, guard what has been entrusted to your care. Turn away from godless chatter and the opposing ideas of what is falsely called knowledge, which some have professed and in so doing have wandered from the faith" (1 Timothy 6:20).

In Jeremiah 27 we see that Babylon had its mediums, sorcerers and diviners. Also in Jeremiah 7 and 44 we find "the Queen of Heaven," the title for the Babylonian god Ishtar. In Revelation we again see Babylon: "Fallen! Fallen is Babylon the Great! She has become a home for demons and a haunt for every evil spirit. . . . For all the nations have drunk the maddening wine of her adulteries" (Rev. 18:2).

In much of the feminist literature I've read, there is almost always a fierce rebellion shown against the "patriarchal" God of the Bible. In Jeremiah, God's wrath towards the "Queen of Heaven" is unfathomable. Caitlin Matthews asserts: "The Goddess has restored to women their innate pride in themselves. . . . Nothing is going to delay the Goddess's second coming, whether in the guise of Sophia or under any other form."[25] Has Babylon, Satan's mistress, reawakened?

> For the sin of rebellion is like the sin of divination, and arrogance, the evil of idolatry.
>
> 1 Samuel 15:23

For your information:

The Quest magazine, in which Corinne McLaughlin's article appeared, is a publication of The Theosophical Society. This society is based on a highly developed system of occultism derived from mystery religions and Hindu philosophy. An article in this magazine was used by Rev. Jim Kok to expound on his ideas about prayer. His article on prayer, entitled "Making Your Garden Grow," appeared in *The Banner*, 2-18-91. Because of my research, I knew that *The Quest* was an occult magazine and obtained a copy. Inside the front cover it read: "Ancient Wisdom for a New Age." Books such as "*The Encyclopedia of Witches and Witchcraft, The Goddess Reawakening, The Tarot, Shamanism, The Wholeness Principle, The Kabbala* (Cabala), are encouraged reading. Being concerned, I wrote *The Banner*. However, they would not print my response.

In viewing a video from Calvin College, featuring Professor Ralph Honderd on Wellness Motivation, I was bewildered as to why he would recommend Herbert Benson's book, *Beyond the Relaxation Response*. Benson is from Transcendental Meditation and is well known in New Age circles. His book promotes the use of occult techniques for meditation–deep breathing exercises, chanting, visualization, etc. God is seen as an energy force (as taught in Hinduism, witchcraft, etc.).

Also, Dale Cooper, Chaplain of Calvin College, in his video "A Time to be Silent: Christian Meditation," suggests that we can breathe God in and out implying God is an energy force. For, how can we breathe a personal loving Father in and out?

Notes:

1. McLaughlin, Corinne, "The Mystery of the Veiled Mother of the World," *The Quest*, Summer 1990, pg. 56.
2. *Ibid.*
3. King, Francis X, *Mind & Magic* (London, England: Dorling Kindersley Ltd., 1991), pg. 204.
4. Lindsey, Karen, "Spiritual Explore," *Ms.,* Dec. 1985, pg. 38.
5. *Ibid.,* pg. 42.
6. Starhawk, Miriam, *The Spiral Dance, The Rebirth of the Ancient Religion of the Great Goddess* (San Francisco: Harper & Row), 1979, pg. 48.
7. *Ibid.,* pg. 144.
8. *Ibid.,* pg. 9.
9. *Ibid.,* pg. 144.
10. Harris, Maria, *The Dance of the Spirit* (New York: Bantam Books, 1989), pg. 42.
11. *Ibid.,* pg. 118.
12. *Ibid.,* pg. 119.

13. Neff, Mary K., "God the Mother," *The Theosophical Digest*," March 1990, pg. 10 (and other sources).

14. Cady, Susan & Taussig, Hal & Ronan, Marian. *Wisdom Feast, Sophia: Sophia in Study and Celebration* (San Francisco: Harper & Row, 1986), pg. 185.

15. Ferm, Deane William, reviewing *Wisdom Feast* in *The Christian Century*, October 14, 1987.

16. Matthews, Caitlin, *Sophia, Goddess of Wisdom* (Hammersmith, London: Grafton Books, 1991), pg. 330-331.

17. Merton, Thomas, *New Seeds of Contemplation* (Norfolk, CT: New Directions, 1961), pg. 141.

18. *Ibid.,* pg. 138.

19. *Ibid.,* pg. 294-295.

20. Carroll & Dyckmen, *Inviting the Mystic, Supporting the Prophet* (New York: Paulist Press, 1981), 15.

21. *Ibid.,* pg. 19.

22. Fox, Matthew, *Creation Spirituality* (San Francisco: Harper & Row, 1991), pg. 64.

23. *Ibid.,* pg. 100

24. Andrews, Susan, "Agony, Passion, and Hope: The Future of the Presbyterian Church, A Pastor's Perspective," *McCormick Perspectives* April, 1991.

25. Matthews, Caitlin, *Sophia, Goddess of Wisdom* (Hammersmith, London: Grafton Books, 1991), pg. 332.

Appendix E

An Open Letter
From: Neal Punt
To: Jack Reiffer and Cliff Christians
Re: Protest from the Hessel Park Council
May 28, 1991

Dear Jack and Cliff,

I think enough of both of you to take the time to tell you why I think the
the protest you carried with you to classis was ill-advised. The protest appears to lack an appreciation for the history and the real concern of the appeal.

The appellants felt that the theology that permeates all of Madeleine
L'Engle's books (a claim made by L'Engle) is in conflict with the standards
for books to be placed in the Orland Church Library. The difficulty could be
attributable to L'Engle's theology, to the current standards for books to be
placed in Orland Park's library, or to the appellant's misunderstanding of
what L'Engle says in her books.

The elders, relying almost <u>exclusively</u> on secondary sources, repeatedly
told the appellants they were misreading L'Engle. With each rejection of
their concern the appellants dug more deeply into the <u>original</u> works of
L'Engle. The materials submitted to classis show that the appellants pleaded
with the elders to look at L'Engle's books instead of relying on what others
were saying about her books.

The elders steadfastly maintained that L'Engle's books met the criteria
for books to be placed in their church library. Finally the appellants concluded that EITHER: the elders did not know what L'Engle was teaching in
her books; or, the elders, in violation of their oath of office, were willfully
defending as Christian certain basic, essential teachings and practices that
were unbiblical and contrary to the confessional standards of the Christian
Reformed Church.

When this matter first came to the attention of the classical committee
neither the elders nor the appellants were willing to try to work out their

differences with the help of the church visitors. Due to the elders' misunderstanding of the purpose of an appeal we (the classical committee) were able to "force" both parties to try to work out their differences with the help of the church visitors. This is the means by which this matter should, and I believe could, have been resolved.

When, for whatever reason, the matter was not resolved with the help of the church visitors the appellants had the right to present their appeal to the January 1991 meeting of classis.

In the light of the above history I do not think the grounds in Hessel Park's protest are valid. Consider:

> Ground 1. The classis acted inappropriately in making any judgment about the orthodoxy of the writings of Madeleine L'Engle. The teaching and preaching ministries of the churches certainly need to analyze of a host of influences in the lives of the people of God; but it is not appropriate for the assemblies to do this work, except when there are charges regarding those who have signed our form of subscription.
>
> The double request at the end of the appellants' material was as follows (page 10): ". . . we are asking Classis to declare the writings of L'Engle to be heresy. . . . we are also asking Classis to suggest that her books be removed from the OPCRC library." The first request was out of order. The second was the only question of merit before the classis.

How easy and totally inconsiderate and unjust it would have been for classis to simply rule the first request out of order. Knowing both of you as I do, I think that ordinarily you would be among the last to treat persons, who have what they consider to be a real concern, in such a legalistic way. However just their cause might be, it is practically impossible for non-clergy persons to submit an appeal in such good order that the "experts" in classis could not find some pretext for declaring their appeal out of order if they were minded to avoid the matter at issue. We may not so treat members of the church no matter how conveniently classis could have legally done so.

Therefore the advisory committee, at the very beginning of their report, set forth what they considered to be "the central issue." If any council member in the entire classis, the appellants, or the elders of Orland Park thought that the advisory committee misunderstood "the central issue" of the appeal they had time to prepare their objections and argue against adopting the report at the January 1991 meeting of classis.

The advisory committee concluded, and the appellants agreed, that "the central issue" of the appeal "is whether or not L'Engle's books ought to be classified as those of a Christian writer." The elders, in complete contradiction to their protestation, namely, "Judging L'Engle as to whether she is 'Christian' or not is abhorrent to the reformed Christian"–had continuously attempted to demonstrate that L'Engle is "a Christian author." They did so in their written response to the appeal as well as in their many communications to the appellants.

The supporting documents, provided by the elders and distributed with the agenda, demonstrate that for more than a year the elders had defended L'Engle's unorthodox teachings as basically "Christian." L'Engle's supposed essential orthodoxy was the elders' basis for keeping her books in the church library. It was the elders' intentional and continuing defense of what the appellants considered to be L'Engle's false doctrine that, from day one, was the essence of their complaint against the elders.

It very seldom happens that a classis is called upon to make a judgment about the orthodoxy of the writings of an author who has not signed the Form of Subscription. It was completely "appropriate for" classis "to do this work" in this particular instance for one reason and only one reason. The elders contended throughout the entire time of disagreement that L'Engle's theology was basically consistent with the essential tenets of the Christian faith. Because the elders used this evaluation as the basis for keeping L'Engle's books in the church library, classis was compelled to judge whether this basis was valid or not.

The evidence presented to classis indicates that an affirmative answer to the question "Is the book true to Biblical teachings and the doctrinal position of our church?" is among the criteria for every book that is placed in the Orland Park Church library. Having this criteria and then placing L'Engle's books in the library is to say that these books are "true to Biblical teachings and the doctrinal position of our church.' Because this conclusion cannot be reasonably denied, it was drawn by the appellants, concurred in by the advisory committee and accepted by the vast majority of the delegates at classis.

The appellants had provided the elders with specific references demonstrating that L'Engle's books in basic, essential doctrines are not "true to biblical teachings and the doctrinal position of our church." With this evidence before them for more than one year, the elders of Orland Park were either unwilling or unable to show that the appellants were misreading L'Engle. The advisory committee concluded that the appellants were not misreading L'Engle. Even though the appellants complaint was published in the agenda no council or individual delegate of classis presented any evidence to demonstrate that the appellants were misreading L'Engle.

No author should even hope to be more fairly and justly treated than to have those making judgment about what he or she has written by citing the author's published works, referencing specific passages viewed in the light of the extended context, without relying on so much as one secondary source to draw their conclusion. Classis had every right and the sacred duty to make these judgments from published works of L'Engle because the elders continued to claim that the appellants were misreading L'Engle. Classis was obligated to, and clearly did, adjudicate precisely this limited aspect of the tension between the elders and the appellants.

Hessel Park's protest goes on to say that the removal or non-removal of the books from the library was "the only question of merit before the classis." The removal or non removal of the books does not speak to the substance of the disagreement between the elders and the appellants. This is seen first of all in that the appeal asks that "Classis . . . suggest that her books be removed." If this had been the essence of their appeal the appellants would have asked classis to do much more than make a suggestion. According to the appeal itself the proposal, asking classis to make this suggestion, was mentioned only because many people are being deceived by L'Engle. This was only one of many possible ways in which the <u>effects of the basic problem</u> could have been in some measure ameliorated.

Furthermore, the paragraph immediately preceding the one from which Hessel Park quoted the "two requests" explicitly states, "Taking her books out of the library <u>will not solve the problem</u> if they [the elders] still consider her writings to be Christian" (emphasis added). Clearly, the problem, according to the printed appeal, was that the elders considered "her writings to be Christian." The advisory committee correctly surmised that this was the heart of the issue. How utterly cruel it would have been for classis to jump on this proposed "suggestion," a proposal made offhandedly by the appellants, and thereby avoid the heart of the problem that the appellants in good faith had placed before classis.

> Ground 2. The only substantive matter in the entire appeal that was properly before classis was the question whether or not Orland Park was in violation of its own rules for the church library. That this was the issue was suggested also by the opening sentence of the original appeal: "We are appealing to Classis Chicago South a decision given by the elders to retain books written by author Madeleine L'Engle in our church library." This should have been the focus of the advisory comittee's work and of the discussions of classis.

> Instead, the attempts by Orland Park to explain, both in writing and on the floor, how they did indeed justify retaining the books, were ignored by classis. A wide range of books is evidently allowable under their understanding of their existing guidelines.

I doubt that any delegate to classis would dispute anything stated in the first paragraph of this second ground. But the point is precisely this–if Orland Park was "not in violation of its own rules for the church library," then the elders were in fact telling the members of the Orland Park Church that

L'Engle's books placed in their church library are "true to Biblical teachings and the doctrinal position of our church."

On the basis of the evidence provided by the appellants, confirmed by the advisory committee, and researched by myself and I am certain by other delegates also, the vast majority of delegates found that to say the books in question are "true to Biblical teachings and the doctrinal position or our church" is patently untenable.

Neither at the January meeting of Classis nor in the protest has the Council of Hessel Park demonstrated that classis ignored Orland Park's attempt to "justify retaining the books." The protest simply makes this bare, unsubstantiated charge. I doubt that you can find in the elders' "writing," or that you heard at the meeting of classis, any attempt to justify retaining these books, other than the attempt to say that these books meet the exceedingly restrictive criteria for the placement of books in the Orland Park library. This attempt certainly was "the focus of the advisory committee's work and of the discussions of classis."

Perhaps the gist of the second ground in Hessel Park's protest is that the elders have the exclusive right to determine what books are allowable under their existing rules. If it is understood that the elders may interpret their own rules in any way they see fit, without seriously considering what the rules actually say, then there is no point whatever in having such rules.

> Ground 3. Classis failed in its primary calling to help resolve the differences existing between the appellants and their consistory. Instead of taking the ordinary vote, to sustain or not to sustain the appeal, classis adopted the findings of its advisory committee as a form of advice to the consistory and the appellants. The parties are left to decide for themselves what this means for their various positions; this is a dangerous and indecisive way for classis to try to help.

An advisory committee was appointed to give guidance to classis "to help resolve the differences existing between the appellants and their consistory." This guidance did not have to be limited to advising a classis to sustain or to not sustain the appeal together with the grounds for such an action. Classis' "primary calling" is to address the substance of the matter at issue when an appeal is presented to it.

Precedent for this is found in the January 1985 Minutes of our classis. The Lethbridge CRC Council (actually it was Jelle Tuininga) appealed the decision of the Evergreen Park Council to not sustain the five charges levelled against me. The advisory comittee of that classis reviewed the matter. They worded the refutation of each of the five charges differently than the B.P. Council had, thereby reflecting what the advisory committee considered to be the substance of the issue. That advisory committee never suggested and classis never expressly said "we sustain the appeal" or "we do not sustain the appeal." Most appeals are too complex to simply say one party is completely right and the other is wrong.

Although it was never expressly so stated, the substance of what classis said in 1985 indicated that Lethbridge's appeal was not sustained. Lethbridge appealed the decision of classis, not the decision of the Evergreen Park, to Synod. Classis, not Evergreen Park, had to and did defend its decision before Synod.

Because classis had clarified the issue by adjudicating the substance of the matter, Synod 1985 had an easier decision to make. It could and did decide to "not sustain the appeal" of Lethbridge against the decision of classis.

Although Classis January 1991 did not expressly so state, the substance of what classis said indicated that the appeal was sustained. By addressing the substance of the appeal, rather than by dismissing it on the basis of some technicality, classis provided very significant help to "resolve the differences existing between the appellants and their consistory," without presumptuously telling the elders what they must do or not do.

There were many ways in which the tensions at Orland Park could have been avoided when the complaints regarding L'Engle's books were first registered. The books could have been removed. The criteria for placing books in the library could have been changed. A special section in the library could have been designated indicating that the books in this section do not meet the published criteria for books to be placed in the church library.

Any of these and many other constructive possibilities will be available to resolve the tensions that still exist if everyone involved would graciously, openly, forthrightly, and genuinely accept the declaration that was "decisively" made by classis, namely, that the books in question "do not conform to the policies established [currently in force] for books to be placed in the Orland Park CRC Library."

With the advisory committee report's clear understanding of the cause of the differences that existed between the appellants and the elders, and with the classis' decisive yet very wisely strictly limited declaration about the current situation, people of good will have a good foundation on which to rebuild the unity that belongs to the church. But if people intentionally disregard the work that classis has struggled to accomplish, what possibility is there for resolving the tensions peacefully?

Hessel Park's protest has the potential of doing a great deal of harm by encouraging the elders of Orland Park and other persons to disregard what classis has made clear. To me the protest is like handsful of dust intentionally thrown in air so that, as a result of it, every one must say "Nothing is clear."

The protest does nothing but throw dust in the air because no one can interpret the significance of it. Does it mean that Hessel Park does not agree that L'Engle denies the essential biblical doctrines singled out by classis? Is it Hessel Park's contention that the appellants, the advisory committee and delegates to classis have misread L'Engle? (If so, where is the proof for that?) Does Hessel Park protest or object to classis action because they feel classis violated some procedural matter? Or, worst of all possibilities, does the protest mean that the Hessel Park Council believes that even though these books deny the basic doctrines singled out by classis, neverthless such books are "true to Biblical teachings and the doctrinal position of our church?"

For these reasons I find the registering of a protest by Hessel Park ill-advised. Even though it is permissible, it strikes me as being somewhat discourteous to submit a protest to an assembly knowing that there can be no response to it or questioning of its validity by that assembly. I fail to see how the protest, as it stands, can contribute to the healing process that must take place.

How much better, if their conscience forbids Hessel Park to accept classis' clarification of the issue and decision, to appeal classis' action to synod! That certainly is their prerogative and would lessen the possibility of some very serious and continuing misunderstandings.

Cordially,

Neal Punt

Background Information - From among other "essential biblical truths" Classis Chicago South (1/16/91) singled out these, formally declaring that L'Engle denies:

1) that the atonement was a sacrificial payment for sin
2) that Jesus is uniquely divine
3) that anyone (including Satan) will be finally lost
4) that the Bible is essentially different from any other piece of literature

Classis noted that L'Engle claims she is building her theology in all the stories she writes.

PS–I present this as an "open letter" since it deals with public matters. I do so, so that I can feel free to send it to others. If either of you care to respond to this letter, I will, in fairness to you, provide you a list of those to whom I have sent a copy.

FORM OF SUBSCRIPTION

We, the undersigned, Professors of the Christian Reformed Church, Ministers of the Gospel, Elders and Deacons of the Christian Reformed congregation of .... of the Classis of .... do hereby, sincerely and in good conscience before the Lord, declare by this our subscription that we heartily believe and are persuaded that all the articles and points of doctrine contained in the Confession and Catechism of the Reformed Churches, together with the explanation of some points of the aforesaid doctrine made by the National Synod of Dordrecht; 1618-'19, do fully agree with the Word of God.

We promise therefore diligently to teach and faithfully to defend the aforesaid doctrine, without either directly or indirectly contradicting the same by our public preaching or writing.

We declare, moreover, that we not only reject all errors that militate against this doctrine and particularly those which were condemned by the above mentioned Synod, but that we are disposed to refute and contradict these and to exert ourselves in keeping the Church free from such errors. And if hereafter any difficulties or different sentiments respecting the aforesaid doctrines should arise in our minds we promise that we will neither publicly nor privately propose, teach, or defend the same, either by preaching or writing, until we have first revealed such sentiments to the Consistory, Classis, or Synod, that the same may there be examined, being ready always cheerfully to submit to the judgment of the Consistory, Classis, or Synod, under the penalty, in case of refusal, of being by that very fact suspended from our office.

And further, if at any time the Consistory, Classis, or Synod, upon sufficient grounds of suspicion and to preserve the uniformity and purity of doctrine, may deem it proper to require of us a further explanation of our sentiments respecting any particular article of the Confession of Faith, the Catechism, or the explanation of the National Synod, we do hereby promise to be always willing and ready to comply with such requisition, under the penalty above mentioned, reserving for ourselves, however, the right of appeal in case we should believe ourselves aggrieved by the sentence of the Consistory or the Classis; and until a decision is made upon such an appeal, we will acquiesce in the determination and judgment already passed.

Appendix F

ACCREDITATION STATUS

Regent College is accredited by the Association of Theological Schools in the USA and Canada.

As noted above, the College is also affiliated with the University of British Columbia. In effect, this means that the College meets the criteria for affiliation established by the Senate of the University of British Columbia, but does not imply any scrutiny or approval of the course offerings of the amliate by the University Senate. Nor does affiliation imply automatic transfer of course credit between the two institutions. University criteria for affiliation with theological colleges are documented in the *1992-93 Calendar* of the University of British Columbia, p.45.

THEOLOGICAL POSITION

We accept wholeheartedly the revelation of God given in the Scriptures of the Old and New Testaments and confess the faith therein set forth and summarized in such historic statements of the Christian church as the Apostles' Creed and the Nicene Creed. We here explicitly assert doctrines that are regarded as crucial to the understanding and proclamation of the gospel and to practical Christian living.

1. The sovereignty and grace of God the Father, Son and Holy Spirit in creation, providence, revelation, redemption and final judgment.
2. The divine inspiration of Holy Scripture and its consequent entire trustworthiness and supreme authority in all matters of faith and conduct.
3. The universal sinfulness and guilt of human nature since the fall, bringing everyone under God's wrath and condemnation.
4. The substitutionary sacrifice of the incarnate Son of God as the sole ground of redemption from the guilt, penalty and power of sin.
5. The justification of the sinner by the grace of God through faith alone in Christ crucified and risen from the dead.

6. The illuminating, regenerating, indwelling and sanctifying work of God the Holy Spirit in the believer.
7. The unity and common priesthood of all true believers, who together form the one universal Church, the Body of which Christ is the Head.
8. The expectation of the personal, visible return of the Lord Jesus Christ.

The above points constitute the theological statement of the World Evangelical Fellowship, modified for inclusive language in #3.

Appendix G

THE BATTLE TO DESTROY TRUTH

Donald Hettinga, Professor of English at Calvin College, Grand Rapids, Michigan, has recently authored the book, Presenting Madeleine L'Engle *(Twayne Pub., New York, 1993). He acknowledges Calvin College for giving him a sabbatical leave and Calvin College Alumni for its "generous financial support" to complete his work.*

Hettinga correctly observes that L'Engle has "antagonized Christian audiences more than non-Christian audiences." That "throughout her career, she has been under almost continual challenge from Christians. . ." (p. 16). There is good reason for this. L'Engle vehemently denies and rejects every essential Biblical teaching traditional orthodox Christianity has held to and instead, provides her own "gospel." She consistently mocks the beliefs of those Christians whom, as Hettinga so willingly points out, she terms as "the extreme Evangelical right."

At the January 16, 1991 session of Classis Chicago South, Classis adopted an Advisory Report which declared that Madeleine L'Engle denies the substitutionary atonement, the unique divinity of Jesus Christ, the unique authority of the Bible in all matters of faith and practice, and that some will be eternally separated from God. Classis also advised that it would be part of wisdom for the Christian community to ferret out the allegations of occultism.

In spite of Classis' declaration, of which Hettinga was well aware, his work is an unsubstantiated, but vigorous defense of L'Engle's Christianity. He portrays myself and others who are critical of L'Engle's writings, "those who perceive the heresy of her beliefs," as being incredibly naive and narrow-minded. Hettinga takes pride in making those "Christian critics" look like they actually delight in the "celebration of her disbelief" (pp. 16-17). This defense for L'Engle is tragic for Hettinga, Calvin College, the Christian community at large and for L'Engle herself.

To those who do not have sufficient knowledge of New Age (Eastern/occultic mysticism) concepts, their ramifications and how they conflict with Scripture, his book might seem an accomplished effort to discredit those who have exposed L'Engle's writings and her personal ties to the New Age Movement. However, it is the critical information he purposefully does not address, that is needed in order to fully understand the implications of what L'Engle is teaching.

Some of the deep concerns over L'Engle's works are cited by Hettinga, but quickly glossed over without any refutation. For example, he writes: "And there have been those who label her as a New Age spiritualist with an emphasis on the Bible as story and her belief that God can be perceived in all parts of creation" (p. 16). Listed in his notes to document this statement was the title of Rev. John F. De Vries' article "How the New Age Infiltrates" (*The Outlook*, November, 1990).

Rev. De Vries, a Christian Reformed pastor, is well acquainted with Eastern religions due to his personal experiences and work in India. He has co-authored the excellent book, *Satan's "Evangelistic Strategy" For This New Age*. De Vries' article contained many quotes from L'Engle's non-fiction works which clearly showed how her beliefs coincide with New Age thought. He traced these beliefs back to the four lies Satan used to deceive Eve.

Instead of refuting De Vries' article, Hettinga lets his statement stand as authoritative, leaving the reader to assume De Vries' assessment to be ridiculous. After all, the Bible does contain stories, and God's handiwork can be seen in all creation. At least, one might think this is what L'Engle is espousing from the little bit of information given. He neglects to quote the many passages in which L'Engle claims that the Bible is myth (containing an iconic truth);[1] nor does he point out her acceptance of the New Age theory that "all of creation is God's body."[2] The reason for this is not because he hasn't read the books in which these statements are found.

Hettinga also refers to an article in *The Banner*, sarcastically entitled, "Church Critics Battle L'Engle Heresy" (January 21, 1991, p. 21). This article was the result of an interview between myself and *Banner* reporter Ruth Moblard De Young. [I feel it is important to note that the documentation I showed De Young and stated was absolutely necessary to include in the article to show why many Christians were speaking out against L'Engle's works, was left out. In its place, false statements and misleading information were given, leaving the distinct impression that we were just book-burning censors. *The Banner* refused to print all the corrections necessary to amend their error, after I asked them to do so.]

Complaining about my allegation of L'Engle's use of occult practices, Hettinga writes; "there have been those who have indicted her inclusion of what *they* classify as 'occult practices': 'telepathy' and the use of runes, scrying, astral travel, psychic healing, and the use of a medium with a crystal ball (p. 16, emphasis added). But what he fails to inform his trusting readers, is that *occultists* identify these practices to be *occult* practices as well.

It is truly amazing that Hettinga does not recognize that these are occult practices. For whatever reason, he chooses to ignore facts, and thereby misleads his readers. You can find these practices in almost any book of witchcraft, magic, or study of the occult. *The Concise Lexicon of the Occult* authored by practicing witch Gerina Dunwich (Carol Publishing Group, New York, 1990) contains all the practices cited above.

Even in *Webster's Dictionary*, scrying is defined as "Divination" and is so used throughout L'Engle's book, *Swiftly Tilting Planet*. In the second chapter of his book, Hettinga reviews *Swiftly Tilting Planet* and talks about scrying. However, he never mentions the fact that it is divination and that this psychic ability is viewed by L'Engle as a gift from God that should be accepted as something good. Hettinga does not seem to be bothered by the fact that God condemns divination in all its forms (Deuteronomy 18:9-12).

Interestingly, Hettinga critiques only L'Engle's "fiction." He not only acknowledges the use of scrying, but also of telepathy, astral travel (which is called "tessering" or time travel), runes, kything (according to L'Engle, mental telepathy and a whole lot more–it includes communication with the dead), Native American healing–which is known as shamanism (witchcraft/ psychic healing), etc. Unfortunately, he says nothing negative about these practices. He gives them credence and acceptance.

It is one thing for a Christian author to include these practices in their writing with the intent of exposing their error. It is quite another thing for a "Christian author" to portray them as gifts of God and good, as long as you don't use them for evil purposes, as L'Engle does in both her non-fiction and fiction.

This is what is considered by occultists to be the difference between white and black magic. They believe that there are latent powers within us that can be tapped into. When used for good, these powers are called White Magic. When used for evil purposes, it is Black Magic. However, whether used for evil or good, God calls occult practices and beliefs "detestable practices" (NIV, Deut. 18:9-12). He makes no distinction. It is "white magic" L'Engle is promoting.

A well-known leading authority on New Age and other religions, J. Gordon Melton, explains that "psychic powers" come from universal energy, an energy that supports and permeates all of existence. This energy is given many names, some of which are "prana, mana . . . holy spirit, the chi, mind, and the healing force" (*New Age Almanac*, Visible Ink Press, Detroit, MI, 1991, p. 304).

In her book, *Walking on Water: Reflections on Faith and Art* (non-fiction, Harold Shaw Pub., Wheaton, IL, 1980), L'Engle writes: "In so-called 'primitive' societies there are two words for power, mana and taboo: the power which creates, and the power that destroys; . . . Odd that we have retained in our vocabulary the word for dangerous power, taboo, and have lost mana" (p. 82). She warns that this power can be dangerous for those who use it wrongly, as many occultists do. It is this power or force that, according to L'Engle, enables us to do anything Jesus did in his lifetime (p. 86). How does one achieve these powers? Through the Eastern/occult techniques of meditation (altering one's state of consciousness in order to contact this "higher power") (p. 194).

Many people think of occultism as strictly being Satanism or black magic, not realizing that occult simply means hidden or having to do with secret philosophies.

The New Encyclopaedia Britannica (1989 edition, Vol. 25, p. 75) maintains that "those aspects of occultism that appear to be common to all human societies," are "divination, magic, witchcraft, and alchemy." Included under the heading of occultism are the books of Jewish mysticism–the Kabbala, and Theosophy, "a blend of Western occultism and Eastern mysticism" [Hinduism, etc.] which "proved to be a most effective propagator of occultism. . . ." Both Kabbalism and Theosophy contain those aspects of occultism first described. It is interesting that Gnosticism (opposed by John and Paul in the New Testament), was kept alive through these and other esoteric orders.

Many Christians are unaware that certain aspects of all the above mentioned categories of the occult are intertwined. And, at their core, they teach the same thing–that all humans have the power (or divine source) within themselves to attain perfection. (Note: This includes Satanism.) But most importantly, Christians need to understand that those involved in Theosophy, Kabbalism and other esoteric orders not only call themselves occultists, but also consider themselves Christian and their religion to be just a different strain of Christianity.

In esoteric schools of thought, the universal or cosmic energy force J. Gordon Melton described, is referred to as "the Cosmic Christ." This force or "Christ" is what supposedly guides the evolution of man into godhood. (For reference see Martin, Walter, *The New Age Cult*, Bethany House Publishers, Minneapolis, MN, 1989, p. 125.) It is this redefining of Christianity, lack of understanding (at first) of what is all taught in these systems, along with a rejection of the infallibility and total authority of Scripture, that is causing many to fall into believing a whole different gospel–a gospel that is the ultimate enemy of Jesus Christ; a gospel that is silently but surely creeping into the Christian Reformed Church, as well as mainline denominations.

The Christian Research Institute has described the New Age Movement as "The most common name used to portray the growing penetration of Eastern and occultic mysticism into Western culture" (*The New Age Cult*, p. 18). J. Gordon Melton acknowledges that "Evangelical Christians correctly perceive the New Age Movement as the continuation of older occult movements such as spiritualism and theosophy . . ." (*New Age Almanac*, p. 313).

L'Engle endorses all of the above mentioned categories of the occult, as we shall see in this and next issue. It is through both her adult non-fiction works and children's "fantasy" novels that she has preserved the "ancient wisdom" or "secret doctrine" condemned by God Himself. As L'Engle herself admits: "If I wanted to write a statement of what I believe, I'd go off and get ordained. I'm a storyteller. I think my talent is for story. As a story teller, my first job is to tell a story. The theology is underneath if you want to find it. You can say more in story than you can in a sermon" (*The Door*, December, 1986, p. 25).

Teachers and others have tried to discount the accusations of New Age/occultism against L'Engle by saying it's just fantasy or fiction. However, these practices are the norm to occultists and very real. Like Hettinga, they do not show how both her fiction and non-fiction promote occultism. It's time we did so.

In chapter four of his book, ironically entitled "For Heaven's Sake," Hettinga describes what happens in L'Engle's fiction novel, *An Acceptable Time* (Farrar, Straus, Giroux, New York, 1989). Because he again hits me personally in this chapter, I think it only appropriate to use it to respond to his faulty accusation. This is what Hettinga claims:

> *L'Engle articulates a Christian doctrine of sacrificial love though, characteristically, she does so by ranging outside of Christian orthodoxy for the elements of her fiction. Though this strategy may not endear her to those Christian critics who in their suspicions of time travel, druids, and other fantastic elements accuse her of perpetuating some kind of New Age heresy, it does keep the novel from being a didactic tract* (p. 105).

As proof for what he has stated, he cites in his notes, "For an example of this type of accusation, see Claris Van Kuiken, "Sojourning Into Darkness," *Christian Renewal*, 23 March , 1992, 8." (This is rather strange since in my article all I mentioned was what Classis Chicago South had declared and adopted at its January 16, 1991 meeting.) Well, let's see how L'Engle promotes occultism in both her fiction and non-fiction alike.

An Acceptable Time is perhaps one of the most vivid as to its occultic nature with its emphasis on druid worship, communication with the dead, the use of runes, ogam (ogham) stones, astral projection, psychic healing, goddess worship, and more. It is also one of the most deceptive for those unaware of God's condemnation of the occult.

With a twist, L'Engle has a bishop, of all people, proclaiming that druids were "a lot less esoteric and occult than modern medicine" (p. 130). (Druids, were the priests of the Celts who used divination, believed in many different gods, committed human sacrifice, etc.) Again, this book portrays the idea that as long as used for good, occult practices are acceptable (hence the title??). The bishop concludes that "We've lost many gifts that were once available" (p. 55). These "gifts" which are presented as coming from God, are communication with the dead, divination, psychic healing, astral travel, and other occult practices.

The bishop, whose last name is ironically, Colubra, ("Latin for snake" p. 15) calls Samhein, "a holy time," which is when "the gates of time swing open most easily . . ." (p. 67). It is known as the time when the veil between the living and those who have died is the thinnest and communication with the deceased is supposed to be easiest.

According to *The Concise Lexicon of the Occult,* Samhein is: "One of the four Grand Sabbats, also known as Halloween, and celebrated on October 31st. Samhein is the most important of all the Witches' Sabbats. It is the ancient Celtic/Druid New Year, and also the time when spirits of deceased loved ones and friends are honored. At one time in history, many believed that it was the night when the dead returned to walk among the living. *The divinatory arts of scrying and runecasting are Samhain traditions among many Wiccans*" (p. 158, emphasis added).

It is during the time of Samhein that the bishop and another main character, Polly, communicate with druids who lived 3,000 years ago. The druids, Karralys and Anaral, have special healing powers (psychic powers) and Anaral has the ability to read Ogam stones. (Ogham is "Rune-casting; an ancient Celtic system of divination based on the casting and reading of line patterns or characters carved into or painted on small stones, beans pieces of wood or bones," *The Concise Lexicon of the Occult,* p. 128.) Despite this, Hettinga proclaims in his book, that "Karralys, Anaral, Polly, the bishop, Dr. Louise, and the Murrys *all acknowledge God whether they call him Christ or the Presence,* and all behave unselfishly, sacrificially" (p. 108, emphasis mine). But just what is the Presence?

A conversation between Polly and the druid girl Anaral gives us a subtle glimpse:

> *"This goddess," Polly mused, "and the Mother. Are they one and the same?*
>
> Anaral punched down the risen dough. "To me, and to Karralys, yes. To those who are not druids–Tav, for instance–the goddess is the moon, and the Mother is the earth. For some, it is easier to think of separate gods and goddesses in the wind, in the oaks, in the water. But for me, it is all *One Presence,* with many aspects, even as you and I have many aspects, but we are one" (*An Acceptable Time,* p. 235, emphasis mine).

It is important to note that Anaral and Polly find a silver circlet head-piece with a crescent moon in the middle and place it on their heads. This is extremely significant since this is a prominent piece to be worn in witchcraft by the Queen or High Priestess. It represents the Goddess whom witches worship (as told and shown in *The Complete Book of Witchcraft* by Raymond Buckland, Llewellyn Pub., St. Paul, MN, 1990, pp. 34-35).

On the back cover of *The Truth About Witchcraft Today* it is stated that "The practice of Wiccan magic is not evil, it is not supernatural. It is the creation of positive personal and global change through the natural energies found in each of us and in the Earth. It is a religion based on harmony with Nature Forces and all aspects of the Divinity." Now, please reread Polly and Anaral's conversation.

In witchcraft, it is believed that mystical (magical) powers come from an ultimate energy source or force (as I have already explained). This energy force has two sides, male and female. Scott Cunningham explains that "The Goddess is the female force, that portion of the ultimate energy source which created the universe." Wiccans associate the Goddess with the moon. "Some call the Goddess Diana in Her lunar aspect." The Goddess, he continues "is also associated with the Earth. The entire planet is a manifestation of God-dess energy. . . . Wiccans may revere Her in this aspect as Gaea, Demeter, Astarte, Kore, and by many other names." Most Wiccans "know the God-dess in three aspects . . . the Maiden, the Mother, and the Crone." "The triple aspects also relate to the phases of the Moon. The Maiden corresponds to the New and waxing Moon, the Mother to the Full, and the Crone (also called Hag or Wise Grandmother) to the waning Moon" (*The Truth About Witch-craft Today*, pp. 72-73).

Cunningham also tells us that Wiccans believe the Goddess is "every-where . . . in the Earth, the Moon, and within themselves" (pg. 73). In Witch-craft, the God is the male force of "the primal divine energy . . . represented by the Sun" (pg. 75). Many Wiccans devote themselves entirely to the goddess, while others devote themselves equally to both.

In her non-fiction book, *A Stone for a Pillow*, L'Engle explains that the "crescent moon was a symbol of worship of the goddess, Ishtar or Ashtaroth, and other female deities, like Diana, whose symbol was the moon. . . . In countries where the crops followed the phases of the moon, where earth was mother, the worship of the moon goddess was natural. . . ." Criticizing Prot-estantism for overemphasizing the "masculine, patriarchal God who some-times seems to have more of the attributes of Zeus with his bolts of lightning . . ." she claims we need not be afraid of the symbol of the moon and that we need to "regain the feminine, intuitive, the nurturing element in ourselves, and our understanding of the Godhead . . ." (Harold Shaw Pub., Wheaton, IL, 1986, pp. 182-182).

What is the Presence? It is the energy force that occultists believe to be within all of us, and which is also known as the Cosmic Christ as I have previously stated. Hettinga's statement that Karralys, Anaral, Polly, etc. all acknowledge God whether they call him Christ or the Presence means *all paths lead to Divinity*. (Note: The Presence is referred to often in occult literature.) At the risk of being labeled a "witch-hunter," which I have already been accused of by some in my own church and denomination and which Hettinga himself implies on pg. 44 of his book, I claim L'Engle does promote witchcraft, as well as Kabbalism, Theosophy and Gnosticism, as we'll see later.

In *An Acceptable Time*, Polly also muses that "one name for the goddess was Sophia, Wisdom. A divine mother who looks out for creation with intelligence and purpose" (p. 226).

L'Engle endorses the occult science of alchemy in her newest non-fiction work, *The Rock That Is Higher* (Shaw Pub., 1993). Alchemy had three aims: "an attempt to turn base metals into gold with the aid of the Philosopher's Stone, to search for an elixir that could prolong life indefinitely; and to acquire methods of creating life artificially."[3] However, it was also *"symbolically, a mystical art for the transformation of consciousness."* And, "as a mystical art, it draws on various spiritual traditions, including the *Hermetica, Gnosticism, Islam, the Kabbalah, Taoism, and yoga*"[4] (emphasis mine). She writes:

> My [L'Engle's] bishop told me that when the wise men gave their gifts to the Christ child, they were giving him their magic; they were magic; magicians; alchemists; and they gave up their power to the one they recognized as Lord. At the same time that I heard this, I was reading a novel in which alchemy played an important part, and which postulated that for the true alchemist what was far more important than turning base metal into gold was reconciling male and female, what was called "the chymical wedding" (p. 28).

In the New Age book, *Sophia, Goddess of Wisdom*, author Caitlin Matthews, "an ordained Priestess of the Fellowship of Isis, a worldwide confederation of Goddess spirituality" explains the occult concept of "The Chemical Wedding" and then describes alchemy as "an art which seeks to realize the eternal perfection which constitutes creation: the Mistress who redeems creation is Sophia" (Mandela, a division of HarperCollins, Hammersmith, London, 1991, pp. 254-255).

Throughout a *Rock That Is Higher*, L'Engle teaches the New Age/occult theory that we are all both female and male or what is known as androgyne. This is seen in witchcraft and also in the Chinese concept of the yin-yang—the union of opposites—male and female, good and evil, light and dark—all is one. So "God" is both male and female, good and evil. Therefore, Satan is just the other side of God. L'Engle further claims that Jesus "is also the true princess, and the true princess is within each one of us, too" (p. 240) And who is the princess? L'Engle tells us that "In the Book of Wisdom in the Apocrypha, hagia Sophia" is "the true princess . . ." (p. 248).

In India, alchemy is a union of male (the god Shiva) and female (the god Parvati) principles; the result is "an enlightened being."[5] This is supposedly obtained by such techniques as yoga. It's not surprising then that L'Engle promotes "mind-expansion" and "altered states of consciousness" in *A Rock That Is Higher* (p. 234), as well as the Eastern/occult techniques of meditation in many of her other non-fiction works such as *And It Was Good* (p. 135), and *Walking on Water: Reflections of Faith and Art* (p. 194).

L'Engle admires and promotes the works of psychologist/occultist Carl Jung. *Harper's Encyclopedia of Mystical and Paranormal Experience* states: "Carl G. Jung's interest in alchemy grew out of his intense interest in Gnosticism, and his desire, as early as 1912 to find a link between it and the processes of the collective unconscious that would pave the way for the re-entry of the Gnostics' sophia (wisdom) into modern culture. He found such a link in alchemy, which he saw as analogous to individuation, the process of becoming whole." According to Jung, alchemy was "a spiritual process of redemption" where the light of the Godhood and nature became one (p. 7).

Jung believed that in its highest mystical sense, "alchemy represents the transformation of consciousness to love, personified by the hermaphrodite, the union of male-female opposites who are joined into a whole" (*ibid.,* p. 7). (In Gnosticism, the Holy Spirit is considered female.) In simpler terms, man saves himself and becomes "God." Carl Jung, whose works are heavily promoted in New Age literature, acknowledges that he was forced to write some of his works by and through discarnate entities (demons) (Jung, *Memories, Dreams, Reflections* , Vintage Books, division of Random House, Inc., NY, 1961, pp. 190-193).

Caitlin Matthews credits the work of Carl Jung in *Sophia, Goddess of Wisdom*, as "One of the major factors which have paved the way for the New Age." And, that "Jung's comprehensive gnosis stretched from Classical mythology through to Gnosticism and Alchemy" (pp. 320-321). She recognizes that "The face of the Goddess is being restored to us in many forms, not least that of Sophia, Goddess of Wisdom, who has preserved and sustained the Goddess' ancient love for the creation. She is not just the planet earth or Nature, though some see her so; she also is the Lady of our physical, creative and spiritual life" (p. 336).

Matthews confidently says: "Those born in this century are now prospective citizens of the New Age, an era where spiritual orthodoxy will be replaced by spiritual adventure, where a greater responsibility for personal behavior and environmental awareness will be paramount. It is an era where the Divine Feminine will lead the way and where women will rediscover and enter their power" (p. 320).

Her prediction seems to be coming true at an incredibly fast rate and Madeleine L'Engle is one of its major sources. This fact is documented more thoroughly in *Trojan Horse, How the New Age Movement Infiltrates the Church* by Samantha Smith and Brenda Scott and to which I contributed research and some of my own composition (Huntington House Pub., Lafayette, LA, 1993).

Now, here is a point to ponder: In *A Rock That Is Higher* , L'Engle claims: "For people who have to have an enemy, the new enemy is the New Age (whatever that is; I'm still not sure). The books I've read which are against the New Age tell me more about the people who are against it than about the New Age itself. From what little I have found out about it, it strikes me as being a twentieth-century form of Gnosticism, with a touch of Mary Baker Eddy, and I am not particularly interested. I was sent one book by a New Age guru and tried to read it; I didn't find anything terrifying in it; I simply found it so dull that I couldn't finish it" (p. 182).

In this same book, L'Engle quotes a friend of hers as saying: "Madeleine . . . I don't think your enemies are the New Agers, I think they're the Anti-New Agers" (p. 184). With her usual undocumented and unsubstantiated strategy of making those who have spoken against New Age look ridiculous, L'Engle lets her readers believe that those who are speaking out against the New Age are the ones who are against Christ! She devotes almost a whole chapter to it. Unfortunately, many will fall for this deception. In reality, it shows L'Engle's position quite well.

One of the best summed up comparisons of Christianity to New Age thought I've read was written by J. Gordon Melton:

> The Evangelical Christian perspective centers around a personal God who has offered salvation to sinful humans through the life, death, and resurrection of Jesus Christ, a real man who was also the unique incarnation of God. The revelation of God in Christ as recorded in the Bible is believed by Evangelical Christians to be the very word of God in written form.
>
> In contrast, the New Age perspective is generally centered around an impersonal divine energy or principle which undergirds all that exists, from which everything, including human being, has been derived, and in which everything participates. It is this affirmation of the ultimate as a divine pattern and force (instead of a personal deity) which gives rise to the belief that each person is god or, more precisely, each person is essentially divine. The New Age ideology precludes a belief in a personal savior such as Christians believe Jesus to be. Many New Agers do believe certain people, of whom Jesus was one example, more fully reveal the divine reality in which everyone participates. In other words, New

Age theology denies the unique divinity of Jesus, *an essential
building block of traditional Christianity* (emphasis mine, *New
Age Almanac*, p. 313).

In my next article, I will be examining Professor Hettinga's defense of
L'Engle against the "accusation" of universalism, "a belief that every person
will be saved, regardless of his or her belief in Jesus Christ." And, how
L'Engle redefines Christian terminology, promotes Kabbalism and Theosophy and rejects essential Biblical doctrines, including the unique divinity of
Jesus Christ–an essential block of Christianity, without which Christianity
crumbles.

Notes:

1. For an example of this, see L'Engle, *A Stone For A Pillow*, Harold Shaw Publishers, Wheaton, IL. 1986, pp. 80-82.
2. L'Engle, Madeleine, *And It Was Good* , Harold Shaw Publishers, Wheaton, IL.
   1983, p. 82.
3. Drury, Nevill, *Dictionary of Mysticism* , Prism Press, Dorset, Rev. ed., distributed in the USA by Avery Publishing Group, Inc., Garden City Park, NY, 1992,
   p. 9.
4. Guiley, Rosemary Ellen, *Harper's Encyclopedia of Mystical and Paranormal
   Experience* , Harper & Row Publishers, San Francisco, p. 5.
5. *Ibid.,* p. 7.

Appendix H

THE BATTLE TO DESTROY TRUTH, PART II

To L'Engle's eyes the story of much of theology has been one of reductive miscomprehension; ever since God appeared to humanity, he has been misunderstood. . . .
Donald Hettinga, *Presenting Madeleine L'Engle*, p. 19

No matter how many eons it takes, he will not rest until all of creation, including Satan, is reconciled to him, until there is no creature who cannot return his look of love with a joyful response of love.
Madeleine L'Engle, *The Irrational Season*, p. 97

In his book, *Presenting Madeleine L'Engle*, Calvin College Professor, Don Hettinga asserts that "the doctrinal issue that most frequently raises the ire of Christian critics is that of her alleged universalism." "Again and again," he sympathetically sighs, "the question arises after her lectures or in the middle of interviews" (p. 17).

L'Engle's response to these questions, he states, is "that she isn't a universalist, that she is, instead, 'a particular incarnationalist,' who 'can understand God only through one specific particular, the incarnation of Jesus of Nazareth' " (p. 17). Hettinga does add that this response is not exactly clear since some of her comments do seem to be saying she is a universalist and others seem to say she is not. He provides a few of L'Engle's more subtle examples of these contradictory statements from her non-fiction works, *A Stone For A Pillow* and *Walking on Water: Reflections on Faith and Art* and concludes that the confusion is due to her "emphasis on the loving nature of God." He then writes:

> For God to fail, for him to damn part of creation, would mean that Satan and not Christ had the victory over death. The Day of

Judgment will not be a forensic judgment, a judgment of criminals: "The judgment of God is the judgment of love, not of power plays or vindication or hate" (*Stone*, 117). Because the whole Creation groans, the whole Creation will be redeemed, "not just the small portion of the population who have been given the grace to know and accept Christ. All the strayed and stolen sheep. All the lost little ones" (*Stone*, 117). (Hettinga is quoting *A Stone For A Pillow* on page 18 of his book.)

Instead of acknowledging the multitude of Bible passages that make it very clear that not all persons will be saved, Hettinga continues to defend L'Engle's view: "If L'Engle's theology is confusing here, perhaps it is so also because of her unwillingness to limit God in any way. Language, imagination, science, and theology all are inadequate to capture the essence of God. . . . To L'Engle's eyes the story of much of theology has been one of reductive miscomprehension; ever since God appeared to humanity, he has been misunderstood and limited by those to whom he has appeared . . ." (p. 18).

Did Jesus' disciples misunderstand what Jesus taught them? Is the Bible correct when it says: "God is just: He will pay back trouble to those who trouble you and give relief to you who are troubled, and to us as well. This will happen when the Lord Jesus is revealed from heaven in blazing fire with his powerful angels. He will punish those who do not know God and do not obey the gospel of our Lord Jesus. They will be punished with everlasting destruction and shut out from the presence of the Lord and from the majesty of his power . . . ?" (2 Thessalonians 1:6-10). What then are we to do with Romans 1 and 2 which speak of the wrath of God and His righteous and just judgment, or chapters two and three of 2 Peter?

What about L'Engle's belief that all will be reconciled to God again, including Satan, a statement that Hettinga did not see fit to include in his defense of her? What does he do with Romans 16:20, "The God of peace will soon crush Satan under your feet," or Matthew 25:41,46 and Revelation 14:9-11? Sadly, he does nothing. Hettinga finishes his circular, unwavering and unBiblical defense of L'Engle with this flippant answer: "Thus, for L'Engle, the writing of stories is ultimately an exercise of faith, but that exercise inevitably produces friction with some readers because, as she notes, 'every new question is going to disturb someone's universe' " (pp. 18-19).

It is time to cut through all this rhetoric and closely examine what L'Engle is teaching in *A Stone For A Pillow* and other non-fiction works. We need to see how she rejects and redefines the substitutionary atonement and the last judgment and leads her readers to accept another Jesus and a "different gospel" (2 Corinthians 11:6).

In *A Stone For A Pillow*, Madeleine L'Engle begins her ridicule of the substitutionary atonement with a personal story of how, while serving on jury duty, she read the book *Revelation and Truth* by Nicholas Berdyaev, a Russian theologian. (Note: L'Engle had the title backwards; it's *Truth and Revelation*.) Berdyaev's book told her that "one of the gravest problems in the *Western* world today is that we have taken a forensic view of God" (p. 11, emphasis added). Explaining that forensic has to do with crime, L'Engle conveys the message that we in the Western world have fallen into a "gloomy and unscriptural misapprehension" about God. We have viewed God too much like an angry judge sentencing a criminal; a God "who assumes that we are guilty unless we can placate divine ire and establish our innocence" (p. 12).

She continues to tell her readers about her participation in a teenage talk show where a panel of high school students was asked to describe what God looked like. She was "horrified to hear them describe a "furious old Zeus-figure with a lightning bolt in his hand. A forensic god." L'Engle asks her readers if this "angry god, out to zotz us" could have "cared enough about us to come to us as Jesus of Nazareth, as a human, vulnerable baby." Next, she questions the Biblical truth of God's amazing love as found in 1 John 4:10: "This is love; not that we loved God, but that he loved us and sent his Son as an atoning sacrifice for our sins." L'Engle asks: "Did Jesus have to come and get crucified, because only if he died in agony could this bad-tempered father forgive his other children?" (p. 12).

Well, L'Engle says she "got into a good discussion, then. The teen-agers did not really like their cartoon god. They were ready and willing to hear another point of view." So L'Engle gladly gave them her view. She "talked about astrophysics and particle physics and the interdependence of all the Creation" (p. 12).

Within the first few pages of her book, L'Engle has prepared the reader to accept an altogether different concept of the atonement by questioning the wrath of God. Then, ten pages further into her book, she slices out the heart of the gospel: the substitutionary atonement, the purpose and work of our Lord Jesus Christ. Listen carefully:

> In a vain attempt to make people see God as an avenging judge, theologians have even altered the meaning of words. Atonement, for instance. A bad word, if taken forensically. A young friend said to me during Holy Week, "I cannot cope with the atone-ment." Neither can I, if the atonement is thought of forensically. In forensic terms, the atonement means that Jesus had to die for us in order to atone for all our awful sins, so that God could forgive us. In forensic terms, it means that God cannot forgive us unless Jesus is crucified and by this sacrifice atones for all our wrongdoing. But that is not what the word means! I went to an etymological dictionary and looked it up. It means exactly what

it says, at-one-ment. I double-checked it in a second dictionary. There is nothing about crime and punishment in the makeup of that word. It simply means to be at one with God (*A Stone for a Pillow*, p. 22-23).

Some of you may have been taught that because of the substitutionary atonement, sinners can once again be at-one with God. This meant that reconciliation with God was possible "by grace . . . through faith" in the blood of Jesus Christ (Ephesians 2:8, Romans 3:25). That He willingly laid down His life of His "own accord" and was "sacrificed once to take away the sins of many people" making "atonement for the sins of the people" (John 10:17-18, Hebrews 9:28, 2:17). This concept of being at-one with God does not reject the substitutionary atonement, so the at-one-ment L'Engle speaks of has to have a different meaning. It helps to know what L'Engle was reading while serving on jury duty.

In *Truth and Revelation*, Berdyaev promotes the concept of transcendental man, the "Adam Kadmon of the Kabbalah." He states that "Truth is revealed in various ways in accordance with degrees of consciousness" and that the "supra-consciousness corresponds to transcendental man" (Geoffrey Bles Ltd., London, W.C., 1953, pp. 17, 27). In the Kabbala (the occult books of Jewish mysticism), the aim of humankind is to realize union with the Divine.

Symbolizing this union is a diagram called the Tree of Life which depicts ten different levels or spheres of spiritual reality in man and the cosmos. These ten stages are called Sephirot (emanations of God). The Tree of Life is sometimes shown superimposed on the body of Adam Kadmon, who is "the Archetypal Man" and metaphorically "the body of God" (Drury, Nevill, *Dictionary of Mysticism*, Rev. ed., Avery Publishing Group Inc., Garden City Park, New York, 1992, p. 3).

In the Kabbala, we find the New Age concept of adrogyne (also taught in witchcraft and Eastern religions as shown in the first part of this article). Adam Kadmon is both male and female. The right side of the Tree of Life is female; the left is male. Adrogyne is a recurring theme in *A Stone For A Pillow* and many of L'Engle's other works. The purpose of the Tree of Life is to show "the descent of the divine into the material world, and the path by which people can ascend to the divine while still in the flesh." It is through contemplation and meditation (techniques similar to Eastern yoga disciplines), that the Kabbalist ascends the Tree of Life to attain "enlightenment" or godhood (Guiley, Rosemary Ellen, *Harper's Encyclopedia of Mystical & Paranormal Experience*, pp. 307-308).

What was L'Engle reading? Berdyaev's belief that "salvation can be understood as the attainment of a perfection like divine perfection, as a movement upwards towards completeness. . . . It is simply that in man the divine principle is revealed" (*Truth & Revelation*, p. 122).

Holding in disdain the Biblical teachings of The Last Judgment, Berdyaev asks if Christianity could "abandon the expectation of the Last Judgment" (*Truth & Revelation*, p. 126). At least, the "forensic" view of it. What is needed, he pleads, is a deeper, hidden meaning of the Last Judgment as the mystics perceived it. For "belief in hell is disbelief. It is to have greater faith in the devil than in God" (*ibid.,* p. 130). L'Engle concurs with Berdyaev's belief about hell in *A Stone For A Pillow* and concludes that the last judgment is not a "forensic judgment," but rather, "God's judgment is atonement, at-one-ment, making us one with the Lord of love" (pp. 60, 62).

L'Engle has just redefined the Last Judgment and the Atonement to mean basically the same thing, a final at-one-ment with God. Therefore, all humanity will eventually be oned with God. All will be "redeemed." Similarly, New Age guress Shirley Maclaine describes the atonement in her book, *Out on a Limb* as, "At-one-ment with the original creator or with the original creation" (Bantam Books, New York, p. 107).

You will also find this identical redefining of the atonement in the works of Alice Bailey (June 16, 1880-Dec. 15, 1949), who was a member of the occult Theosophical Society. She wrote, through her spirit guide (demon) whom she called Djwhal Khul, or "the Tibetan," a set of twenty books which were published by The Lucis Trust (formerly known as Lucifer Publishing). Among these are: *Discipleship in the New Age, Letters on Occult Meditation, Treatise on White Magic, The Reappearance of the Christ,* and *Education in the New Age.*

The first "spirit guided" or "channeled" book was *Initiation; Human and Solar.* In this work, two pages are dedicated to the redefining of the atonement. The discarnate entity teaches through Bailey: "The whole evolution of the human spirit is a progressive at-one-ment. In the at-one-ment between the Ego and the personality lies hid the mystery of the Christian doctrine of the Atonement. . . . As evolution proceeds progressive at-one-ments occur. . . . The whole process is therefore for the purpose of making man consciously one..with his higher Self . . . with his Spirit or 'Father in Heaven' " (Lucis Trust, New York, 1951, pp. 18-19). It is important to note that in this book the Trinity is redefined as "The Father: Will or Power, The Son, Love-Wisdom, the Christ principle, and The Holy Spirit: Active Intelligence." This is called "the constitution of man" (p. xv, emphasis added). Therefore, man is part of the Trinity. Man is God.

What is also revealing is to compare L'Engle's gospel next to *A Course in Miracles*, a "New Age Bible" supposedly dictated by Jesus Himself to Helen Schucman, a Columbia University professor. It's not mere coincidence that *A Course* mirrors L'Engle's assumption, "ever since God appeared to humankind he has been misunderstood," and her redefinitions of the atonement and last judgment.

This counterfeit "Jesus" claims that "The Apostles often misunderstood" the crucifixion and "out of their own fear they spoke of the 'wrath of God' as His retaliatory weapon" (Foundation For Inner Peace, Tiburon, CA, 1975, Vol. 1, p. 87). Contrary to the Scriptural teaching that we are "saved from God's wrath through him" (Romans 5:9), this "Jesus" says, "I was not 'punished' because you were bad. . . . God does not believe in retribution." The Last Judgment is, therefore, "a final healing rather than a meting out of punishment" (*ibid.,* 32, 30).

A Course also redefines the resurrection as a "reawakening," or "rebirth," a shift in perception or change of mind about who we are and the meaning of the world (p. 65, *A Manual for Teachers*). In her non-fiction book, *The Summer of the Great Grandmother*, L'Engle shares this view of the resurrection: "Gregory and Macrina never doubted the Resurrection, but they thought of it neither as a vague continuing in unending time, much as we are in mortal life, nor as an awakening of the dead body from the grave, old bones and flesh reassembling themselves to make the same flawed body that died. Rather, they thought of it as a radical change of all that we have come to think of as ourselves" (Harper & Row, San Francisco, 1974, p. 123).

Leading New Age authority J. Gordon Melton describes God as: "The mystical consciousness or awareness frequently called by such names as higher consciousness, self-realization, Christ consciousness, or New Age awareness" (*New Age Almanac*, Visible Ink Press, Detroit, MI, 1991, p. 304). In New Age thought, Jesus of Nazareth realized his full potential (divinity) and resurrected his Christ-hood Self or "Christ consciousness," as we all can do. L'Engle writes: "So let there be no question; I believe in the *resurrection of Jesus of Nazareth as Jesus the Christ,* and the resurrection of the body of all creatures great and small, not the literal resurrection of this tired body, this broken self, but the body as it was meant to be, the fragmented self made new; so that at the *end of time all Creation will be One* (*The Irrational Season*, Harper & Row, San Francisco, 1977, pp. 108-109, emphasis mine).

A Course of Miracles teaches: "Forgiveness, salvation, Atonement, true perception, *all are one.*" The Last Judgment, the Atonement and the Resurrection mean a final, universal healing to "wholeness" or "rightmindedness" to the "reality" that we are all Christs. For, "The name of Jesus is the name of one who was a man but saw the face of Christ in all his brothers and remembered God. So he became identified with Christ, a man no longer, but *at one with God.* "Is he the Christ? Oh yes, along with you!" (*A Manual For Teachers*, pp. 82-83, emphasis mine).

L'Engle feels it is "challenging and freeing" to believe that "we are not called to be Christians, we are called to be Christs" (*And It Was Good*, p. 51) Are we all Christs? Is this what L'Engle is actually saying? And is this what Calvin College, via Professor Hettinga, is defending and promoting? Let's continue dissecting *A Stone For a Pillow*.

Moving along through *A Stone For A Pillow,* one begins to feel increasingly uncomfortable in making judgments of any kind as to who has "the truth." L'Engle asks: "Are we looking for evidence that our Christian group is the group, with the truth, or are we looking for at-one-ment?" (p. 67). She can't "understand why the idea of emptying hell upsets some people so. To be upset about it is to think forensically . . ."(p. 178-179). There's that word *forensic* again–a word that L'Engle continuously uses to make one feel guilty for believing that "heaven" is "for Christians only" (p. 166).

Insultingly, L'Engle says she laughed when she read from a supposed Christian best-seller in which the author identified people who worship Satan and had included Teilhard de Chardin. (Of course, she doesn't give the name of the book or quote the author. It is most likely that the wording L'Engle used is quite different than that of the author.) Fiercely defending the works of Teilhard de Chardin, L'Engle turns the accusation around: "When someone accuses Teilhard de Chardin of being a Satanist, then whoever is making the accusation does not see the real Satan-worshipper who worships destruction and hate, and works for the annihilation of Christian love" (pp. 74-75).

French Jesuit priest and mystic Pierre Teilhard de Chardin is considered by both New Age and Christian authors alike to be a "father of the New Age Movement." According to *Harper's Encyclopedia of Mystical & Paranormal Experience*, his "religiously oriented concepts of cosmic evolution are influential in New Age thought." It also explains that: "One of Teilhard's greatest contributions to religious thought was 'his emphasis on the cosmic Christ, a shift from the dominant redemption orientation of Christianity to a creation orientation' " (Guiley, Rosemary Ellen, Harper San Francisco, 1991, pp. 604-605).

Blending science (Darwin's theory of evolution) and religion, he "identified the cosmic Christ as a dimension of the evolving universe" and believed that this psychic energy (cosmic Christ) could produce the transcendent, "ultrahuman." Out of this came his theory that "humankind is psychically connected to all other life forms and has the power to be a co-creator [with God] in the evolutionary process . . ." (*ibid.,* p. 606). The goal of this evolution of human consciousness was a convergence toward Christ, the "Omega Point" at which would come the unity and "collective salvation of the world." Here again, we see a theory of At-one-ment where all will become "Christified."

Just prior to her defense of Teilhard, L'Engle continued her assault on traditional Christianity claiming that she has "met far too many people who have had to spend years in the difficult task of unlearning bad Sunday school teaching," who "found it almost impossible to get rid of the image of an angry God out to punish them" (p. 63). This image includes the "heresy that Jesus came to save us from the wrath of God the Father" because of all our "horrible sinfulness" (*The Irrational Season*, p. 87).

What God does L'Engle say we should we believe in? "If we shed our idea of God as being someone Out There, separate from all that has been made, and begin instead to think of God as within all Creation, every galaxy, every quantum, every human being, then we cannot hold ourselves 'out there' either." "If God is in and part of all creation, then any part can be a messenger, an angel. . . ." "It will be a long time before we who call ourselves Christians will understand that *God is One, that God is All* . . ."(*A Stone*, pp. 86, 98, 214, emphasis mine).

Think about this. If God is One and All is God, if God is in and part of everyone and all Creation, and if atonement means that all creation will be at-one with God, isn't everything God? Contributing author Sri Madhava Ashish answers this question in a book about the founder of the Theosophical Society, occultist Helen P. Blavatsky, and her channeled work, *The Secret Doctrine*. Madhava Ashish saw clearly that if "Man is at one with the universe; and that is the same as saying that man is at one with God. Man is God, or God is man; it makes little difference which way one looks at it" (*H. P. Blavatsky and the Secret Doctrine*, edited by Virginia Hanson, The Theosophical Publishing House, Wheaton, IL, 1971, p. 51).

Theosophical adherent Shirley Nicholson is also in full agreement with L'Engle's view of God. She explains that the Theosophical view of God is in opposition to a God apart from the world. "Rather, the One Life permeates, supports, and gives life to everything that arises from it. . . . We, too, are part of the One. In addition, in the depths of our consciousness we are one with the Essence which permeates all, which is also our own inner being. In delving within in meditation to find the inmost self . . . we somehow mysteriously merge with the supreme Self of all and for a time become conscious in some degree of our oneness with the divine life. . . . Such is the teaching that underlies the theosophical statements about the brotherhood of all people. . . . There is overwhelming evidence from the most diverse sources that we are interconnected, that we are all part of one whole, sharing at all levels. . . . We are the stuff of the universe" (*Ancient Wisdom–Modern Insight*, The Theosophical Publishing House, Wheaton, IL, 1985, pp. 24-25).

While L'Engle speaks of a God that is within all creation, she constantly reiterates that religion is divisive, but God is not. "Religion," she insists, has to become a "unifying and not a divisive word." She believes, "Religion is devisive when it becomes fanaticism–an insistence that we know all the answers, and that anybody whose answer differ from ours is damned" (*Stone*, pp. 70, 139).

L'Engle is not only speaking of minor (or even major) differences within mainline denominations. She includes differences between Christianity and Buddhism, Hinduism, ancient Egyptian religions, every religion. She is seeking the New Age goal of a one-world religion. There is only one problem with her cure for "divisiveness." Can you guess which narrow-minded, intolerant, "smug sheep" religion will not be able to accept her view of "Christianity?" Who then is "the echthroi," the Greek word L'Engle uses to describe "the enemy . . . who would separate us from the stars and each other, un-Name, annihilate"? Who believe in a "forensic" Creator who would punish those who reject him? (*Stone*, pp. 215-216). Hopefully, you know the answer.

Why can L'Engle say so sarcastically, "For me, Gandhi is a Christ figure. I'll be perfectly happy to go wherever he goes. If you want to call that hell, that's your problem"? How can she say, "Christ can speak to me through the white china Buddha who sits on my desk at Crosswicks . . ."? (*Stone*, pp. 166, 168). Or that, at times, "Buddha is a better Christ figure than the crucifix"? (*Trailing Clouds of Glory, Spiritual Values in Children's Books*, Westminister Press, Philadelphia, PA, 1985, p. 106).

Does Professor Hettinga understand that what L'Engle espouses is similar to having Gideon tell the Israelites that God could speak to them through Baal? That Baal could be a God figure? God commanded Gideon to tear down the altar of Baal (Judges 6:25). Through Jehu, God destroyed Baal worship in Israel (2 Kings 10:28). God does not tolerate "any gods to be alongside me" (Exodus 20:23). This is the angry, forensic, "tribal god" (L'Engle's words) that L'Engle cannot tolerate.

To soften the shock of such statements, L'Engle almost always adds a cushion. For instance, she adds: "I am no more likely to become a Buddhist than my parents were likely to turn to Islam when they framed those lovely verses from the Koran' (*Stone*, p. 168). However, she expounds, "There is no limit to the ways in which Christ can speak to us, though for the Christian he speaks first and most clearly through Jesus of Nazareth" (*Stone*, p. 169). What Christ can speak not only through Jesus, but through Buddha, or Krishna or any other figure?

As J. Gordon Melton points out in his description of God: "Jesus, and the other significant religious teachers like Buddha or Krishna, were particularly transparent as bearers of the Divine, or Christ Principle" (*New Age Almanac*, p. 304). The Cosmic Christ, the Christ Consciousness, the Christ Principle, are all names for the same force that evolves us into godhood. If you recall, Love is another name for the Christ principle as seen in *Human: Initiation and Solar* by Theosophist, Alice Bailey. L'Engle believes in a God that is "Love Itself."[1] *A Course in Miracles* describes God as Love Itself (p. 112-114, Vol. 2). Love, in New Age literature, is another name for "the energy force." (For added information to support this fact, see Walter Martin's, *The New Age Cult*, Bethany House Publishers, Minneapolis, MN, 1989, pp. 26-27).

The introduction of chapter two in Hettinga's book begins with this quote by L'Engle: "Then by some chance, I'm not sure how or why, I stumbled on a book of Einstein's . . . and in Einstein I found my theologian" (p. 21). Towards the end of *A Stone For a Pillow*, L'Engle stresses "the interdependence of all life, all Creation," and the "language of particle physics," and "subatomic particles." She muses over Einstein's theory of relativity, $E=mc^2$

(energy equals mass times the speed of light squared) (pp. 183, 194-195). Confusingly, she parallels $E = mc^2$ with symbols that draw us closer to God. She then quotes Revelation 13:18 where 666 is the number of the Beast and in total contradiction to Scripture (Rev. 19:19-20), claims that "numbers can be redeemed, and ultimately, 666 will return to God" (p. 195).

Please keep in mind that in *Today's Christian Women* magazine, L'Engle is quoted as saying, "I know nothing about the New Age Movement, nor do I care to" (Sept./Oct. 1991).

It is on page 191 of *A Stone For a Pillow* that L'Engle reveals she is well acquainted with the New Age Movement by quoting from the New Age labeled book, *The Tao of Physics*, by leading New Age physicist Fritjov Capra. Noting that Capra quotes from the Upanishads (books of Hinduism), L'Engle writes: There appears to be a tacit assumption that the world of particle physics and the world of eastern mysticism (Hinduism, Buddhism) are compatible, but not the worlds of particle physics and Christianity. This is not only blindness on the part of those who claim this, it is a misunderstanding of Christianity. Christianity is an Eastern religion. It is to our shame that we have westernized it, imposed on it our forensic thinking" (p. 192).

Remember what L'Engle said about a *forensic* view of God and the atonement in the Western world? She has literally just turned Christianity into Hinduism. As Rev. John F. De Vries wrote in his article "How the New Age Infiltrates:" "I believe that L'Engle is an excellent example of the subtle and clever way in which New Age teaching (and ancient paganism) worm their way into the church." (*The Outlook*, November 1990, p. 11).

In *The Tao of Physics*, Capra blends Hinduism, Buddhism and Taoism with the science of subatomic physics, particle physics, etc. . . . Capra explains that while feeling the rhythm of his breathing, he had a beautiful experience. "I suddenly became aware of my whole environment as being engaged in a gigantic *cosmic dance.* . . . As I sat on that beach my former experiences came to life; I 'saw' cascades of energy coming down from outer space, in which particles were created and destroyed in rhythmic pulses; I 'saw' the atoms of the elements and those of my body participating in this *cosmic dance of energy*; I felt its rhythm and I 'heard' its sound, and at that moment I knew that this was the Dance of Shiva, the Lord of Dancers worshipped by the Hindus" (Batamn New Age Books, New York, 1984, p. xix, emphasis mine).

The Aquarian Guide to the New Age explains that Capra "explored various altered states of consciousness" and that the Dance of Shiva is "believed by Hindu mystics to underlie the whole of manifestation." It also tells us that Capra's "new view" is "a very old view . . . precisely the same world view as that of the ancient mystics" (Campbell, Eileen and Brennan, J.H., The Aquarian Press, 1990, p. 77).

L'Engle echoes Capra's view of the universe and of the cosmic dance: "This me, like all of creation, lives in a glorious dance of communion with all the universe. In isolation we die; in interdependence we live" (*Stone*, 90). In her work, *And It Was Good*, she writes: "The Great Dance, the ancient harmonies, weaving and interweaving to make the pattern perfect. Often it is difficult to see that there is any pattern. We are too small to see the richness of the whole. *But all of creation is pattern, from the Great Dance of the galaxies to the equally Great Dance of the submicroscopic, subatomic particles, existing only because they are dancing together*" (Harold Shaw Publishers, Wheaton, IL, 1983, p. 191, emphasis mine).

In *Ancient Wisdom–Modern Insight*, Shirley Nicholson quotes Fritjof Capra to show how the views of science and Eastern mysticism are merging and relates that, "drawing parallels between modern physics and the mystic's view of reality emphasis mine, is very much in keeping with theosophy" (p. 42). Theosophy teaches a "holistic" view of the universe where everything is seen as a complex set of whole systems, all "intricately connected and interdependent and reflective of the [bigger] whole" (*New Age Almanac*, p. 363). This is called the "Grand Pattern of patterns" (*Ancient Wisdom– Modern Insight*, p. 34).

In the December 3, 1982, issue of *Commonweal* magazine, L'Engle reviewed the New Age labeled book, *Dancing of the Wu Li Masters*, by another leading New Age physicist, Gary Zukav. She wrote: "The comparison of the language of some of the quantum physicists and that of the medieval mystics is fascinating. emphasis mine, It is easy to tell from the books which have spoken most deeply to me where my own mind is turning at the moment" (Volume 109: Issue 21, p. 666). Zukav's book also asserts that there is a great cosmic dance of energy of which we are all a part. Already years ago, L'Engle was promoting New Age authors and their vision of a holistic universe where all creation is evolving into a state of perfection.

L'Engle's emphasis on the interdependence of all Creation, particle physics, quantum mechanics, etc. is the promotion of Eastern mysticism/occultism as seen in Theosophy which has been "the major advocate of occult philosophy in the West and the single most important avenue of Eastern teaching to the West" (J. Gordon Melton, *New Age Almanac*, Visible Ink Press, Detroit, MI, 1991, pg. 16). L'Engle uses a term from astrophysics that describes this interdependence of all creation. It is called the "the butterfly effect" (*Stone*, p. 42). Hettinga notes the concept of "the butterfly effect" on page 24 of his book, and mentions that L'Engle draws on Einstein's theory of relativity and the quantum theory (p. 23), but again, does not explain their connection to New Age thought.

Because I am dealing with such a controversial and crucial matter, here is some added information J. Gordon Melton presents in his *New Age Almanac*: "Most emphasis mine, New Agers identify God with the Ultimate Unifying Principle that binds the whole together. . . . *Using metaphysical speculations derived from Albert Einstein's identification of matter with energy, they will occasionally reduce all reality to energy. . . . Thus, some New Agers are pantheists, identifying God and the universe as one reality.* People participate in god as individualized manifestations of that Ultimate Unifying Principle and as channels delivering the universal energy to the world" (p. 304, emphasis mine). Is it any wonder that L'Engle calls Einstein her theologian? Incidentally, it has been documented that Albert Einstein's niece has said that he kept a copy of Helen Blavatsky's work, *The Secret Doctrine* (see above reference), on his desk at all times.[2]

In her book, *And It Was Good* (and others), L'Engle presents the New Age concept of co-creation. In Hinduism, the world as we see it, evil (sin), etc. . . . is illusion or maya. Because we are a part of God, we can, with our minds by the energy force within us, create a different reality. We can literally "transform" this world back into a Garden of Eden. L'Engle postulates: "Reality is not something we observe; something out there, as some people used to think that God was something out there. Reality is something we participate in making as co-creators with God" (p. 86).

Known for proudly shouting "I am God," Shirley MacLaine, one of the most popular New Age advocates in the West, sums up L'Engle's gospel: "Basic to New Age subatomic discoveries is the concept that in the subatomic world–the stuff of the universe–everything, every last thing, is linked [interconnected]. The universe is a gigantic, multidimensional web of influences, or information, light particles, energy patterns, and electromagnetic 'fields of reality.' Everything it is, everything we are, everything we do, is linked to everything else. There is no separateness. *This understanding brings us to the most controversial concept of the New Age philosophy; the belief that God lies within, and therefore we are each part of God. Since there is no separateness, we are each Godlike, and God is in each of us. We experience God and God experiences through us. We are literally made up of God energy, therefore we can create whatever we want in life because we are each co-creating with the energy of God–the energy that makes the universe itself*" (*Going Within, A Guide for Inner Transformation*, Bantam Books, New York, 1990, p. 100, emphasis mine).

Repeatedly denying the purpose of the substitutionary atonement, and mocking those who turn Jesus "into a wimp who has come to save us from a furious father,"[3] L'Engle adds toward the ending of *A Stone For A Pillow*: "If the totally interdependent, interconnected world of physics is true, then this oneness affects the way we look at everything. . . . It radically affects the way we look at the cross. Jesus on the cross was at-one with God, and with the infinite mind, in which Creation is held. The anguish on the cross has to do with this at-one-ment in a way which a *forensic definition of atonement cannot even begin to comprehend*" (p. 209, emphasis mine).

The forensic definition of the atonement is that Jesus died to pay the penalty for sin! What the Bible teaches so explicitly and what we believe, is what L'Engle unequivocally denies and rejects. The New Age Movement is an attack upon the person and work of Jesus Christ; His unique divinity and the price He paid for our sins, the substitutionary atonement. You will find in New Age literature, an intense disgust for those who claim Jesus to be the only way of salvation from sin. They are viewed as the narrow-minded, intolerant and bigoted people who will stand in the way of world peace.

However, the New Testament clearly testifies that Jesus is indeed "the one and only Son of God," the creator of all things (John 1:1-18, 3:16, 14, 18; Hebrews 1) and that Jesus Christ was and always will be "our great God and Savior" (Titus 2:13). We also know from Scripture that as the world hated Jesus Christ, it will hate and persecute those who follow Him (John 15:18-25).

A Stone For A Pillow closes with this chilling thought. L'Engle claims that when ". . . Lucifer and Michael are again friends . . . there will be no more echthroi [enemy]" (p. 239).

In *Walking on Water: Reflections on Faith and Art*, L'Engle expounds on her belief that Satan will be reconciled to God, that 666 will ultimately be redeemed and that Lucifer and Michael will be friends again. Using a quote from Dostoyevsky's *Crime and Punishment*, she cancels out the strong Biblical warning: "If anyone worships the beast and his image and receives his mark on the forehead or on the hand, he, too, will drink of the wine of God's fury, which has been poured full strength into the cup of his wrath" (Revelation 14:9). Denying God's wrath, confusing one to believe we cannot make judgments regarding Scriptural truths, L'Engle deceives her readers into believing that they may receive the mark of the Beast and still be saved! This is what she quotes:

> Then Christ will say to us, "Come you as well, Come drunkards, come weaklings, come forth ye children of shame." And he will say to us, "Ye are swine, made in the Image of the Beast and with his mark, but come ye also." And the wise men and those of understanding will say: "O Lord, why do you receive these men?" And he will say, "This is why I receive them, O ye of understanding, that not one of them believed himself to be worthy of this." And he will hold out his hands to us and we shall fall down before him and we shall weep . . . and we shall understand all things. Lord, thy kingdom come (Harold Shaw Publishers, Wheaton, IL, 1980, p. 68).

God has condemned the detestable beliefs and practices found in the categories of occultism I've described. The prophet Samuel warned Saul who had consulted a medium contrary to God's command: "For rebellion is like the sin of divination, and arrogance like the evil of idolatry" (1 Samuel 15:23– Note: In some Bibles, the word *witchcraft* is used instead of *divination*).

God condemned witchcraft, contacting familiar spirits, etc. . . . because

He knows that this will lead many to follow doctrines of demons. As 1 Timothy 4:1 states so prophetically, "The Spirit clearly says that in later times some will abandon the faith and follow deceiving spirits and things taught by demons. Such teachings come through hypocritical liars, whose consciences have been seared as with a hot iron." Verse 6 says, "If you point these things out to the brothers, you will be a good minister of Christ Jesus, brought up in the truths of the faith and of the good teaching that you have followed. *Have nothing to do with godless myths . . .*" (emphasis mine).

In order to discard essential Biblical truths, L'Engle must destroy the credibility of God's Word. She does so in *A Stone For A Pillow*, in many of her other works and in her lectures, by reducing the Bible to myth. I have reserved for the third part of this article explaining what L'Engle means by the "Mythical Bible" and her contention (and Hettinga's by promoting it), that it is in myth and fantasy that we find the "truth that will make us more free" (*Presenting Madeleine L'Engle*, p. 11).

Notes:

1. L'Engle, Madeleine, *Trailing Clouds of Glory, Spiritual Values in Children's Books*, Westminster Press, Philadelphia, PA, 1985, p. 78.
2. In *Reincarnation: A New Horizon in Science, Religion and Society*, Julian Press, New York, New York, 1984, on page 27, authors Sylvia Cranston and Carey Williams document this fact from *The Journal of San Diego History*, San Diego Historical Society, Summer 1974.
3. L'Engle, Madeleine, "The Mythical Bible," Chicago Sunday Evening Club, Chicago, IL, Program 3501, October, 1991.

Appendix I

BATTLE TO DESTROY TRUTH, PART III

"Adam thus bequeathed us his death, not his sin. . . . We do not inherit the sins of our fathers, even though we may be made to endure their punishment. Guilt cannot be transmitted. We are linked to Adam only by his memory, which becomes our own, and by his death, which foreshadows our own. Not by his sin."
  Madeleine L'Engle, *Ring of Endless Light*, p. 80, fiction.

"Why do we have a life span instead of being like the amoebae? Because of sex. It wasn't until it took two members of a species to produce offspring that a life span came into the evolutionary system. Sex and death came into the world simultaneously."
  Madeleine L'Engle, *The Irrational Season*, p. 40, non-fiction.

"Therefore, just as sin entered the world through one man, and death through sin, and in this way death came to all men because all sinned."
  Romans 5:12

In the second part of "The Battle to Destroy Truth," I concentrated on how L'Engle rejects and redefines the substitutionary atonement and the last judgment to refute Professor Donald Hettinga's defense of L'Engle against the allegation of "universalism." We saw how he dismissed this concern with the excuse that it was L'Engle's "emphasis on the loving nature of God" that was confusing Christians into believing she was a universalist.

Using this same erroneous rationale, Hettinga fortifies L'Engle's complete and utter destruction of the gospel of Jesus Christ. He contends that her "emphasis on the Bible as story," has resulted in the indictment of being a "New Age spiritualist" (p. 16). Is the problem her emphasis on the Bible as story? Or, does she indeed deny, as Classis Chicago South declared, the unique authority of the Bible in all matters of faith and practice?

L'Engle claims the Bible is contradictory, ". . . just as our lives and thoughts are filled with contradictions" (*And It Was Good*, p. 131). This statement alone should be a warning signal for Christians that L'Engle denies the divine inspiration and unique authority of Scripture. She also relates that she reads the Bible in much the same way as she reads fairy tales. "But," she clarifies, "fairy tales are not superficial stories. They spring from the depth of the human being. The world of the fairy tale is to some degree the world of the psyche. . . . Never confuse fairy tale with untruth" (*A Stone For A Pillow*, p. 81). This prepares L'Engle's listeners for her presentation of a "Mythical Bible."

Hettinga provides one short excerpt from L'Engle's interview, "Before Babel," which strongly insinuates the Bible is no different than any other "primitive myth" that "contains truth." He doesn't explain it or refute it. Instead, he continues saying: "One of L'Engle's interests throughout her career has been to retell stories that appear in the Bible." She has done so in poetry and drama, "but it is in her fiction . . . that she is most successful in her re-creations. In these works she uses her powers of narrative to flesh out stories that were told in the Bible and to speculate on what might have been." She drops her characters into "a world of myth" (pp. 111-112).

It is quite evident from his book, that Hettinga feels it is perfectly legitimate for a "Christian author" to place the Bible on the same shelf as other myths, legends, fantasy and fairy tale. How is it that L'Engle is granted the license to add to and subtract from Scripture, presenting ideas in both her non-fiction and fiction that are in complete opposition to it?

In *A Stone For A Pillow*, (and in many of her other works and lectures), L'Engle uses confusion, constant questioning, and intimidation to manipulate her audience. She carries this to the point of seducing one into believing that if they accept any portion of the Bible as being literally true, they have been deceived by one of Satan's lies: "That limited literalism which demands that the Bible's poetry and story and drama and parable be taken as factual history is one of Satan's cleverest devices" (p. 81).

Furthering her cause, she implies that if a person refuses to accept the Bible as myth, they are being used by Lucifer: "Alas, Lucifer, how plausible you can be, confusing us into thinking that to speak of the Bible as myth is blasphemy. One definition of myth in the dictionary is parable. Jesus taught by telling parables. Did Jesus lie? Blaspheme?" (*ibid.,* p. 82). But, "don't let the word myth be upsetting," L'Engle entices. "Far from being a lie, myth is a way for us to see beyond limited fact into the wonder of God's story. . . . So let's not give Satan pleasure" ("The Mythical Bible," Chicago Sunday Evening Club, Chicago, IL, Program 3501, p. 1).

Who would want to be Satan's scapegoat? Who would want to believe they were calling Jesus a liar? Oh, how twisted her statements are. It was the crafty serpent, Satan himself, who deceived Eve by questioning what God had said and providing her with a different version of "the truth" (Genesis 3:1).

Unfortunately, most of the time there is just enough truth in what L'Engle purports so that many swallow all of what she dishes out, hook, line and sinker. It is true, for instance, that Jesus taught in parables and that one definition of myth is parable. However, Jesus also told us when He was speaking in parable. She is also correct in saying that we shouldn't take every word or sentence in the Bible literally. Jesus sometimes used hyperbole (i.e., the camel going through a needle's eye) to bring across a point He wanted made. But she takes one giant leap into falsehood when she asserts that we cannot take any part of the Bible literally.

Christians who defend the Bible as factual history are accused by L'Engle of "Biblical idolatry." For the "marvelous mysteries" of the Bible "cannot be understood in the language of literalism and inerrancy" ("The Mythical Bible," p. 4). We can't "have the Bible," L'Engle pouts, "God gives us the truth, we don't "have it." For anyone to claim they do, is to L'Engle, coming very "close to sin" (*ibid.,* p. 3). She insists that "what is destroying our myths today . . . are literalism and fear" (*ibid.,* p. 4).

In the first chapter of his book, "Living by Story," Donald Hettinga writes about L'Engle's use of "intuition in the writing process" and "the use of the subconscious which requires a function of memory that she labels 'anamnesis,' a function that enables her to write out of her 'child self' " (pp. 13, 15). He continues explaining, "The risk of entering 'the deep black waters of the subconscious mind' is genuine, but so is the reward. That intuitive darkness is 'that part of us which is capable of true prayer, poetry, painting, music'; it is only by entering it that any of us 'have any hope of wholeness' " (p. 14). It is "our fear of our subconscious minds, our intuitive selves" that keeps us from becoming "whole," from becoming one with God (*And It Was Good,* p. 85). Is this how we become whole, by entering the darkness of the subconscious mind?

According to L'Engle, "The Bible doesn't give any answers, it just tells more stories" (*The Door,* Dec., 1986, p. 24). Where, and to whom then do we look for our salvation?

In her sermon, "The Mythical Bible," aired on the popular television show, The Chicago Sunday Evening Club, L'Engle presented her belief that it is in myth that we find the truth Jesus promised would set us free. She also remarked: "Myths, like dreams, are grounded in the subconscious" (p. 4).

Since, as Hettinga indicates, L'Engle's writings are also written with "the use of the subconscious," what makes her words any less valid than our God's?

I believe one of the reasons so many people fall into believing there is absolutely nothing wrong with comparing the Bible to myth or story is because of L'Engle's affirmation that the Bible is indeed true, and that myths are just expressions of truth. Also clouding the issue is her confession that the Bible is "the living Word of God" (*And It Was Good*, p. 166). How can she equate the Bible with myth and at the same time claim it is the living Word of God?

This may seem contradictory, but in New Age thought, it makes a great deal of sense. This brings us back to the New Age concept of co-creativity. When New Agers/occultists speak of creativity, imagination, myth, and intuition in the context of being co-creators with God, these words have a much deeper meaning than you and I would normally perceive them to have. As *The New Age Guide* states: " 'Creativity' is heard in a context different and more expansive than its traditional usage" (Clancy, John, Sweet Forever Publishing, Eastsound, WA, 1988, p. 91).

L'Engle writes: "The artist must be open to the wider truths, the shadow side, the strange worlds beyond time. . . . God is constantly creating, in us, through us, with us, and to co-create with God is our human calling. When I am writing, on the other side of silence, as it were, and I am interrupted, there is an incredible shock as I am shoved through the sound barrier, the light barrier, out of the real world and into what seems, at least for the first few moments, a less real world. . . . The same thing is true in prayer, in meditation. For disciplines of the creative process and Christian contemplation are almost identical" (*Walking on Water, Reflections on Faith and Art*, p. 185).

As we have already seen in parts I and II, L'Engle promotes Kabbalism and Theosophy and other occult beliefs and practices associated with "white magic." It is important to remember this as we continue.

In New Age thought, Truth (with a capital T), can only be experienced and cannot be based on or reduced to factual knowledge. Therefore, beliefs (or doctrines), are placed on a much lower level of importance and can be continually subject to change. This is why L'Engle can say without hesitation, "My religion is subject to change without notice" (*And It Was Good*, p. 167).

The New Age emphasis is on self-knowledge and inner transformation. The knowledge needed for inner transformation is obtained through various occult techniques of meditation in which one enters into an altered "higher state of consciousness" and receives mystical illuminations. These "divine moments" of "kairos," is what occultists call the "secondary imagination." This is extremely different than what we know as the "primary imagination," a simple association of ideas.

The secondary imagination is also known by occultists as "intuition." Besides meaning "just a gut feeling," some definitions "of intuition include visions, as well as the transmission of information from spirit guides or entities. . . ." Intuition is compared with ESP and is considered "integral to all forms of divination and psychic consultation" (Guiley, Rosemary Ellen, *Harper's Encyclopedia of Mystical & Paranormal Experience*, Harper San Francisco, 1991, p. 285).

Occultist/psychologist Carl Jung suggested that intuition "is not merely a perception, but a creative process with the capacity to inspire and that archetypes, are inborn forms of intuition" (*Harper's Encyclopedia of Mystical & Paranormal Experience*, p. 287). Archetypes, in the psychology of Carl Jung, are primordial images (spirit guides/guardian angels–CVK) found in the collective unconscious. They "appear in mystical visions as sacred or mythic beings and have the power to 'seize hold of the psyche with a kind of primeval force.' . . . Archetypal visions have often been regarded by mystics as personal revelations from an external divine source" (*ibid.*, p. 287). L'Engle promotes Carl Jung's demon-inspired theory of the collective unconscious (racial memory) and "guardian angels" in *Walking on Water, Reflections of Faith and Art and* in many of her other works.

In her channeled book, *A Treatise on White Magic*, Theosophist Alice Bailey teaches through her spirit guide Djwual Khul: "man must progress into the deep realm of pure intuition. He can then tap truth at its source. He enters into the mind of God Himself. He intuits as well as idealizes and is sensitive to divine thoughts. . . . He calls these intuitions later, as he works them out, ideas or ideals, and bases all his work and conduct of affairs upon them" (Lucis Publishing Company, New York, 1951, p. 366).

Bailey also states: "Inspiration is analogous to mediumship" (*ibid.*, p. 179). The definitions of inspiration and creativity are nearly identical in occult terms to intuition. In Western magic, these words are described as: "the act of allowing one's personal daemon or genius to direct one's thoughts and intentions. One can also be inspired by opening oneself to channels of sacred knowledge through communication with angels, archangels, and God" (Drury, Nevill, *Dictionary of Mysticism*, Prism Press, Dorset, 1992, p. 152.) [Note: Under the heading of inspiration is Cosmic Consciousness (Christ Consciousness)].

White Magic, also known as High Magic, "is intended to bring about the spiritual transformation of the person who practices it. This form of magic is designed to channel the magicians' consciousness towards the sacred light within . . . *the aim of High Magic has been described as communication with one's holy guardian angel, or higher self*" (*ibid.*, p. 190, emphasis mine). White magic is the use of the "imagination" to improve the common good.

What does all this have to do with L'Engle's claim that the Bible is myth?

In his interview with acclaimed journalist Bill Moyers, New Age mythology expert Joseph Campbell reveals that "myth comes from the imagination" (*The Power of Myth*, Anchor Books-Doubleday, New York, 1988, p. 72). However, he is not talking about the primary imagination. Campbell is discussing the secondary imagination in which one receives information while in an altered state of consciousness. He elaborates: "Both Freud [Sigmund] and Jung felt that myth is grounded in the unconscious. . . . Since the inspiration comes from the unconscious, and since the unconscious minds of the people of any single small society have much in common, what the shaman (witchdoctor) or seer brings forth is something that is waiting to be brought forth in everyone" (*ibid.,* p. 71).

Moyers questions Campbell: "So when we talk about folk tales, we are talking not about myths but about stories that ordinary folks tell in order to entertain themselves or express some level of existence that is below that of the great spiritual pilgrims." Campbell answers: "Yes, the folk tale is for entertainment. The myth is for spiritual instruction" (p. 71). It is the shaman, says Campbell, ". . . who has had an experience. In our tradition it is the monk who seeks the experience . . ." (p. 73).

"In mysticism, intuition is considered the means by which to achieve direct and immediate truth, and knowledge of the most intimate secrets of life" (*Harper's Encyclopedia of Mystical & Paranormal Experience*, p. 287). And myth, according to Carl Jung and supported by Campbell, is what develops from the "mythic images present at a deep level of the unconscious mind and maybe viewed as an expression of the archetypes of the collective unconscious. . . . The various deities of myth and legend personify common human attributes or universal principles in Nature and the cosmos. Myths often express the spiritual values of a culture and provide a framework of meaning within which members of a society live and function" (*Dictionary of Mysticism*, p. 216).

For Campbell and L'Engle, it is the religious mystical experience that gives rise to the myths in which we can find the truth "that will set us free."

Speaking of Carl Jung's concept of myth, Joseph Campbell asserts that "Anyone writing a creative work knows that you open, you yield yourself, and the book talks to you and builds itself. To a certain extent, you become the carrier of something that is given to you from what have been called the Muses–or, in biblical language, "God." [In Greek mythology, the Muses are ". . . the personification of creative inspiration. The Muses were the nine daughters of Zeus and Mnemosyne, and each had a different specialization" (*Dictionary of Mysticism*, p. 214).

Parroting Joseph Campbell, Hettinga explains L'Engle's importance of story: "Story is a gift, not from the Muse, but from God, and a gift from God requires obedience. 'The artist,' she writes, 'must be obedient to the work' just as Mary was obedient in the Annunciation. When the work says, 'Here I am; compose me, or write me; or paint me,' the duty of the artist 'is to serve the work.' . . . '. . . there is little difference for me between praying and writing' " (p. 13). Hettinga points out that "this view of story necessarily emphasizes the value of intuition in the writing process. Because the reality that L'Engle attempts to apprehend in her fiction surpasses empirical reality, she seeks to write with more than just her intellect" (p. 13). However, he fails to recognize that L'Engle's non-fiction is written in the same manner.

Though she claims her stories are from God, not the Muse, as Campbell illustrates, they are considered the same thing. While L'Engle sincerely believes she is serving "the work" or "God," this is nothing short of serving and listening to the instructions of demons as God commanded us not to have anything to do with occultism. It is interesting to note, that the whole aim of the occult Hermetic Order of the Golden Dawn whose concepts are based on the Kabbala, was to prosecute the "Great Work."

The Great Work is described by leading occultist Israel Regardie, as "the reconciliation of divinity and manhood" (*The Golden Dawn*, Llewellyn Pub., St. Paul, Minnesota., 1971, p. 47). More recently, Donald Kraig, author of *Modern Magick*, defines the Great Work as "The work of achieving enlightenment and unity with Divinity (some people would say unity with your Higher Self)" (Llewellyn Pub., St. Paul, MN, 1988, p. 540).

This is accomplished through the "Active Imagination." This is also the ultimate goal of witchcraft (As described in *The Witches Bible Compleat*, Janet and Stewart Farrar, Magickal Childe Publishing, Inc., New York, 1981). [Note: Included in the many occult practices of the Order of the Golden Dawn are: astral projection, scrying, the use of runes and alchemy–exactly what L'Engle teaches and is viewed as "good" in her works.]

Joseph Campbell professes, "Anyone who brings into his life the message of the Word is equivalent to Jesus" (*The Power of Myth*, p. 267). This is because he believes that ". . . Christ . . . is the being of all of us" (p. 267), and that it is our "higher self" that reveals "Truth" during an altered state of consciousness. The living Word of God of which L'Engle speaks is the revelation that comes during the mystical experience in which one has contacted their "holy guardian angel", "higher Self," or "God." The Bible therefore, is no different than any other myth. And no one can claim they have "the truth," because truth is what each person perceives it to be.

Like L'Engle who writes: "Long before Joseph Campbell and others popularized a mythic view of the universe, that was my view" (Yancy, Philip, ed., *Reality and the Vision*, Word Pub., Dallas, 1990, p. 113). Campbell promotes a different Christ, a different God: "We are all manifestations of Buddha consciousness or *Christ consciousness*, only we don't know it. The word 'Buddha' means 'the one who waked up.' . . . We are all to do that–to wake up to the Christ or Buddha consciousness within us." At least Joseph Campbell is willing to openly admit, "This is blasphemy in the normal way of Christian thinking, but it is the *very essence of Christian Gnosticism* . . ." (*The Power of Myth*, p. 69, emphasis mine).

L'Engle explains that Carl Jung's "concept of racial memory," is "his belief that when we are enabled to dip into the intuitive, subconscious self, we remember more than we know. She adds: "One of the great sorrows which came to human beings when Adam and Eve left the Garden was the loss of memory, memory of all that God's children are meant to be" (*Walking on Water*, p. 19). She asserts that we have to "rethink 'original sin' " and redefines sin as, "lack of at-one-ment" (*A Stone For A Pillow*, pp. 54, 23). No, sin is disobedience to God. Our problem is not that we have forgotten who we are and have to recognize the divinity within us and become one with "the Source."

What is "the truth" L'Engle avows will set us free? Because of her denial of the inherited sinful nature of humanity and the need for a savior to pay the penalty for sin, L'Engle can proclaim in "The Mythical Bible": "From what our present understanding of the universe tells us, everything came from one tiny, tiny, sub-atomic particle. . . . From the opening of this infinitely small particle came all the galaxies, the solar systems, the planets, the oceans, land, green things, creatures, and finally human beings. We are all made of the same matter as stars. . . . *Matter and energy, we are taught, are interchangeable, so the sheer energy of Christ, for love of us, took on the matter of Jesus. This is the myth that is true, that truth which sets us free and gives us life, and life more abundantly, Amen! Alleluia! Amen!*" (p. 6, emphasis mine). L'Engle is espousing the New Age concept of cosmic evolution as was taught by Pierre Teilhard de Chardin (as seen in Part II). L'Engle's truth is found in a "Cosmic Christ" who is found in "another gospel."

Hettinga believes L'Engle's fantasies "offer her a literary vehicle for apprehending the mysteries of God in the universe." He expresses his deep appreciation for her artistic abilities: "Such an imaginative vision, such 'creativity opens us to revelation.' . . . Such a vision sees angels and unicorns, the possibility of other worlds and the mysticism of theoretical physics as being as much a part of God's revelation as the birds of the air and the trees of the field" (*ibid.,* pp. 11- 12).

L'Engle assures us that "We must constantly be open to new revelation which is another way of hearing God with loving obedience" (*Walking on Water: Reflections on Faith and Art*, p. 133). Both Hettinga and L'Engle have paved the way for her "words about God" to be accepted as equally valid as Scripture.

At the closing of *Presenting Madeleine L'Engle*, Hettinga writes that L'Engle's fantasy novels "point to the importance of choosing good over evil, of exercising moral responsibility, of working on the side of love" (p. 150). However, as Rev. John F. De Vries points out so well: "She writes about good and evil, a secure and loving family, joy and hope, and the ultimate victory of love over sin . . . but subtly, in the process, all that will ultimately be destroyed by the heresy which she cleverly works into her writings" ("How the New Age Infiltrates," *The Outlook*, Nov. 1990, p. 11).

L'Engle's works promote self-realization, the reaching of one's full potential through contact with spirit guides and the use of psychic powers. This has been confirmed in the *Encyclopedia of Children's Literature Review* by secular critics as well (Senick, G.J., editor, Gale Research Co., Detroit, MI, 1988). Tragically, for L'Engle, the Bible doesn't give any answers. We can follow the path L'Engle has set before us, searching the realm of myth and imagination, or we can find our Truth in the written Word of God who made the plan of salvation so unmistakably clear. L'Engle, has willfully chosen to reject the beautiful gospel message of our Lord Jesus Christ.

This leaves the haunting question, how have Madeleine L'Engle's teachings, and other authors whose writings are similar to hers, influenced those within the Christian Reformed Church and our Christian schools?

All Scripture is God-breathed and is useful for teaching, rebuking, correcting and training in righteousness, so that the man of God may be thoroughly equipped for every good work.

2 Timothy 3:16

For the time will come when men will not put up with sound doctrine. Instead, to suit their own desires, they will gather around them a great number of teachers to say what their itching ears want to hear. They will turn their ears away from the truth and turn aside to myths.

2 Timothy 4:3-4

Appendix J

Letter from the Board of Trustees

January 10, 1994

Dear Brothers and Sisters:

Greetings in the name of the Lord Jesus Christ.

The trustees of the Christian Reformed Church in North America (CRCNA) have observed with increasing disappointment and concern the various negative statements and charges which are being levelled at the CRCNA and its various agencies. During the past years the various offices and boards of the CRCNA have, in most instances, chosen not to reply to such negative networking simply because it seemed prudent, trusting that people of goodwill would recognize the distinction between truth and distortions of truth or blatant untruths. However, because of the pain that many members experience when the church they love is attacked, we have concluded that a response is necessary lest anyone conclude that the charges are true. Therefore we are sending you this letter.

We are especially eager to address the suggestion made, either directly or by innuendo, that the CRCNA has departed from its confessional position that the Holy Scriptures are our only rule for faith and practice. The assertion is simply not true. Through the years synods of the CRCNA have affirmed the faith of the church in the infallibility of Scripture, and urged upon the church the approach of humble faith in the Word of God. Differences of interpretation surface among those who are equally devoted to the Scriptures and are within the fellowship of the same denomination. To suggest that this automatically means that some uphold the Bible while others do not, is unfair to those who prayerfully struggle to understand the teachings of the Word and is harmful to the fellowship of the body of Jesus Christ we call the church.

306

Therefore, in the name of the Lord, we plead with all who devoutly call on the name of our Savior Jesus Christ to form their judgment about the faith of the CRCNA, not on the basis of false accusations gathered from here or there–statements which are also often either quoted out of context or mis-quoted and twisted to convey a different meaning–but on the basis of the churches' own official confessions and official statements, decisions, and actions. (See *Acts of Synod, 1993,* p. 611)

The CRCNA is being blessed by the Lord with the Spirit's presence in so much of its ministry around the world. There are many reasons to celebrate both the faithfulness of our covenant God and the faithfulness of his people. With you, we are committed to being faithful to him, to his Word, and to the calling that is ours to proclaim and to teach all that he has commanded us as together we engage in evangelism, education, and benevolence.

Cordially in Christ,

Allan H. Jongsma
President, Board of Trustees

Leonard J. Hofman
General Secretary

Peter Borgdorff
Executive Director of Ministries

(See page 308 for response.)

Response

January 27, 1994

Dear Board Member,

As I read through your letter of January 10, 1994, I wondered if you realized the tremendous burden of responsibility you chose to carry when you sent out your appeal to members and former members of the Christian Reformed Church. I wondered if you realized the magnitude of destruction it could bring and felt compelled to write and plead with you to listen to my concerns.

The first paragraph of your letter strongly implies that those who have "leveled" charges against the CRCNA or have criticized its various agencies (or, for that matter, any preacher, professor, or leader in the CRC), are "negative," ill-willed liars. By saying that many have experienced pain when their church is "attacked," *you have indicted those who have made the criticisms as the enemy of the church.* The word attacked has quite a different meaning than the word admonish–which the Lord requires us to do.

You failed to look at the pain experienced by the people who have made the allegations. The pain of seeing a church and denomination they loved all their life straying farther and farther from the truth of God's Word. The pain of being driven out of the CRC by malicious gossip because they took a stand for what their church and denomination had originally upheld and defended. Pain of seeing their relations with family members and friends torn apart because they would not compromise *essential* Biblical truths. The pain of hearing ministers they've known using the pulpit to divide the congregation against them. But most of all, the pain of seeing their Lord and Savior being taken off the throne and spit upon. *The important question here is, what is the cause of pain, not who is feeling pain.*

In paragraph two, you complain that the suggestion has been made, "either directly or by innuendo, that the CRCNA has departed from its confessional position that the Holy Scriptures are our only rule for faith and practice." Yet, you do not provide the documentation for this charge, nor do you give the reasoning behind it. This is irresponsible.

Adding to your defense you write: "Differences of interpretation surface among those who are equally devoted to the Scriptures, and are within the fellowship of the same denomination. To suggest that this automatically means that some uphold the Bible while others do not, is unfair to those who prayerfully struggle to understand the teachings of the Word and is harmful to the fellowship of the body of Jesus Christ we call the church."

While it may be true that these members are equally devoted to Scripture, one has to question the soundness of your statement. Consider, for a moment, what would happen if preachers and professors had differing interpretations on the significance of the substitutionary atonement, the unique divinity of Jesus Christ, the unique authority of Scripture, and eternal damnation. What if some decided to teach the Bible as myth? What if there were those who believed we could use occult techniques of meditation for good? What if some in the higher ranks taught that we cannot judge whether someone's writings were not Christian? Would this be considered departing from the confessional position that the Holy Scriptures are our only rule for faith and practice?

Unfortunately, all the above is already being done, in one way or another. Whether you are aware of this or not, I'm not sure. Do you realize the consequences of your statement and the chaos it produces?

Many are devoted to the Scriptures, but many may also be devoted to a different gospel. While some may not realize what they are doing, others (being deceived), are purposefully and deceitfully teaching a gospel they know is incompatible with what the CRC has always held to. This is what is harmful to the church.

In the third paragraph of your letter, you plead with all those who "devoutly call on the name of our Savior Jesus Christ to form their judgment about the faith of the CRCNA, not on the basis of false accusations, but on the basis of the churches' own confessions. . . ."

Because this statement is directed to those people who haven't made these allegations, you have indirectly said that those you have made these accusations are *not* devoted to Jesus Christ (whether you meant to say that or not). But the most dangerous, unBiblical notion you have laid upon all members of the CRC is that we are not to question any teaching at all unless and until the confessions of the CRCNA have changed. By the time the confessions would change, it would be too late to say anything!

You end your letter claiming we are all "committed to being faithful to him, to his Word, and to the calling that is ours to proclaim and to teach all that he has commanded." . . . Does the Board of Trustees include that to mean defend the gospel and refute false teachings????

You have silenced, sentenced and banished all those who have taken a stand for their faith now, and those who will in the future. You have ignored God's constant warnings to watch out for false brethren and teachings within the church. You have decided to neglect God's command to defend the gospel and refute false teachings. In short, you have chosen to be blinded to the deception that is taking place right now within the CRCNA. The strong delusion God has promised to send is here.

Scripture warns us that in later times some will fall for deceiving doctrines of demons and that there will be world-wide apostasy. This is real, not illusionary. In studying the occult, I've read a number of channeled books. It's unsettling to see that these demonic spirits all teach open-mindedness, tolerance, and absence of judgment, because each person perceives truth differently. This is exactly what many of our leaders are now claiming.

Pride. It was the downfall of humankind from the very beginning. It may very well be the downfall of the Christian Reformed Church of North America. We are in the midst of a spiritual battle, yet many do not have a clue as to what is taking place or why. Unless you can forget about your loyalty to a denomination, and instead remember your first loyalty and love is to Jesus Christ, there is no hope. You, as member of the Board of Trustees of the CRCNA, have taken upon yourself this responsibility; to guide the CRC into the path of Truth. I pray it is not too late to fulfill your mission.

I have enclosed a copy of our family's transfer of membership from the Orland Park CRC. Please read it carefully disregarding any preconceived notions or remarks made about this ordeal. I would appreciate a response to this letter and its enclosed material. I am also very willing to meet with the Board of Trustees if they are willing and see the need to do so.

Sincerely,

Claris Van Kuiken

Note: I write this as an open letter.

cc: All members of the Board of Trustees

enclosure: Transfer of membership

BIBLIOGRAPHY

Madeleine L'Engle–Novels

A Wrinkle in Time. 1962. New York: Dell Publishing, 1973.

A Wind in the Door. 1973. New York: Dell Publishing, 1974.

A Swiftly Tilting Planet. 1978. New York: Dell Publishing, 1981.

A Ring of Endless Light. 1980. New York: Dell Publishing, 1981.

A House Like a Lotus. 1984. New York: Dell Publishing, 1985.

An Acceptable Time. New York: Farrar, Straus, Giroux. 1989.

Many Waters. 1986. New York: Dell Publishing, 1987.

Madeleine L'Engle–Non-Fiction

A Circle of Quiet. 1972. San Francisco: Harper & Row Publishers, 1972.

A Cry Like a Bell. Wheaton, IL: Harold Shaw Publishers, 1987.

A Rock That Is Higher: Story as Truth. Wheaton, IL: Harold Shaw Publishers, 1993.

A Stone for a Pillow: Journeys with Jacob. Wheaton, IL: Harold Shaw Publishers, 1986.

And It Was Good: Reflections on Beginnings. Wheaton, IL: Harold Shaw Publishers, 1983.

Sold Into Egypt: Joseph's Journey into Human Being. Wheaton, IL: Harold Shaw Publishers, 1989.

The Irrational Season. San Francisco: Harper & Row Publishers, 1977.

The Summer of the Great Grandmother. 1974. San Francisco: Harper & Row Publishers, 1974.

Trailing Clouds of Glory: Spiritual Values in Children's Books. Edited with Avery Brooke. Philadelphia, PA: Westminster Press, 1985.

Two-Part Invention: The Story of a Marriage. 1988. San Francisco: Harper & Row Publishers, 1989.

Walking on Water, Reflections on Faith and Art. Wheaton, IL: Harold Shaw Publishers, 1980.

Madeleine L'Engle–Interview, Speeches, Review, Essay

"Madeleine L'Engle: The Door Interview." *Wittenburg Door*, December 1986, 23-29.

L'Engle, Madeleine. "The Mythical Bible." Chicago Sunday Evening Club, Chicago, IL, Program 3501 (Television program, Channel 11), October 1991.

L'Engle, Madeleine. Speech (no title) given at Calvin College, Grand Rapids, MI, September 23, 1987.

L'Engle, Madeleine. "The Plausible Impossible." Speech at Wheaton College, Wheaton, IL, March 30, 1990.

L'Engle, Madeleine. Review of *Dancing of the Wu Li Masters* by Gary Zukav, *Commonweal*, Volume 109: Issue 21, December 3, 1982, 666.

L'Engle, Madeleine. "George MacDonald: Nourishment for a Private World." *Reality and the Vision: Eighteen Contemporary Writers Tell Who They Read and Why*, edited by Philip Yancey, Dallas: Word Publishing, 1990, 111-121.

Chaim Potok–Fiction

The Chosen. 1967. New York: Ballantine Books, 1989.

The Promise. New York: Knopf, 1969.

The Book of Lights. New York: Knopf, 1981.

Christian Critiques of New Age Thought

De Vries, John F. "What is New Age?" *The Outlook*, (Journal of Reformed Fellowship, Inc.), Volume 40: No. 8. September 1990, 8-9.

De Vries, John F. "The Four Spiritual Flaws of the New Age Movement, Part 2." *The Outlook*, (Journal of Reformed Fellowship, Inc.), Volume 40: No. 9. October 1990, 13-15.

De Vries, John F. "How the New Age Infiltrates, Part 3." *The Outlook*, (Journal of Reformed Fellowship, Inc.), Volume 40: No. 10. November 1990, 11-13.

Gods of the New Age. Rivershield Film Ltd. production. See also: Matriciana, Caryl. *Gods of the New Age.* Eugene, Oregon: Harvest House Publishers, 1985.

Groothuis, Douglas. *Revealing the New Age Jesus.* Downers Grove, IL: InterVarsity Press, 1990.

Lutzer, Erwin and John F. De Vries. *Satan's "Evangelistic Strategy" For This New Age.* Wheaton, IL: Victor Books, 1989.

Martin, Walter. *The New Age Cult.* Minneapolis, MN: Bethany House Publishers, 1989.

Rhodes, Ron. *The Counterfeit Christ of the New Age Movement.* Grand Rapids, MI: Baker Book House, 1990.

Scott, Brenda and Samantha Smith. *Trojan Horse, How the New Age Movement Infiltrates the Church.* Lafayette, LA: Huntington House Publishers, 1993.

Van Kuiken, Claris. "A Christ Without a Cross." *Christian Renewal.* Volume 10: Number 2. September 23, 1991, 10-11, 20.

Van Kuiken, Claris. "The Re-emergence of the Goddess: Prayer, Imagination & Feminism." *Christian Renewal.* Volume 10: Number 5. November 11, 1991, 14-15.

Van Kuiken, Claris. "Just Whose Gospel is Going to Russia?" *Christian Renewal.* Volume 11: Number 11. March 8, 1993, 14-15.

Van Kuiken, Claris. "The Battle to Destroy Truth." *Christian Renewal.* Volume 12: Number 1. September 13, 1993, 12-14.

Van Kuiken Claris. "Battle to Destroy Truth, Part II." *Christian Renewal.* Volume 12: Number 2. September 27, 1993, 14-17.

Van Kuiken, Claris. "Battle to Destroy Truth, Part III." *Christian Renewal.* Volume 12: Number 3. October 11, 1993, 12-13,16-17.

Van Kuiken, Claris. "New Hermeneutic or Ancient Wisdom?" *Christian Renewal.* Volume 13: Number 3. October 3, 1994, 14-15.

Other

The NIV Study Bible, New International Version. Grand Rapids, MI: Zondervan Bible Publishers, 1985.

The Holy Bible. King James Version, New York: The World Publishing Company.

Andrews, Susan. "Agony, Passion, and Hope: The Future of the Presbyterian Church, A Pastor's Perspective." *McCormick Perspectives*, April 1991.

Baron, Henry J. "Wrinkle on Trial." *Christian Educators Journal*, Vol. 33: No.1. October 1993, 12-13.

Berkhof, Louis. *Systematic Theology.* Grand Rapids, MI: Wm. B. Eerdmans Publishing Co., 1949.

Berdyaev, Nicholas. *Truth and Revelation.* London, W.C.: Geoffrey Bles Ltd., 1953.

Boogart, Thomas. "Galileo, Fox, and the Reformed Tradition." *Perspectives*, January 1991, 18-20.

Boulton, Wayne G. "The Thoroughly Modern Mysticism of Matthew Fox." *The Christian Century*, April 25, 1990, 428-432.

Brink, William P. and Richard R. De Ridder. *Manual of Christian Reformed Church Government*: Grand Rapids, MI: CRC Publications, 1987.

Bruinsma, Robert W. "Of Dogs and Witches: Dangerous Books in the Christian Classroom." *Christian Educators Journal*, Vol. 33: No. 1. October 1993, 15-17.

Davidson, Gustav. *A Dictionary of Angels*. 1967. New York: The Free Press-Macmillan, 1971.

Gritter, Karen. "Reflections on Spirituality." *The Calvin Seminary Kerux*, Volume XXIV: No. 29. May 17, 1991, 3.

Hettinga, Donald R. *Presenting Madeleine L'Engle*. New York: Twayne Publishers-Macmillan, 1993.

Kalteissen, Karen L. "Fear Not: Selecting Fantasy Literature for the Christian Classroom." *Christian Educators Journal*, Vol. 33: No. 1. October 1993, 6-7.

Kok, Jim. "Making Your Garden Grow." *The Banner*, February 18, 1991.

Krass, Alfred. "One Way: For too long I misunderstood the meaning of Jesus' words." *The Other Side*, Sept-Oct 1993, 16-19.

Kremer, Lillian S. "Chaim Potok." *Dictionary of Literary Biography:Twentieth-Century American-Jewish Fiction Writers*. Volume 28. Detroit, MI: Gale Research Co., 1984, 232-243.

Lagerway, Mary Boreman. "Madeleine L'Engle: A Passion for What's Real." *The Banner*, October 1, 1990, 12-13.

Linscheid, John. "A Thousand Trains to Heaven." *The Other Side*, Sept-Oct 1993, 8-15.

McBryde, Malcolm. "Listen Here, Church." *The Banner*, September 1994, 24.

Monsma, Martin. *The Compendium Guide, Book One*. Rev. ed. Grand Rapids, MI: Zondervan Publishing House, 1958, 17.

Postema, Don. *Space for God*. Grand Rapids, MI: CRC Publications, 1983.

Senick, G. J., ed. *Encyclopedia of Children's Literature Review*. Detroit, MI: Gale Research Company, Volume 14, 1988, 137-142.

Smith, Cathy. "A Wrinkle in Time: A Point of Contention." *Christian Educators Journal*, Vol. 33: No. 1. October 1993, 18-21.

Thibodaux, David. *Political Correctness*. Lafayette, LA: Huntington House Publishers, 1992.

Ursinus, Zacharius and Caspar Olevianus. *The Heidelberg Catechism*. Written in Heidelberg, Germany with the advice and cooperation of the entire theological faculty at the Heidelberg University, published on January 19, 1563.

Van Gilst, Lorna, managing editor. "Living the Metaphors of Grace." *The Christian Educators Journal*. Volume 33: No. 1. October 1993, 5.

Wolterstorff, Nicholas. "The CRC: A Community in Pain." as quoted by Gayla R. Postma. *The Banner*. June 8, 1992, 21.

Sources Relevant to New Age Thought

Atwater, P.M.H. *The Magical Language of Runes*. Santa Fe, NM: Bear & Company, 1986.

Bailey, Alice. *A Treatise on White Magic*. New York: Lucis Publishing Company, 1951.

Bailey, Alice. *Education in the New Age*. New York: Lucis Publishing Company, 1954.

Bailey, Alice. *Initiation: Human and Solar*. New York: Lucis Publishing Company, 1951.

Benson, Herbert. *Beyond the Relaxation Response*. 1984. New York: Berkley Books, 1985.

Buckland, Raymond. *The Complete Book of Witchcraft*. St. Paul, MN: Llewellyn Publications, 1986.

Campbell, Eileen and J. H. Brennan. *The Aquarian Guide to the New Age*. Wellingborough, England: The Aquarian Press, part of Thorsons Publishing Group, 1990.

Campbell, Joseph, with Bill Moyers. *The Power of Myth*. New York: Anchor Books-Doubleday, 1988.

Cady, Susan, Marian Ronan, and Hal Taussig. *Wisdom's Feast: Sophia In Study And Celebration*. San Francisco: Harper & Row Publishers, 1989, 185.

Carroll, L. Patrick and Katherine Marie Dyckmen. *Inviting the Mystic, Supporting the Prophet*. New York: Paulist Press, 1981.

Capra, Fritjof. *The Tao of Physics*. 2nd ed., rev. New York: Bantam New Age Books, 1984.

Capra, Fritjof, and David Steindl-Rast. *Belonging to the Universe*. San Francisco: Harper & Row Publishers, 1991.

Clancy, John, Tovi Daly, Claude Golden, and D.K. Shumway. *The New Age Guide for the Thoroughly Confused and the Absolutely Certain*. Eastsound, WA: Sweet Forever Publishing, 1988.

Cranston, Sylvia and Carey Williams. *Reincarnation: A New Horizon in Science, Religion and Society*. New York: Julian Press, 1984.

Cunningham, Scott. *The Truth About Witchcraft Today*. St. Paul, MN: Llewellyn Publications, 1988.

D'Antonio, Michael. *Heaven on Earth*. New York: Crown Publishers, Inc., 1992.

Dossey, Larry. *Recovering the Soul*, New York: Bantam New Age Books, 1989.

Dossey, Larry. *Healing Words*. San Francisco: Harper & Row Publishers, 1993.

Dossey, Larry. "The Power of Prayer." An interview by Jerry Snider. *Magical Blend*. Issue 42, April 1994, 37-42,82-83.

Drury, Nevill. *Dictionary of Mysticism*. 1985. Rev. ed. Dorset: Prism Press, (distributed in the USA by Garden City Park, NY: Avery Publishing Group Inc.), 1992.

Dunwich Gerina. *The Concise Lexicon of the Occult*. New York: Citadel Press Book-Carol Publishing Group, 1990.

Farrar, Janet and Stewart Farrar. *A Witches Bible Compleat*. 1981. Volume 1, The Sabbats. New York: Magickal Childe Publishing, 1984.

Ferguson, Marilyn. *The Aquarian Conspiracy: Personal and Social Transformation in Our Time*. Los Angeles, CA: Jeremy P. Tarcher, Inc., 1980.

Fox, Matthew. *The Coming of the Cosmic Christ*. San Francisco: Harper & Row Publishers, 1988.

Fox, Matthew. *Creation Spirituality: Liberating Gifts for the Peoples of the Earth*. San Francisco: Harper & Row Publishers, 1991.

Fox, Matthew. *Meditations with Meister Eckhart*. Santa Fe, NM: Bear & Co., Inc., 1983.

Fox, Matthew. "Meister Eckhart, Mystic of Deep Ecology." Mountain Luminary, Volume 6: No. 3. Summer 1991, 1,9.

Fox, Matthew. *On Becoming a Musical Mystical Bear:Spirituality American Style*. New York: Paulist Press, 1976.

Guiley, Rosemary Ellen. *Harper's Encyclopedia of Mystical & Paranormal Experience*. San Francisco: Harper & Row Publishers, 1991.

Hanson, Virginia, editor. *H. P. Blavatsky and the Secret Doctrine*. 2nd ed. Wheaton, IL: The Theosophical Publishing House, 1988.

Harris, Maria. *Dance of the Spirit: The Seven Steps of Women's Spirituality*. New York: Bantam Books, 1989.

Hubbard, Barbara Marx. *The Book of Co-Creation, The Revelation*. Sonoma, CA: The Foundation for Conscious Evolution, 1993.

Jung, Carl. *Memories, Dreams, Reflections*. Rev. ed. New York: Vintage Books-Random, 1965.

Kelsey, Morton. *Transcend*. Rockport, MA: Element, Inc., 1991.

Kelsey, Morton. "In the Spirit of The Early Christians." Interview by Charles H. Simpkinson, *Common Boundary*, Jan/Feb 1992, 18-23.

King, Francis X. *Mind & Magic*. London, England: Dorling Kindersley. Ltd; New York: Crescent Books-Random House, 1991.

Kraig, Donald Michael. *Modern Magick Eleven Lessons in the High Magickal Arts*. St. Paul, MN: Llewellyn Publications, 1988.

LeShan, Lawrence. 1974. *How to Meditate, A Guide to Self-Discovery*. New York: Bantam New Age Books, 1975.

LeShan, Lawrence. "*The Medium, the Mystic and the Physicist: Toward a General Theory of the Paranormal*. New York: Ballentine-Random, 1975.

Lindsey, Karen. "Spiritual Explorer." *Ms.*, December 1985, 38.

Matthews, Caitlin. *Sophia, Goddess of Wisdom*. Hammersmith, London: Mandala, 1991.

Maclaine, Shirley. *Out on a Limb*. New York: Bantam Books, 1983.

Maclaine, Shirley. *Going Within, A Guide for Inner Transformation*. 1989. New York: Bantam Books, 1990.

McLaughlin, Corinne. "The Mystery of the Veiled Mother of the World." *The Quest*, Summer 1990, 56-63.

Melton, J. Gordon. *New Age Almanac*. Detroit, MI: Visible Ink Press, 1991.

Merton, Thomas. *New Seeds of Contemplation*. Norfolk, Conneticut: New Directions, 1961.

Neff, Mary K. "God the Mother." *The Theosophical Digest*, March 1990, 10-15.

Nicholson, Shirley. *Ancient Wisdom-Modern Insight.* Wheaton, IL: The Theosophical Publishing House, 1985.

"Occultism." *The New Encyclopedia Britannica*. Chicago: Encyclopedia Britannica, Inc., Volume 25. 1989, 75-97.

Peck, M. Scott. *The Road Less Traveled.* New York: Touchstone-Simon and Schuster, 1978.

Peck, M. Scott. *Further Along the Road Less Traveled.* New York: Simon & Schuster, 1993.

Prophet, Mark L. and Elizabeth Clare Prophet. *The Lost Teachings of Jesus 2: Mysteries of the Higher Self.* Livingston, MT: Summit University Press, 1986.

Regardie, Israel. *The Golden Dawn.* 5th ed., rev. and enl. St. Paul, MN: Llewellyn Publications, 1988.

Roberts, Jane. *Seth Speaks.* 1972. New York: Bantam Books, 1974.

Savary, Louis M. and Patricia H Berne. *Kything: The Art of Spiritual Presence.* Mahwah, NJ: Paulist Press, 1988.

Schucman, Helen. *A Course in Miracles.* 3 vols. Tiburon, CA: Foundation for Inner Peace, 1975.

Spangler, David. *Reflections on the Christ.* 3rd ed. Findhorn, Scotland: Findhorn Publications, 1981.

Starhawk, (Simos, Miriam). 1979. *The Spiral Dance, A Rebirth of the Ancient Religion of the Great Goddess.* 10th anniversary ed. San Francisco: Harper & Row Publishers, 1989.

Steindal-Rast, David. "Waking to the Poetry of Life." An Interview by Rev. R. Scott Colglazier, *Creation Spirituality*. Volume VIII: Number 6. Nov/Dec 1992, 24-27.

Teilhard de Chardin, Pierre. *The Phennoman of Man.* New York: Harper & Row Publishers, 1959.

Teilhard de Chardin, Pierre. *The Divine Milieu.* New York: Harper & Row Publishers, 1960.

Toms, Michael. *At the Leading Edge: New Visions of Science, Spirituality, and Society.* Burdett, NY: Larson Pub., 1991.

Zukav, Gary. 1979. *The Dancing of the Wu Li Masters: An Overview of the New Physics.* New York: Bantam New Age Books, 1980.

Documents in Case (selected)

January 16, 1990: Recommendation to the Elders of Orland Park CRC concerning the works of Madeleine L'Engle and the church library from Church Education Committee.

January 24, 1990: Letter to Claris Van Kuiken from Gary Vander Bent, Clerk of Orland Park CRC Council.

March 16, 1990 p.m.–Sermon: "Live a Life of Love." Rev. Cornelius De Boer, Orland Park CRC, Orland Park, IL.

March 21, 1990: Letter to Si & Claris from Gary Vander Bent on behalf of the Elders of Orland Park CRC.

April 12, 1990: Letter to Claris Van Kuiken from Rev. John De Vries.

April 12, 1990: Letter to Ken Mels from Rev. John De Vries.

April (no day given), 1990: Letter to Karen & Dean Leensaart, Si & Claris Van Kuiken, Sharon Tiggelaar, from the Elders, Orland Park CRC.

September 11, 1990: Letter from church visitors, Rev. Cal Hoogendoorn and Rev. Tony Van Zanten, to Elders of Orland Park CRC , Si & Claris Van Kuiken, Dean & Karen Leensvaart.

September 16, 1990 a.m.– Sermon: "Examining the Walls." Rev. Gerald Erffmeyer, Orland Park CRC, Orland Park, IL.

September 30, 1990 a.m.–Sermon: "Facing the Opposition." Rev. Gerald Erffmeyer, Orland Park CRC, Orland Park, IL.

October 10, 1990: Letter from church visitors, Rev. Cal Hoogendoorn and Rev. Tony Van Zanten, to OPCRC Elders , Van Kuiken, Leensvaart.

October 28, 1990 a.m.–Sermon: "Facing Tricky Traps." Rev. Gerald Erffmeyer Orland Park CRC, Orland Park, IL.

November 27, 1990: Appeal to Classis Chicago South from Si & Claris Van Kuiken and Dean & Karen Leensvaart.

November 29, 1990: Letter from Church Visitors, Rev. Cal Hoogendoorn (Palos Heights CRC, Palos Heights, IL) and Rev. Tony Van Zanten (Roseland Christian Ministries, Roseland, IL) to OPCRC Elders, Classis Chicago South, Van Kuiken, Leensvaart.

December 4, 1990: Response to appeal from the Council of Orland Park Christian Reformed Church to Classis Chicago South.

December 7, 1990: Letter to Classis Chicago South from Si & Claris Van Kuiken, Dean & Karen Leensvaart (in response to church visitors' letter, 11-29-90).

January 16, 1991: Report of the advisory committee on the appeal of the members of Orland Park Church adopted by Classis Chicago South.

March 5, 1991: Resignation of Howard Stob to the Congregation of the Orland Park Christian Reformed Church & to the Council of Orland Park CRC.

March 25, 1991: Second and final resignation of Howard Stob to Orland Park CRC Council.

May 8, 1991: Protest of classis' decision from council of Hessel Park CRC, Champaigne, IL, to Classis Chicago South.

May 21, 1991: Letter to Elders of Orland Park CRC from Si & Claris Van Kuiken, Dean & Karen Leensvaart, "the appellants."

May 22, 1991: Letter to appellants from Secretary of Elders, OPCRC.

June 4, 1991: Letter to Revs. Erffmeyer & De Boer from Si & Claris Van Kuiken, Dean & Karen Leensvaart, Ken & Ruth Evenhouse, John & Sharon Tiggelaar,

Howard & Jo Stob–all now "the appellants."

June 19, 1991: Letter to the appellants from Elders of OPCRC.

June 24, 1991: Letter to church visitors, Revs. Lamsma & Rick Williams, from the appellants.

May 28, 1991: Open Letter to Jack Reiffer and Cliff Christians (Hessel Park CRC, Champaigne, IL), from Rev. Neal Punt.

September, 1991 (no specific date given): Letter to appellants from Rev. Henry Lamsma and Rev. Rick Williams.

October 11, 1991: Letter to the Consistory of the Orland Park CRC from the appellants.

October 17, 1991: Letter from the Elders of OPCRC to appellants.

November 14, 1991: Letter to Elders of the Orland Park CRC from Church Visitors–Rev. Rick Williams and Rev. Henry Lamsma.

November 20, 1991: Letter to the appellants from the Elders of OPCRC.

November 22, 1991: Letter to Elders of OPCRC from the appellants.

December 6, 1991: Formal charges sent to Classis Chicago South against the Elders of Orland Park CRC from the appellants: Howard & Jo Stob, John & Sharon Tiggelaar, Claris Van Kuiken, Dean & Karen Leensvaart, Ken & Ruth Evenhouse.

December 27, 1991: Letter to Rev. Richard Hartwell, Stated Clerk, CCS, from The Elders, OPCRC.

January 2, 1992: Letter to church visitors–Rev. Rick Williams & Rev. Henry Lamsma from appellants.

January 14, 1992: Letter to the delegates of Classis Chicago South from the Classical Committee: Gary Hutt, Neal Punt, Tony Van Zanten.

February 3, 1992: Appeal from appellants to the 1992 Synod of the Christian Reformed Church, Grand Rapids, MI.

May 5, 1992: Letter to Howard Stob from Donald F. Oosterhouse, Grand Rapids, MI.

June 2, 1992: Transcript of meeting between the appellants and judicial code committee from synod.

September 4, 1992: Letter to the reconciliation committee from Howard Stob: "THE ISSUE AS I SEE IT."

September 15, 1992: Letter to the reconciliation committee appointed by Synod 1992: Rev. Lugene Bazuin, Dr. Harry Arnold, Rose Van Reken, with Position Paper & report of the advisory committee from Howard Stob (for all the appellants).

November 18, 1992: "Confidential" response To Appellants' Position Paper–from Consistory of the Orland Park CRC to Synodical Reconciliation Committee (with cover letter dated November 27, 1992).

December 18, 1992: Letter to reconciliation committee from Howard Stob (for all the appellants).

January 15, 1993: Letter to the reconciliation committee appointed by synod in response to the elders' answers to position paper.

March 5, 1993: Letter to synodical pastoral committee from the appellants.

June 6, 1993 p.m—Sermon: "Is This Church Healthy?" Rev. Gerald Erffmeyer, Orland Park Christian Reformed Church, Orland Park, IL.

March 10, 1993: Letter to Howard Stob from Pete Schipma.

March 29, 1993: Letter to Leonard J. Hofman, General Secretary of Synod from reconciliation committee: Rev. L.A. Bazuin, Dr. H. G. Arnold, Mrs. R. Van Reken.

April 5, 1993: Letter to Pete Schipma from Howard & Jo Stob, Dean & Karen Leensvaart, John & Sharon Tiggelaar, Ken & Ruth Evenhouse, Claris Van Kuiken.

June 22, 1993: Letter to Rev. George Vander Weit, (Troy, MI), from Rev. Neal Punt, (Evergreen Park, IL).

June 26, 1993: Letter same as above to the delegates from Classis Chicago South going to Synod.

June 29, 1993: "On Schlissel, Kuipers, Flikkema, and Church Library Books." *The Banner* , pg. 14.

June 30, 1993: "Confidential" letter from Orland Park Christian Reformed Church to Classis Chicago South Interim Committee.

July 8, 1993: Letter to Mr. Howard Stob from Rev. Leonard J. Hofman, General Secretary of the CRCNA granting a judicial hearing—adopted.

August 28, 1993: Letter to Rev. Richard M. Hartwell, Sr., Stated Clerk, Classis Chicago South from the appellants in response to elders' confidential letter.

September 15, 1993: Letter to the delegates of Classis Chicago South from Pete Schipma, Clerk, (as done in consistory, September 7, 1993).

October 21, 1993: Judicial Hearing at Calvin CRC, Oak Lawn, IL.

October 24,1993 p.m.—Sermon: "Circle of Reconciliation." Rev. William Lenters (Hope CRC, Oak Forest, IL) preaching at Orland Park CRC.

December 22, 1993: Letter requesting transfer of membership from Si & Claris Van Kuiken to the council of Orland Park CRC .

January 10, 1994: Letter from the Board of Trustees of the Christian Reformed Church of North America, Grand Rapids, MI, to members of all CRC churches.

April 1994: "Conservatives Respond to Christian Reformed Trustees' Attack on "Negative Networking." Letter by Claris Van Kuiken printed in *The Reformed Witness*, Hudsonville, MI, Volume 3: Number 1, 8.